The Geography of Cinema – A Cinematic World
Edited by Chris Lukinbeal and Stefan Zimmermann

MEDIA GEOGRAPHY AT MAINZ

Edited by

Anton Escher
Chris Lukinbeal
Stefan Zimmermann

Volume 1

The Geography of Cinema – A Cinematic World

Edited by Chris Lukinbeal and Stefan Zimmermann

Franz Steiner Verlag Stuttgart 2008

Cover illustration: „The Pope of Broadway" depicts Anthony Quinn on the Victor Clothing Company Building, 242 South Broadway, Los Angeles, California. Mural by Eloy Torrez, assisted by Bob Grigas, 1985. Photography by Chris Lukinbeal.

Bibliographische Information der Deutschen Bibliothek
Die Deutsche Bibliothek verzeichnet diese Publikation in der Deutschen Nationalbibliographie; detaillierte bibliographische Daten sind im Internet über <http://dnb.ddb.de> abrufbar.

ISBN 978-3-515-09199-2

Jede Verwertung des Werkes außerhalb der Grenzen des Urheberrechtsgesetzes ist unzulässig und strafbar. Dies gilt insbesondere für Übersetzung, Nachdruck, Mikroverfilmung oder vergleichbare Verfahren sowie für die Speicherung in Datenverarbeitungsanlagen.
© 2008 Franz Steiner Verlag, Stuttgart
Gedruckt auf säurefreiem, alterungsbeständigem Papier.
Druck: Laupp und Göbel, Nehren
Printed in Germany

Geographers usually see themselves in a tradition of Alexander von Humboldt and we would like to highlight his position that everything in our world is interdependent. Deriving from that assumption geography has to be seen as an unlimited science, a discipline that knows the borders but has none.

Anton Escher, Chris Lukinbeal and Stefan Zimmermann,
Tempe and Mainz, January 2008

CONTENTS

Preface 9

INTRODUCTION

Chris Lukinbeal / Stefan Zimmermann
A Cinematic World 15

Deborah Dixon / Leo Zonn / Johnathan Bascom
Post-ing the Cinema:
Reassessing Analytical Stances Toward a Geography of Film 25

THE AUTHOR

Joseph Palis
An Unmapped People and Places:
Cinema, Nation and the Aesthetics of Affection 51

Gerd Becker
Nouri Bouzid's *Bezness* as a Visual Study on the Glance:
Reflections on Exploring the Scientific Potential of Non-verbal Cinema 59

Deborah Dixon
'Independent' Documentary in the U.S.:
The Politics of Personal Passions 65

THE TEXT

Marcus A. Doel
From Animated Photography to Film: the Formation of Vernacular
Relativity in Early English Films (1895–1908) 87

David B. Clarke
Spaces of Anonymity 101

Christopher M. Moreno / Stuart Aitken
Space Operas and Cultures of Addiction:
The Animated Tale of Philip K. Dick's *A Scanner Darkly* 115

Susan P. Mains
'English Fever': Documenting the Caribbean Diaspora in *The Colony* 137

Mita Banerjee / Peter W. Marx
Ally Lives Just Next Door...
German-U.S. Relations in Popular Culture 155

Stefan Zimmermann
Landscapes of *Heimat* in Post-war German Cinema 171

THE READER

Christina Beal Kennedy
Living with Film: An Autobiographical Approach 187

Contributors 205

PREFACE

Most of the essays in this volume derived from an international symposium, *The Geography of Cinema – A Cinematic World*, at the Institute of Geography at the Johannes Gutenberg-University Mainz in June 2004. While special sessions on cinema and the media have occurred at conferences in Europe, the UK, the U.S. and Australia, this symposium was the first to gather some of the leading scholars in cinematic geography from around the world. The objective of the symposium was to explore the burgeoning subfield of film geography and chart new research trajectories (Figure 1). We, the organizers, also sought to close the gap between film studies and geography while broadening the existing knowledge base of both.

A highlight of the symposium included the showing of documentary films at Caligari FilmBühne in Wiesbaden[1] produced by faculty and students at the Institute of Geography at Johannes Gutenberg-University in Mainz. Also shown at the theatre was Susan Main's preliminary work on documenting diaspora and stories of Jamaican migration to the UK. Rather than just presentations on current research and group discussions, this event encouraged geographers to engage film production, digital media and documentary filmmaking. This event was the impetus for later documentary projects in Arizona[2] and at San Diego and Northridge, California[3].

We are grateful that nearly all of the sixteen scholars invited were able to attend and present their latest research. Scholars came from Germany, the United Kingdom, United States, Jamaica and the Philippines. We are indebted to the Centre for Intercultural Studies[4] of the Johannes Gutenberg-University Mainz, who deemed this event worthy of financial support. Some of the essays from the symposium were published in Erdkunde (2006, volume 60, number 4; see Figure 2) and other essays were requested from authors who were at the symposium for

1. http://www.wiesbaden.de/caligari, a historical neo-Gothic syle theater that opened in 1926.
2. The *Mediated Geographies: Critical Pedogogy and Geographic Education* project produced a series of student based documentary, all of which are located on the project website: http://geography.asu.edu/lukinbeal/mediated.html. One of Ari PALOS' documentaries (the project's consultant) is discussed in this book in Deborah Dixon's chapter on independent U.S. documentary films.
3. These projects were presented at the 2007 annual meeting of the Association of Pacific Coast Geographers (http://www.csus.edu/apcg/). Some of these documentaries will be a part of an upcoming special issue of *Aether: The Journal of Media Geography*.
   Aether: The Journal of Media Geography is a new online journal that started publishing in the fall of 2007. Many of the particpants from this symposium are on its editorial board and have written essays for its first volume. For more information see: www.aetherjournal.org
4. Zentrum für Interkulturelle Studien (ZIS)

Figure 1. Programme The Geography of Cinema – A Cinematic World

---

Symposium: *The Geography of Cinema – A Cinematic World*

24. – 26. June 2004

Chair: Alfred Hornung und Anton Escher

Thursday 24<u>th</u> June, Institute of Geography

Deborah Dixon / Stuart Aitken: The Geography of Cinema
Marcus Doel: "Animated photography and vernacular relativity: engineering space and time in early English films"
Deborah Dixon: Framing Border Landscapes
Mita Banerjee & Peter W. Marx: "Ally lives just next door..." German-US-American relations in popular culture.
Christina Kennedy: Place, Emotion and Experience: an Autobiographical Approach to the "Reel"

Friday 25<u>th</u> June, Caligari FilmBühne (Wiesbaden)

Bernd Kiefer: The Caligari: a place of visual pleasure
Susan Mains: Translating Mobility: Documenting Diaspora and Stories of Jamaican Migration
Helge Weichmann: Geographic Fieldwork in Film – Marrakech
Wolfgang Natter: Place and Space in Community-based filmmaking: The Geographies of Appalshop (Kentucky)
Stephanie Schimo: Nare – A Life between saucepan and notebook
Joseph S.E. Palis: Mapping the Heart of Brazil in Walter Salles "Central Station"

Saturday 26<u>th</u> June, Institute of Geography

Gerd Becker: *Nouri Bouzid's* Film Bezness as a visual study on the gaze
Stuart Aitken: Leading Men to Violence and Creating Spaces for their Emotions
Dave Clarke: Moving pictures / stopping places: hotels and motels on film
Christopher Lukinbeal: "Runaway Hollywood"
Stefan Zimmermann: Landscapes of "Heimat" in post-war German cinema
Final discussion

Figure 2. Essays deriving from the Symposium which have been published in Erdkunde

---

AITKEN, S. and DIXON, D. 2006: Imagining Geographies of Film. In: *Erdkunde* 60 (4), 326–336.

ESCHER, A. 2006: The Geography of Cinema. A Cinematic World. In: *Erdkunde* 60 (4), 307–314.

LUKINBEAL, C. 2006: Runaway Hollywood. Cold Mountain, Romania. In: *Erdkunde* 60 (4), 337–345.

LUKINBEAL, C. and ZIMMERMANN, S. 2006: Film Geography. A New Subfield. In: *Erdkunde* 60 (4), 315–325.

inclusion in this book. Also, one essay from the symposium has since been published in Gender, Place and Culture (Stuart AITKEN 2006, "Leading Men to Violence and Creating Spaces for their Emotions," 13, 492–507). The essays by David Clarke and Marcus Doel represent larger projects that have gone on to engage hotels and motels in film and the transition of animated photography into film. Rather than a compresive compendum that seeks to sum up the totality of a new subfield, this book aims to foster further interest and dialogue about geographic research on cinema.

This book represents the first of a new series to be offered by Franz Steiner Verlag. The series, "Media Geography at Mainz", will be edited by Anton Escher, Chris Lukinbeal and Stefan Zimmermann. Two future volumes are already in the works including, Gerd Becker's "Eying the Globe – Science and Visuality" and Stefan Zimmermann's "Deserts, Palm Trees and Bazaars – The Cinematic Geography of the Orient". All books will be published in English and we welcome inquiries related to possible book length manuscripts related to media geography.

We deeply appreciate the editing and editorial comments that Tina Kennedy and Kathrin Samstag made on the penultimate draft of this book.

Chris Lukinbeal, Anton Escher & Stefan Zimmermann,
Tempe and Mainz, August 2008

INTRODUCTION

Chris Lukinbeal / Stefan Zimmermann

A CINEMATIC WORLD

> *With cinema, it is the world
> which becomes its own image, and
> not an image which becomes the world*
>
> (DELEUZE 1986, 57).

INTRODUCTION

Gillian ROSE (2003) recently asked the question, "how, exactly, is Geography 'visual'?" The assumption is that, if we are a visual discipline, we already understand 'the visual.' The use of visuals abound in geographic practice whether in research, remote sensing, GIS, animated maps, photographs, film and television, or charts and graphs. In our teaching, visuals are so commonplace in lectures and presentations that it seems odd to witness a pedagogic event without them. Whether through the use of PowerPoint, slides, the Internet or documentaries and feature films, the visual dominates our educational practices. Many geographers assert that the ocularcentrism of geography is a primary modus operandi towards geographical knowledge. But how does the visual structure geographical knowledge? ROSE (2003, 2001) asserts that visuality refers to what we see, how we see, and what we are able to see. Visuality is of particular importance because power relations always saturate it. This is not to say that geography has not questioned the visual, or visuality; quite the contrary. Much work has been done on visuality as it relates to the construction and depiction of social difference, power relations, subjectivity and identity formation, as well as how it impacts the body. Decoding hierarchies, exposing practices of inclusion and exclusion, and revealing how visuality naturalizes ideologies and our view of the 'other,' remain active arenas of geographic inquiry.

We suggest that much geographic research on film has focused on the content of the visual, or what is seen and unseen (cf. DOEL and CLARKE 2007). While this is a very important aspect of querying exactly how geography is visual, it does not fully address all the modalities of film geography. In this introduction, then, we wish to explore aspects of geographic visualities as they relate to film geography. We assert that a pure focus on visuality limits the purview of film geography. Film is an assemblage of sight and sound, of texture and (e)motion, memory and experience. Moving beyond the sensory subjectivities of voyeurism and voyages, film is, paradoxically, also an assemblage of simulacra and of representational, non-representational, haptical, affective and performative practices. While other assemblages and modalities of exploring film geography are found throughout this book and elsewhere, our aim here is to develop a dialogue that embraces new opportunities for inquiry into cinematic geographies; while, at the same time, not jettisoning traditional cultural geographic theories and practices that provide foundational frameworks.

In this introductory essay, we address ROSE's challenge by discussing three aspects of the visual in the world of cinematic geography. These aspects include the content of what is seen, the form of seeing and the affect of what is seen.

WHAT IS SEEN – THE CONTENT

Authors in this collection use different theoretical approaches when addressing the content of what is seen in film. These approaches range from humanistic, positivistic, and text-centered, to poststructural and psychoanalytic.

The chapter by DIXON, ZONN and BASCOM provides an overview of different approaches that have been used to analyze the content of film by elaborating on an organizational framework of author-centered, text-centered, and reader-centered approaches. Rather than dismissing structural theories that underlie much of the initial inquiries into film geography, their aim is to illustrate how structural and poststructural theories illustrate larger ontological and epistemological debates that challenge how the visual constructs geographic knowledge. Where humanistic inquiry seeks to expose the emotional force and fabric of textual-subject relations between place, film, and viewer (as in Tina KENNEDY's chapter), BECKER's chapter uses a positivistic perspective to counter the dominance of the written word in documenting ethnographies; thereby, allowing researchers to learn from feature films how to tell more accurate and effective visual stories of cultures in place. Marxist and neo-Marxist inquiries work to expose dominate ideologies (that are naturalized within documentaries, feature films and television shows) and to articulate counter hegemonic narratives that seek to resist and subvert established 'ways of seeing.' These approaches are seen in DIXON's chapter on Independent U.S. Documentary Films, and, to a lesser extent, in Joseph PALIS's chapter.

Drawing from poststructural inquiry, BANERJEE and MARX's chapter, as well as MAINS' chapter explore how film and television articulate the 'other' and how race and ethnicity are contested and negotiated identities in a globalized era of transcontinental flows of people and cultures. Both chapters show how film and television work to 'fix' identities and reinforce cultural norms of inclusion and exclusion, promoting marginalized mediated spaces in which ethnic identities are reified as the 'other' to mainstream homogenous inclusive myths. However, as BANERJEE and MARX, as well as MAINS, explain, subterranean and overt challenges to mythic media representations show that identity is relational and constantly under negotiation. In his chapter, ZIMMERMANN shows how films from a particular genre, Heimat, played a key role in the transition of Germany national identity during post World War II. Heimat films worked to provide a national identity, founded on traditional cultural values that allowed Germans to take pride in their heritage, and, at the same time, helped heal the wounds of the recent destruction of their cities. Through a return to the rural idyllic, folklore, and sentimental bonds with landscape, the Heimat genre reveals how the affective power of film can move beyond the individual to the cultural.

Drawing from psychoanalysis and poststructural theories, CLARKE's chapter, as well as that of MORENO and AITKEN, challenges the social-spatial dialectic and moves beyond, within and outside the fixed scalar boundaries of body, individual, society and culture. Non-representational, unconscious spaces are not fixed within the scale of the mind or body; rather, movement, action, reaction and behavior flow freely across scales. CLARKE suggests that hotels, as non-places or resting points where the accelerated circulation of global flows stop to recharge, provide for chance encounters that produce a unique type of subjectivity, an inconsequential togetherness, an anti-church of sorts. MORENO and AITKEN further challenge us to rethink how film, space, and the scales of the body move freely because of addiction. Thereby, this fluidity produces new geographic configurations that we previously may not have considered.

A focus on the content of what is seen configures film as social texts, objects worthy of geographic inquiry. Whatever form social texts take, their symbolic qualities inform, challenge and negotiate social-spatial meaning. In their book, *Engaging Film,* CRESSWELL and DIXON (2002) argue that the textual metaphor has become hegemonic within film geography primarily because it is a powerful and appropriate means through which to engage cultural and social politics of meaning (re)production.

'Text' refers to a signifying practice associated with types of cultural production including the written word, painting, landscape and film. Textual analysis is a hermeneutical method focused on assumption and inquiry, where we query a 'text' guided by a hypothesis. The creative interaction, or hermeneutical circle of going back-and-forth between the interpreter's theoretical framework and the text being studied, leads to meaning and understanding. Diffusion of this hermeneutical method to geography followed the "linguistic turn" in the social sciences.

Applying the notion of 'text' to other forms of cultural production assumes that they are metaphorically like texts. This leads to two different questions: First, is 'text' a good paradigm for film geography? Second, how is the textual metaphor overlaid onto the content of what is seen? Extrapolating from RICOEUR's (1971) work, the textual metaphor is a valid means of inquiry for four reasons. First, written discourse and social life have similar characteristics. As such, meaning is constructed through the act of writing just as agency reifies the built environment (cf. COSGROVE 1984). Second, intention and reception of any text often fail to coincide. Similarly, actions can become detached from agents and can have effects beyond the scale of their intent. This can happen for both the 'text' under inquiry and the 'text' being constructed (cf. DUNCAN and DUNCAN 1988). Third, interpretation of texts and cultural events vary with location, culture and era. In other words, the ethical issue of essentialism, where one's views speak for others, remains a fundamental issue regardless of whether the item being studied is a text, event, or action (SMITH 2002). Fourth, textual meaning is unstable and fluid because it is interpreted. Similarly, social institutions and actions are also unstable and fluid because meaning is constituted through the relative position of the interpreter. Relativism, or the fact that interpretation is relative to the interpreter, is an issue regardless of the method of inquiry. ROSE (2001) takes this a step further when suggesting that discourse analysis can take two forms: the first focuses on the contested meanings within a text (the text-centered approach). The second examines the articulation of discourse in social practices, institutions and technologies that produce texts (the author-centered approach). DIXON, ZONN and BASCOM offer a third, reader-centered, approach. Here, rather than dismissing the issue of relativism, they argue that this approach empowers the reader-viewer by granting them the authority to appropriate, resist or transform the meanings within social texts. This exposes the fact that relativism is not about coming to a consensus about one 'true' meaning or understanding; rather, it is a discursive process wherein negotiation of social meanings are conceived as heterogeneous rather than homogenous. The textual metaphor, overlaid onto the content of what is seen, is paradigmatic because it is a method rather than a theory. Readings can be from a diversity of theoretical positions allowing film geography to develop a truly discursive environment in which to prosper.

The textual metaphor, however, has its limits. For example, an alternative model of inquiry into film geography may follow a production-product-distribution-consumption model in which the text is primarily, but not wholly, constituted by the product. This alternative model of inquiry centers on film as part of a cultural economy that produces cultural goods for global consumption. According to SCOTT (2005, 3), "the cultural economy can be broadly defined as a group of sectors ... that produce goods and services whose subjective meaning, or, more precisely sign-value to the consumer is high in comparison with their utilitarian purpose." Under this rubric, the cinematic world is mutually constitutive of social texts and extra-textual processes. In their examination of the global dominance of the Hollywood film industry, MILLER et al. (2005, 5) argue, "unlike textual reductionists, we do not assume that it is adequate to interpret a film's internal qualities or the supposed 'positioning' of mythic spectators." DIXON's chapter, on independent documentary films in the U.S., presents an author-centered textual analysis in which extra-textual processes, concerning the role of state funding of documentary films, are explored. She argues that the state, through funding, defines documentaries and reifies the idealized notion of rural spaces by focusing on hard-working individuals. As such, society is positioned within President Johnson's notion of a Great Society that frames marginalization within a neoliberal discourse.

While methodological in nature, the textual metaphor may reinforce specific epistemological and ontological formations. CRESSWELL and DIXON (2002) argue that a focus on text and context within the textual metaphor resembles, and may even reinforce, the normative belief that film is a re-presentation of reality. By connecting film with representation, a binary is constructed wherein the 'reel' is a second-hand experience and the 'real' is a primary experience. This binary reinforces the belief that film is of secondary importance to direct geographic studies in the field. This binary further reinforces a hegemonic order within geography, delimiting what is an acceptable and unacceptable mode of inquiry. Only recently has film geography begun to overcome this arbitrary normative belief. LUKINBEAL and ZIMMERMANN (2006, 322) challenge the deterministic logic of the binary stating:

> We eschew the representational determinism that film geography is synonymous with re-presentations of some ontological stable "authentic" reality. Drawing from CRANG et al. (1999, 2), we posit that film geography always exceeds the cinematic technologies which produce representations because film is "constituted by the social relations, discourses and sites in which these technologies are embedded." The technologies that capture, encode and represent the world are always embedded in social and cultural practices that are temporally and spatially specific. Representations are not the polar opposite of reality especially when it comes to film and cinema. Cinematic images are always socialized just as technologies are always socialized.

CLARKE (1997) succinctly argues that cinema is simulacral rather than representational. CRESSWELL and DIXON (2002, 3–4) contend that films are not "mere images of unmediated expressions of the mind, but rather the temporary embodiment of social processes that continually construct and deconstruct the world as we know it." LUKINBEAL (2004, 247) expounds upon this idea stating, "visual media are today's cognitive maps (JAMESON 1984, 1988, 1992) or social cartography (BRUNO 1997, 2002) of meaning creation and identity formation." Therefore, the simulacrum does not conceal truth; truth conceals that there is none (BAUDRILLARD 1988). This leads us to back to our opening quotation by DELEUZE (1986, 57) which explains that the world is not imaged, imagined or re-presented by cinema, but rather the world becomes its own image, "a real without origin or reality: a hyperreal" (BAUDRILLARD 1983, 2). Querying cinema as simulacra leads us away from the content of what is seen and begins to questioning the form of the seen.

THE FORM OF WHAT IS SEEN

Cinema makes no claims that it is anything but a mechanical re-production. Rather than re-producing the 'real' or re-producing what is 'seen', cinema produces a 'reality-effect' – a simulacrum of the real. Cinema is a machine for constructing different relations between space and time. What is seen in a landscape amounts to a representational form that affords the subject apparent mastery over space by aligning vision with truth. In this sense 'seeing is believing' and the 'seen' is a fixed, centered, and all embarrassing gaze. Seeing is not objective; rather, it is a practiced appropriation of space constituted through learned 'ways of seeing,' or scopic regimes ingrained by social and cultural norms. Scopic regime, a term coined by Christian METZ (1977), seeks to differentiate 'vision' from 'visuality.' Whereas 'vision' is often considered a universal and natural, subject-centered phenomenon, 'visuality' emphasizes that ways of looking are not natural; rather, they are socially constructed. Further, scopic regimes have a history wherein specific regimes become hegemonic during specific cultural eras. Both ZIMMERMANN's and DOEL's chapters, for instance, focus on the synchronic nature of scopic regimes within German culture (ZIMMERMANN) and the form of film itself (DOEL).

DOEL argues that there is a significant omission within film geography on the study of the form of film itself. While much has been written on the content, or function of film, form has its own spatial and temporal characteristics that are distinct from, yet related to, function. Focusing on the formative years of film, DOEL traces the geographies of film's scopic regime as it transitioned from animated photography into narrative cinema. Under the scopic regime of animated photography, public interest was tautological in that audiences wanted ultra-realism, life-like animation, or re-presentations of actual life. During this period, film sought to re-produce true movement – to *animate* photography. Misrepresentation of natural movement produced negative reviews from trade journals. Film was evaluated on its ability to re-present motion. Because of this, film was sold by the foot with purchasers showing concern about paying for any footage that was not truly animated. DOEL argues that, with continuity editing and narrative space decades away, time was inscribed "synchronically within the scene, rather than being fashioned diachronically between scenes through editing" (DOEL, current volume). The shift in film's scopic regime occurred when cinema stopped "re-presenting an actual or staged instant" and started to function "as an apparatus that could both manipulate and manufacture space and time. In so doing, animated photography ceased being a *referential* medium, bound to the *Real*, to become a simulacral medium, free to fabricate a reality-effect" (DOEL, current volume). Film ceased functioning as representational (imaging the world) and became simulacral (a world becomes its own image). The essential element of film, then, "is not the framed image" or the content "but that which comes *between* the frames: *the cut*" (DOEL, current volume).

With animated photography, the focus is on the seen on the visual and re-presentational. With narrative cinema, the focus shifts to the scene, visuality and simulacra through use of montage. HEATH (1981) argues that classic narrative space provides a solution to coordinating the problem of space and time relations in film. Classic narrative space became the dominant scopic regime of film which sought to mend the tension between quattrocento space (a central, fixed all embracing point of view) and the inherent movement of film which threatened the fixity of the gaze. He refers to the practice devised to convert 'seen' (fixed) into 'scene' (mobilized) via a manner which "contains the mobility that could threaten the clarity of vision" (HEATH 1981, 36) by constantly re-centering the observer's point of view. CLARKE's and DOEL's (CLARKE and DOEL 2005, 2006, 2007; DOEL and CLARKE 2007) excellent work on the transition within film's scopic regime shows that initially viewers were uncomfortable with point-of-view shots and continuity editing and found them 'unnatural.' Over time, however, this new visuality was naturalized and a new scopic regime accepted.

THE AFFECT OF WHAT IS SEEN

Ari PALOS, a documentary filmmaker (cited in DIXON's chapter), commented that film is not simply visual, but, rather, an assemblage of both the audio and visual (cf. LUKINBEAL et al. 2007). Where others have focused on the affective visual nature of film (AITKEN 2006; CARTER and MCCORMACK 2006), we argue that audio is equally essential to affect in film. Audio guides affective response. It saturates film and sutures the 'seen' into the 'scene'; gives space depth through emotive becoming, and guides the unconscious experiential musings of the mind – turning the voyeur into a voyager of spaces seen and unseen. It calls on our subjectivity to react to seen, heard, felt, and experienced memories and emotions. The assemblage of audio-video takes us on a voyage through ourselves as much as through the film's narrative. This voyage positions us in a dialectics of cinema's 'reality-effect' and our affective relation to our own reality. Music, within film, often produces and guides affective response. Imagine the different effects and affect of blending peaceful, contemplative classical music with the camera's movement through a pastoral rolling hills landscape, to combining heavy metal, pulsating, music with a car chase; or gothic music with a dark; seedy urban landscape. Furthermore, music and the visual assembled in unexpected ways can lead to startling affective responses. Quentin TARANTINO's films, for instance, frequently juxtapose songs from popular culture with violence thus producing strange, divergent, affective spaces. Music also can be central to montage, producing emotionally laden reality effects wherein the syncopation of the music effectively sutures the visual into an affective scene.

A focus on the affect of what is seen *and* heard is not about untangling the emotive from meaning or the subjective from objective; rather, it is about how affect leads us to certain responses. This focus takes us down certain logical pathways that lead us to structure what the author, text, or reader's role is in relation to what the film means to us rationally; while, simultaneously, exploring how affect functions unconsciously on subjectivity, self identity and social identity. Affect works through and beyond us – producing responses at larger scales, or across networks – as our affect affects others. A film's affect provokes tension, contestation, and emotional responses because it does not separate subject (the viewer) from object (the content and form of the visual / audio). Cinema, therefore, is a haptical mobilization, an (e)motional journey that leads us to questions our identity and its relation to values, experiences, and knowledge (BRUNO 2002). Affect moves beyond reflect(ion) to engage the content and form of the visual, as well as our own subjectivity, beyond the reality-effect that film affords. According to CARTER and MCCORMACK (2006, 236), film's affect moves beyond an individual's relative interpretation because it is a "matter of the production and circulation of affects prior to yet also providing the grounds from which distinctive intensities of feeling emerge." While the focus on film geography has been on the representational analytics that "rehearse or disrupt particular discursive codes and scripts" it also "involves a consideration of how they amplify the passage and transition between affect and emotion" (CARTER and MCCORMACK 2006, 236).

In her reader-centered approach to film, KENNEDY's chapter engages film's affective nature through an autobiographical analysis of the role that film played in the formative, childhood years of her life. By positioning herself relationally, rather than objectively, with cinema; KENNEDY is able to explore how affect produces a series of geographies that interconnect her life in film, with film, and because of film.

CONCLUSIONS

Through focusing on three modalities of the visual, we seek to show how film geography is an expanding field of study that moves past re-presentational praxis. Where a focus on the content of what is seen challenges us to probe the relation between visuality and the production of geographical knowledge, a focus on the form of the seen investigates how visualities produce and institute scopic regimes. In focusing on the affect of what is seen, we move within, through, and outside form and content to engage the interdependent nature of film, self, and society. By examining cinema's form, content and affect, we also move beyond representation into simulacra, transcend fixed scales of inquiry, and open dialogues that challenge naturalized scopic regimes, ideologies, myths and truth. Where the visual sees the world of cinema, visuality opens us to a cinematic world.

REFERENCES

AITKEN, S. (2006): Leading Men to Violence and Creating Spaces for their Emotions. *Gender, Place and Culture* 13 (5), 491–507.
BAUDRILLARD, J. (1988): *Baudrillard, Selected Writings,* ed. Mark Poster. Stanford.
BAUDRILLARD, J. (1983): *Simulations*. New York.
BRUNO, G. (1997): Site-seeing: Architecture and the Moving Image. *Wide Angle* 19 (4), 8–24.
BRUNO, G. (2002): *The Atlas of Emotion: Journeys in Art, Architecture, and Film*. New York.
CARTER, S., and D. MCCORMACK (2006): Film, Geopolitics and the affective logics of intervention. *Political Geography* 25, 228–245.
CLARKE, D., and M. DOEL (2005): Engineering space and time: moving pictures and motionless trips'. *Journal of Historical Geography* 31, 41–60.
CLARKE, D. (Ed.) (1997): *The Cinematic City*. New York.
CLARKE, D. and M. DOEL (2007): Shooting space, tracking time: the city from animated photography to vernacular relativity. *Cultural Geographies* 14 (4), 589–609.
CLARKE, D., and M. DOEL (2006): From Flatlands to Vernacular Relativity: The Genesis of Early English Screenscapes. LEFEBVRE, M. (Ed.): *Landscape and Film*. New York, 213–243.
COSGROVE, D. (1984): *Social Formations and Symbolic Landscapes*. Totawa, N.J..
CRANG, M., P. CRANG and J. MAY (1999): Introduction. CRANG, M., P. CRANG and J. MAY (Eds.): *Virtual Geographies: Bodies, space and relations*. London, 1–20.
CRESSWELL, T., and D. DIXON (2002): Introduction: Engaging Film. CRESSWELL, T. and D. DIXON (Eds.): *Engaging Film: Geographies of Mobility and Identity*. Lanham, Maryland, 1–12.
DELEUZE, G. (1986): *Cinema 1: The Movement-Image*. London.
DOEL, M. and D. CLARKE (2007): Afterimages. *Environment and Planning D: Society and Space* 25, 890–910.
DUNCAN, J. and N. DUNCAN (1988): (Re)reading the landscape. *Environment and Planning D: Society and Space* 6, 117–126.

HEATH, S. (1981): *Questions of Cinema*. London.
JAMESON, F. (1984): Postmodernism, or The Logic of Late Capitalism. *New Leftist Review* 146, 53–92.
JAMESON, F. (1988): Cognitive Mapping. NELSON, C. and L. GROSSBERG (Eds.): *Marxism and the Interpretation of Culture*. Urbana, Illinois, 347–357.
JAMESON, F. (1992): *The Geopolitical Aesthetic: Cinema and Space in the World System*. Bloomington.
LUKINBEAL C. and S. ZIMMERMANN (2006): Film Geography: A New Subfield. *Erdkunde* 60 (4), 315–325.
LUKINBEAL, C. (2004): The Map That Precedes The Territory: An Introduction To Essays In Cinematic Geography. *GeoJournal* 59 (4), 247–251.
LUKINBEAL, C., C. KENNEDY, J.P. JONES, J. FINN, K. WOODWARD, D. NELSON, Z. GRANT, N. ANTONOPOLIS, A. PALOS and C. ATKINSON-PALOMBO (2007): Mediated Geographies: Critical Pedagogy and Geographic Education. *Yearbook of the Association of Pacific Coast Geographers* 69, 31–44.
LUKINBEAL, C. (2004): The Rise of Regional Film Production Centers in North America, 1984–1997. *GeoJournal* 59 (4), 307–321.
METZ, C. (1977): *The Imaginary Signifier: Psychoanalysis and the Cinema*. Bloomington.
MILLER, T., N. COVIL, J. MCMURRIA, R. MAXWELL and T. WANG (2005): *Global Hollywood 2*. London.
RICOEUR, P. (1971): The model of the text. *Social Research* 38: 529–562.
ROSE, G. (2001): *Visual Methodologies: An Introduction to the Interpretation of Visual Materials*. London.
ROSE, G. (2003): On the Need to Ask How Exactly, Is Geography "Visual"? *Antipode* 35 (2), 212–221.
SCOTT, A. (2005): *On Hollywood: The Place, the Industry*. Princeton.
SMITH, L. (2002): Chips off the Old Ice Block: *Nanook of the North* and the Relocation of Cultural Identity. CRESSWELL, T. and D. DIXON (Eds.): *Engaging Film: Geographies of Mobility and Identity*. Lanham, Maryland, 94–122.

Deborah Dixon / Leo Zonn / Johnathan Bascom

POST-ING THE CINEMA: REASSESSING ANALYTICAL STANCES TOWARD A GEOGRAPHY OF FILM

INTRODUCTION: FILM AS SOCIAL TEXT

The geographic literature on the significance of film, as a mode of social discourse and the utility of film research to academia, has undergone substantial change in recent years. Invigorated by recent theoretical debates on the character of 'representation' from within and beyond the discipline, this sub-field is now considered an appropriate arena within which more general concerns over the relationship between the imagined and the material – the 'reel' and the 'real' – can be given concrete form (DOEL 1993; AITKEN and ZONN 1994; NATTER 1994; DIXON and JONES 1996; DOEL and CLARKE 1996; HANNA 1996). The explicitly pedagogical essays that constituted geography's engagement with film a few decades ago (for example, MANVELL 1956, and WRIGHT 1956, on the use of film as a teaching tool) have been displaced by a proliferation of geographic analyses that take as their focus of inquiry the role of film in: 1) the imposition of dominant ideologies (GOLD 1985; AITKEN 1991, 1993; BOWDEN 1994; HOPKINS 1994; KRIM 1994); 2) the articulation of moments of resistance (NATTER and JONES 1993; ROSE 1994); 3) the production and consumption of intersubjective meanings (ZONN 1984; ZONN and AITKEN 1994); and 4) the negotiation of identities (AITKEN and ZONN 1993, 1994). Within this broad reconceptualization, films are no longer considered an expression of the mind, but rather as constituted within, and therefore the embodiment of, a social totality: they are *social* texts. To put this in more process-orientated terms, it has become axiomatic that films are the product of, and in turn reproductive of, broader social relations of power.

In this paper we explore the axiomatic character of this reconceptualization of film as a social text, noting the shift that has occurred in regard to the perceived theoretical status of film, but we also study some of the often overlooked ramifications *of* this shift. In particular, we focus on the various ways in which geography's current engagements with film rely, in large part, upon diverse forms of structuralism – an ontological presumption embedded even within those approaches considered most 'postmodern'. In doing so, our intention is not to summarily dismiss such engagements as intrinsically structuralist and thereby incorrect, but rather to point out that an assessment of the analytic assumptions undergirding their deployment requires an *exposition* and / or *illustration* of the ways in which diverse approaches are indeed embedded within more abstract debates regarding ontology and epistemology. Furthermore, in uncovering some of the assumptions underlying a geography of film we can point more clearly toward those approaches that are presently *under*developed; approaches that embed themselves within *post*structuralist conceptualizations of the world.

Our own reading of the current theoretical landscape is itself guided by those strands of poststructuralist thought that problematize: first, the 'subject's' ability to perceive the 'real' processes at work in society, as opposed to mere 'representation'; and second, the 'subject's' ability to 'represent', or articulate, those findings, without asserting a totalizing framework. As such, we introduce an initial note of caution in regard to the identification of diverse approaches to a geography of film: that is, one cannot presume such approaches to be the mere reflection of broader-scale disciplinary paradigms. From a poststructuralist stance, all investigative approaches are productive of particular assumptions regarding the status of 'truth', 'reality' and 'explanation' – these assumptions, however, often cut across the largely nominal divides marked by paradigmatic boundaries. For example, a 'modernist' commitment to locating and representing truths has recently been subject to much critique (see, for example, SOJA 1989, 1991; FOLCH-SERRA 1990; PHILO 1992; SHAPIRO 1992; and NATTER and JONES 1993, among others). Such critiques undermine not only a humanistic focus on essences, but also political economy's search for the 'real' causes of oppression in the world. Furthermore, while diverse analyses draw inspiration from that body of literature labelled 'postmodernism', there occasionally remain distinct traces of essentialism, a characteristic usually associated with political economy (see, for example, MASSEY's 1991 critique of HARVEY, and HARVEY's rebuttal 1993). Our point here is not that the accepted labels given to particular bodies of literature are incorrect, but rather that the theoretical debates currently taking place are far too nuanced for such labels to be useful. As researchers from various sub-fields engage and re-engage in these meta-theoretical debates, we should be aware of the fact that the assumptions underpinning diverse investigations of the world endeavors cut across, and produce divisions within, accepted disciplinary paradigms. This differential 'borrowing' of concepts and premises is as much a feature of landscape analysis (see, for example, BARNES and DUNCAN 1992) as it is of film analysis.

Given our intent to articulate the ramifications arising from the diverse forms of structuralism underlying geography's present engagement with film, the methodological question that arises at this point is: on what grounds do we locate key analytical stances toward a geography of film? In contrast to the potentially misleading character of a paradigmatic ordering of film research, we recognize the utility of an organizational framework based on an 'Author-Text-Reader' (A-T-R) model. This framework takes account of the common distinction many researchers have drawn, and continue to draw, between the particular 'moments' of a film's history. An initial premise made by many researchers is that film, as an object of inquiry, is constituted through the conditions surrounding its production, content, and reception by an audience. This does not mean that subsequent analyses are limited *to* a particular moment, but rather that each approach interprets the component parts of the model according to their analytic assumptions, weighs their significance in regard to the goal of inquiry, and focuses on that moment deemed to be of greatest relevance. Consequently, geography's engagement with film as an object of inquiry has largely settled out into three analytic stances, namely author-centered, text-centered and reader-centered, approaches.[1]

Our method of choice, therefore, is to organize analytic stances according to this A-T-R model, and secondly to utilize them in three separate 'readings' of a particular film, *Powaqqatsi: Life in Transformation*.[2] More specifically, the theoretical assumptions underpinning these analytic stances will be drawn out through an illustration of the reading that ensues from such approaches, and through an exposition of the underlying ontological and epistemological assumptions that permit these modes of reading to take place. This leads us not only to identify the diverse forms of structuralism apparent in the three major analytic stances constituting geography's current engagement, but also to explore the research 'limitations', or borders, established within each form. It is from a *post*structuralist vantage point, we hope, that alternate analyses of the ways in which social 'power' operates within film, and more generally how these myriad power relationships construe the world at large, can be articulated.

AUTHOR-CENTERED APPROACHES: FILMING CAPITAL AT WORK

An author-centered reading of film focuses on the conditions surrounding its production, and rests on the presumption that there exists a *readily communicated* meaning within that textual form. As noted in the introduction, this does not mean that the analysis is limited *to* this moment, but rather that once the premise has been made that meaning has an *origin*, the methodological focus of inquiry is guided by the need to ascertain the conditions from which particular meanings emerge. It is at the moment of production, then, that key ontological and epistemological assumptions are being made. Furthermore, in placing the focus of inquiry on this moment an analytic trajectory is established wherein the two other components of the model (content and reception) are interpreted according to how particular meanings are subsequently embedded within a text, and read by an audience.

1. Much of the interest in how to "read" film, as well as other popular modes of communication, has come from the realm of literary theory. Hence it should not be too surprising to find that geographers have repeatedly turned toward the Author-Text-Reader model used within this discipline. For an excellent review of this model and its explicit and implicit appropriation by geographers see NATTER and JONES (1993): Signposts Toward a Poststructuralist Geography, in JONES, J.P., NATTER, W. and SCHATZKI, T. (Eds.) *Beyond Modernity? Postmodernism, Politics and Space*. New York.
2. *Powaqqatsi* is a feature-length documentary film comprised of a montage of magnificently photographed images of an array of human activities in the First and Third World, all set within a wide range of physical and cultural landscapes. It is the second film in a planned trilogy by the American director Godfrey REGGIO, the first being the critically acclaimed *Koyaanisqatsi*, the third is entitled *Naquoyqatsi*. *Powaqqatsi* eschews a traditional documentary format – plot, characters, dialogue and narration – and consists instead of a series of images produced via a visually stunning array of shooting techniques, including acceleration, reverse action, microscopy and aerial shots. These movements are underscored by Philip Glass' often eerie but engaging acoustic arrangements. At the close of the film a translation appears: "Po.waq.qa.tsi (from the Hopi language, *powaq* sorcerer + *qatsi* life) n., an entity, a way of life that consumes the life forces of other beings in order to further its own life."

Such an approach has usually been associated with a humanistic conception of the individual, wherein the meaning imparted to a text is perceived to have its origin in an original, autonomous, mind; film is a product of the *auteur*. In this section we present the rather unorthodox argument that the presumptions of this approach are also present within a political economic reading of 'reality' and its 'representation'. We do so by suggesting that both approaches are underpinned by a 'modernist' imperative to impart, channel and direct the 'real', or 'true', meaning of a text. From within humanism, we can interpret that truth to be the ideals of the auteur. From within political economy, the meanings embedded within popular films are mere 'representations', serving to naturalize hegemonic, capitalist, discourses produced in the 'real' world, or merely distract the attention of viewers from the 'real' problems facing society (BURGESS 1985; AITKEN 1991; HOPKINS 1994; KLAK 1994; KRIM 1994). The role of the researcher is to expose the truisms hidden behind a text's ideological facade, thereby revealing the fetishistic[3] quality of representation in general (NICHOLSON 1991; GODFREY 1993; BOWDEN 1994). Such an endeavor bears a marked resemblance to the role of the humanist critic, locating and articulating the 'real' intent of the author for all to see. In this section, therefore, we undertake an authorial reading of *Powaqqatsi* in order to demonstrate the readiness with which a political economic analysis of the 'real' and the 'reel' can indeed accommodate this focus on a readily communicated meaning embedded within the text.

According to the director of *Powaqqatsi*, Godfrey REGGIO, the intent behind its production was to communicate the destructive and dehumanizing impacts of capitalist development – the message of the film – more *directly* to the audience via the use of diverse, non-traditional, shooting techniques. For REGGIO, this direct, more emotive form of communication is more likely to ensure the reception and retention of such a message precisely because it is transmitted in a more visually and acoustically diffuse manner. As he puts it:

> What you give up is the specificity of one thought, one idea, unmistakably getting your point across, which people can agree or disagree with. But what you do get is the richness of an experience that can stay in the conscious and the unconscious mind and can be continually revisited and serve as a source of inspiration for the viewer (quoted in DEMPSEY 1989, 21).

If we read the meaning of *Powaqqatsi* as commensurate with the message of its author, then, both the content and the format of the film must be taken into account. The first half of the movie, for example, is a paean to the moral and aesthetic value of traditional third world peasant societies: religion, hand labor, craftsmanship, and the rapprochement between village and nature are all valorized as elemental to a life in balance. The pace of the movie is slow, the camera, it seems, savoring each beautiful frame for as long as possible. "Try slowing it down", suggests REGGIO,

---

3. Fetishistic in this sense of the term refers to Marx's commentary on commodities, whereby they are dissociated from their material production and presented as 'abstract' things determined only by their price on the market. So too, the actual relations of power within which films are produced are hidden by the visual imagery invested in it. Most films play the role of visual ideologies, lulling the non-expert reader into a false sense of security.

"so that, in effect, it becomes monumentalized. In freezing a moment, you create a monument..." (quoted in DEMPSEY 1989, 22). In contrast, the second half explodes into action as the camera pans by activity after activity, some joyful, some comic, some nightmarish. The underlying music shifts to a pronounced and beat-insistent tone as we view the increasingly disturbing juxtapositions of people and things in what now appears to be an urban jumble. What emerges, however, is no horror show but an enticing, if somewhat confusing and ultimately dangerous, place to be: "[T]he Beast doesn't come as a baglady, it comes as a seducer, it comes bejewelled" (REGGIO, quoted in DEMPSEY 1989, 19).

In accord with this authorial intent, our reading of *Powaqqatsi* goes on to distinguish three spheres of socio-spatial 'reality' within the film. Each of these spheres we read as signifying the social regimentation, alienation and exploitation produced under a rapidly expanding capitalist economy: first, traditional peasant economies; second, the rapidly urbanizing Third World cities; and third, the dehumanized First World cities.

To begin, we see the Third World as a place of texture, rhythm, continuity and innocence. Early in the film we see below-the-waist shots of swirling dresses of dancing Altiplano women, while later we see the beautiful headdresses of the same women as we get only a suggestion of the fact that there is a rhythmic flow. Toward the end of the film the camera is pulled back and we see the group of ten or twelve women in its entirety as they slowly dance in a circle, the complete costumes swirling in rhythm, with facial expressions clear and intent. The camera focuses on a child's face at several junctures, and then, after a long pause, it slowly pans across the faces of many children standing shoulder to shoulder. Their expressions vary from indifference to curiosity to a rare smile. The camera focuses on hands that are hoeing a field, then shifts to an areal view of terraced fields with a few scattered huts – this is a mode of existence in harmony with the natural environment. In contrast, the parasitic tendrils of the global economy reach into this rural idyll and transform individuals into an anonymous, regimented, assemblage of limbs – labor in the abstract – as the camera sustains a long montage, scored percussively by GLASS, of slow-motion images of begrimed, sweating laborers carrying sacks of dirt away from a deep mine and its debris-formed and steep terraced slopes. The workers' toil seems endless and of little purpose.

The second socio-spatial sphere of activity is filmed in the metropolitan centers of core capitalist economies where livelihoods are conditioned by intensely competitive social relations of production. Human beings are conspicuously absent here and the social structure has shifted from reliance on face-to-face communication to mediated and indirect forms of interaction. In one image an abandoned and stripped car sits in the median of a highway while shadows of cars, ghost cars of the past and future, speed by in opposite directions. In another hypnotic scene a seemingly endless train of identical cars whip right to left past the camera, a solitary tree set just to the other side of the tracks. The pacing of images begins fairly rapidly then accelerates to a near frenzy: this discrete time-space compression takes us into the vortex of the modern city.

The third sphere of activity is shot in the metropolitan centers of developing countries where the two previous worlds are not only in collision, one is actively subsuming the other. It is in this setting that capitalism appears most voracious in its appetite for larger and larger quantities of human labor. Traditional cultural ties between people and to nature are dislodged as a direct consequence of the intensified demands placed on society and the physical landscape by the dominant capitalist regime of accumulation. The scenes present a sense of unbalance or turmoil, a kind of social entropy. An elderly Filipino woman walks with a package balanced on her head, while behind her a group of young men and women, perhaps high school age, are jogging in unison. Clad in homogenous uniforms and indifferent faces, they overtake her. Change is coming, and it is generic, powerful and inexorable. In another scene, a girl is driving a cart pulled by two mules in heavy vehicular traffic. She beats the mules almost continuously with a stick, but they go no faster. In another scene a young, robed boy walks alongside the road with a sense of purpose and direction. Slowly and inexorably a truck approaches from behind. The truck is churning up dust as it moves, and as it passes the boy the cloud slowly envelops him. Yet, as he slowly disappears he never loses his demeanor. When we can no longer see him, the music stops. A few moments from the very close of the movie, he materializes from the cloud as the truck passes, his step unaltered.

Within this mode of reading, we are presuming that *Powaqqatsi* presents to the viewer *real*-life processes: we are *witness* to the cultural, social and physical impacts of capitalism on the Third World, subsuming all in its seemingly endless quest for profit. The Avant Garde format of the movie is clearly a product of artifice, but the essence of the message is merely *enhanced* through such means: our awareness of the capitalist system and its consequences is heightened through this artistic medium. As such, *Powaqqatsi* adequately fulfills the role of "art as mode of explanation" demanded by one extremely influential strand of political economic thought, articulated by MARCUSE, HORKHEIMER and ADORNO. For MARCUSE (1972), culture is the arena within which contradictions within capitalism are articulated and resolved through ideological apparatus' such as the production of Art.[4] He argues that the 'transcendental' ideals of happiness and beauty celebrated in Art are merely the product of bourgeoisie ideology – the false message imparted by Art is that such ideals are present *in reality*. He writes,

> ... [the bourgeois epoch's] decisive characteristic is the assertion of a universally obligatory, eternally better and more valuable world that must be unconditionally confirmed: a world essentially different from the factual world of daily struggle for existence, and yet realizable by every individual for himself 'from within', without any transformation of the state of fact. It is only in this culture that cultural activities and objects gain that value which elevates them above the everyday sphere. Their reception becomes an act of celebration and exaltation (MARCUSE 1972, 75).

4. While the examples used by MARCUSE, HORKHEIMER and ADORNO to distinguish High and Low culture (i.e., Art versus popular vehicles such as film) are inappropriate to our argument, the impetus behind this categorization of texts remains valid. According to the director of *Powaqqatsi*, this film is indeed intended to be an art form, rather than popular entertainment (see DEMPSEY 1989).

Art glides over the misery of the working class, and persuades those who have access to its thrall that all is well. According to HORKHEIMER and ADORNO (1973), Avant Garde Art breaks this ideological function. The audience is no longer presented with an image that reinscribes a normal relationship between them as subjects and the capitalist form of society: through its very artificiality, Avant Garde Art draws attention to its social origins, forcing the viewer to reevaluate their accepted, taken-for-granted, role in society.

Within this political economic positioning of the role of film as a mode of social discourse, there is simultaneously a rejection of the individualism present in an authorial approach to the text, and a privileging of the individual's capacity to become aware of, and comment on, their 'true' place in society. HORKHEIMER and ADORNO are articulating a particular, structural view of the social world, in which the notion of an autonomous 'mind' is rejected in favor of a materialist explanation of subjectivity. Materialist, in this sense, refers to the presumption that ideas, or attitudes / beliefs are not immanent categories of the mind. They are, rather, dependent upon the input of data from a knowable world composed of intersubjective meanings, inherited values, institutionalized roles and social norms. While such norms and mores are not the *direct* product of the economic base of society, the 'real' place of the individual in society, and the way in which that individual conceives of their role in society, hinges upon their relationship to the mode of production. This particular theorization of the production of subjectivity has been expanded considerably by ALTHUSSER (1971, 233), who writes:

> In ideology men ... express, not the relation between them and their conditions of existence, but the way they live the relation between them and their conditions of existence: this presupposes both a real relation and an 'imaginary', lived relation. Ideology ... is the expression of the relation between men and their 'world', that is, the (overdetermined) unity of the real relation and the imaginary relation between them and their real conditions of existence.

We can read *Powaqqatsi*, therefore, to be an instance wherein the author's ideological commentary on capitalism, and the 'real' social structure produced under capitalism coincide. Such a normative rendering of the film, however, depends upon a presumption shared by both humanism and this particular form of political economy; that is, a belief in the freeing powers of thought and language, such that individual's have the capacity to appreciate and comment on their own and others' 'true' place in society.

In drawing out the analytic assumptions underpinning this approach we can locate a certainty in regard to the *objective* status of the researcher and the *factuality* of capitalist domination which, from a poststructuralist standpoint, poses considerable limitations. As recent reviews point out, for example, the presumption of a dichotomy between 'reality' and mere 'representation' allows the researcher to take an authoritative position outside of the world they are claiming to research (DEUTSCHE 1990, 1991; JONES 1995). DEUTSCHE (1990, 133) problematizes this characterization of the 'real' and the 'reel' by pointing toward its accompanying strategy of *exclusion*, in that the grandiose claim that only one approach accurately re-presents reality necessarily denies the legitimacy of all other modes of explanation:

> A commanding position on the battleground of representation – one that denies the partial and fragmented conditions of vision by claiming to 'perceive' a total truth – is an illusionary place whose construction, motivated by wishes, entails hallucinations and hysterical blindness. It is a position constructed in a form of knowledge that produces total – unfragmented – subjects.

DEUTSCHE's comment on the difference between 'perception', which is the process of assembling material phenomena into recognizable forms, and 'vision', which is a socially constructed way of looking at the world, problematizes *any* claim toward accurate reflection of the real world. The image and the act of viewing are relations highly mediated by wishes, fantasies, etc. Within her conceptualization, there is no easy epistemological assumption that reality can be perceived once the ideological obfuscations of capitalism have been removed.

We can further problematize the ontological certainty underpinning this form of political economy by exploring the limitations placed on the concept of 'representation' within this approach. The term is used to indicate an image or symbol that, through its emplacement within a mode of communication, is presumed to provide either an accurate or false rendering of reality. Just as the researcher can, through the representational form of language, articulate an accurate or false portrayal of 'reality', so other producers can reveal, or obfuscate, that 'reality' through a variety of representational mediums such as film. The underlying presumption here is that language and other forms of communication are either transparent reflections of reality (accurate representations) or deliberately opaque (false representations). If we consider this conceptualization in explicitly semiotic terms, then the presumption being made is that a 'real' world object (the signified) is safely and securely rendered by a particular 'representation' (the signifier), and that there can be no confusion as to what that representation is indeed referring to.[5] This unproblematic link between signified and signifier can be considered the 'natural' state of affairs. Falsification occurs when the 'natural' link between signified and signifier is hidden, or dismissed; the signified is represented by the 'wrong' signifiers, which can now be considered (mis)representations (KLAK 1994; KRIM 1994).

The problematic nature of this ontological stance becomes clearer when we consider the ramifications of just such a claim to accurate representation. In regard to *Powaqqatsi*, if capitalism (the signified) is indeed truly rendered through the signification of it as exploitative, regimentative and inauthentic, then we must

---

5. This emphasis on the arbitrary association between signifieds and signifiers ensues from the work of SAUSSURE. In contrast to a traditional focus within semiotics on the origins of language – wherein it was presumed that the link between a word and its real world referent had been established in ancient times – SAUSSURE articulated the theory that each language was in fact a system to be analyzed in light of its structural character. SAUSSURE argued that words and other signs derive their value not from their referencing of real world objects, but from their difference to other signs. The real world objects labelled as 'trees', for example, could equally well be referenced by any other term. The word 'tree', therefore, derives its value from the difference that can be noted between it and another term such as 'shrub'. Within this approach, the focus of inquiry is directed toward the conventions by which the word 'tree' is maintained as an appropriate term for these real world objects.

presume that other 'realities' depicted in the film, such as *non*-capitalist Third World cultures, are also accurately rendered. If all manner of social ills are laid at the door of an expanding global economy, the construction of a traditional, peasant, rural idyll *must* then be valorized as constitutive of all of the opposite characteristics, i.e., harmony, rhythm and innocence, and of course, authenticity. In conflating all Third World cultures with a 'pure', environmentally harmonious way of life; however, we reiterate the colonial notion that Third World cultures are *non*-modern, *non*-technological – they are *of* the past. The major social cleavage produced and legitimized under colonialism – that between colonizer and colonized, First and Third World – is once again reiterated as *the* initial means of cataloguing humanity.

If the link between Third World societies (the signified) and terms such as 'primitive', 'authentic', and so on, is not a 'natural' one, but is rather the product of particular colonial practices; then the larger principle to be drawn is not that the link between signified and signifier is indeed arbitrary, but that the links that do emerge are themselves the product of, and productive of, social relations of power. With this principle in mind, a poststructuralist examination of the power of 'representation' can follow, as indeed will be shown in later sections. However, semiotics as a body of literature is also productive of its own structuralist logic, and it is this strand of thought that has invigorated our next topic, namely text-centered approaches to a geography of film.

TEXT-CENTERED APPROACHES: ENGAGING THE EXPERT READER

A text-centered approach assumes that the link between signifier and signified is actively constructed and maintained by 'real' world social relations of power. Such an approach, therefore, maintains two presumptions noted in the previous section, namely that there are originary (albeit complex) conditions out of which meaning emerges, and that there is a dichotomy between the 'real' and mere 'representation'. However, in further presuming that the linkages made between the real (the signified) and its representation (the signifier) are the product of artifice, the focus of inquiry shifts toward an examination of the textual strategies used to produce particular meanings. In effect, the text becomes a battleground: on the one side powerful social groups propose to 'accurately' represent reality, while on the other the researcher 'uncovers' the hypocrisy of such claims and points toward the 'true' state of affairs. In engaging the dominant ideologies embedded in textual forms such as film, the researcher becomes an 'expert reader', locating the obvious and the hidden, the true and the false, the message and the subtext. While such an analytic stance has usually been associated with a particular strand of political economy – one which recognizes the power of the symbolic in the constitution of social relations – in this section we go on to argue that it is also a feature of those textual-centered analyses that draw on the concept of 'intertextuality', a term usually associated with poststructuralism. This selective 'borrowing' is, in turn, productive of certain limitations in regard to an investigation of the social world.

The drive to interrogate the embeddedness and 'naturalization' of dominant ideologies in texts such as film has had an immense impact on those analyses which firmly place themselves within a structuralist rubric. In undertaking research on popular media, for example, BURGESS (1990) examines the means by which one side of a binary has been legitimized within the text, such that the audience is 'cued' to interpret meaning in particular ways. Using the work of HALL on the production and consumption of codes of meaning, BURGESS is at pains to point out that while the link between signified and signifier is arbitrary, there is an intent on behalf of the various producers of imagery to 'position' the reader such that they are liable to infer the intended 'message'. 'Framing' devices, intertextual references to other ideas and concepts and so on, have come increasingly under scrutiny by researchers interested in how the media 'works' (DER DERIAN 1992; STAM 1992; Ó'TUATHAIL 1993, 1994; SHARPE 1993; DALBY 1994; MACDONALD 1994). While capitalism has certainly remained a prime suspect in the production of such ideologies, other social structures, such as race and patriarchy, have also been posited as providing the originary moment out of which meaning emerges.

In the battle to uncover the means by which meaning is embedded in a text, an auxiliary tactic has been to actively harness the realm of the symbolic. Within this approach, there is a recognition of the fact that all real world processes are in fact articulated through symbolism, such that the expert reader can never actually succeed in uncovering the 'real' in and of itself. Rather, one can only use a representational form such as language to signify that underlying reality as persuasively as possible. As DANIELS (1989, 200–201) summarizes this pragmatic representation of meaning on behalf of a politically aware academia:

> In acknowledging the iconographic power and even constitution of society and social description, Western Marxists have been both iconoclastic – in attempting to dismantle the illusory power of images to reach an actual or at least authentic world, and idolatrous – in accepting that such a world is no longer tenable and that the appropriate strategy is to harness the power of imagery against capital or at least in a way that will make sense of its workings.

Examples of the latter tactic range from HARVEY's (1989) commentary on *Blade Runner* to NATTER and JONES' (1993) appraisal of *Roger and Me*. Within these analyses, not only are the cultural ramifications of an exploitative capitalism tellingly signified, but also the 'spaces' of resistance to be found within the chosen texts.

The "idolatry" noted by DANIELS can also, however, be found within another approach to film analysis, one that is usually associated with a poststructuralist school of thought. Drawing inspiration from the work of BARTHES and DERRIDA, geographers such as AITKEN (1991, 1993) have pointed out the varied 'subtexts' embedded within symbolic media. Within this conceptualization of 'representation' there is no simple origin to ideology, but rather a host of overlapping discourses that play off each other in new combinations. Importantly, however, these discourses are shaped according to the wishes and demands of the dominant groups in society. In the act of producing, and reading, texts, the meanings that can be achieved through the combination of associations are infinite. The term 'intertextuality' captures this constantly fluid movement from one meaning to another through a wide variety of social texts that make up our world. To put this in semiotic terms, signifiers do not reference underlying signifieds, but rather other signifiers, such that meaning is always in process; meaning is but a temporary stop in a continuing flow of interpretations of interpretations. It is only when a sign is located in a context and read in a context that there is a temporary halt to the endless play of signifier and signifier (BARTHES 1985). Even here, though, context cannot fully control meaning precisely because neither is fully present. Meaning will resonate throughout other contexts, brought into play by the very act of reading.

Given this intertextuality, or fluidity of meaning, the presumption can be retained that social structures operating in the 'real' world govern the production and consumption of such meanings, effectively 'fixing' them in the 'reel' world. In focusing their attention on 'subtexts', film geographers are locating what are perceived to be the results of these power relations, as some associations between signifiers are made to appear 'natural' or commonsensical within the film, thereby rendering them invisible to the non-expert reader. As with a political economic text-centered approach, therefore, images are regarded as the embodiment of real world power relations – the difference being that geographers such as AITKEN (1991, 1993) and ROSE (1994) point to the operation of a host of social structures including capitalism, patriarchy and race. In consequence, there can be no simple delineation of a dominant ideology within texts; there are instead intersecting, conflated and at times oppositional 'subtexts' that must be uncovered if their power is to be defused.

Film analysis, then, becomes a matter not of exposing the original intent behind various 'messages', but rather of deconstructing the ways in which the message itself articulates particular commonsense notions. For AITKEN (1993) and AITKEN and ZONN (1993), deconstruction proceeds via the identification of couplets or binaries. Within these couplets, such as male and female, or good and bad, one side is valued over the other through its association with particular connotations. The valued side is considered fully 'present', in that it is the origin for defining what is *not* it, or in other words, what is the 'other', or mere supplement. Poststructuralist empirics become a matter of breaching the 'closed' character of an intentional meaning or message in order to reveal their artificial (i.e., socially constructed) character. That which has been designated as 'privileged', e.g., the masculine, the rational, the reasoned, and the ordered, must be overthrown via the uncovering within the text of their simultaneously excluded and subsumed others, the feminine, the irrational, the unreasonable, and the chaotic.

By way of application, our own expert reading of *Powaqqatsi* locates those 'hidden' binaries (Figure 1.) proposed by AITKEN and ZONN (1993) amongst others, noting the ways in which various associations have been made within the film between real world objects and particular representations. We begin in a Moroccan setting of desert colors, as the camera follows a woman in flowing bright red robes slowly enters a walled village; the camera stays outside the walls but moves to the left in order to follow her progress. Once she disappears, the camera slowly circles around more walls until another entrance is reached, whereupon it slowly and hesitantly enters. In our rural idyll, the villages consist of enclosure within enclosure, all colored from the brown earth and nestled between the folds of gently rounded hills. The statuesque curves of the terraced fields mirror the meandering rivers below. Everything, it seems, is formed out of circles. The swaying bodies of

Figure 1. Locating the Subtexts in Powaqqatsi

The Supplemental		The Fully Present
female	-------	male
nature	-------	culture
tradition	-------	progress
sexuality	-------	lust
pure	-------	corrupt
community	-------	individuation
freedom	-------	regimentation

women are swathed in flowing garments, while the strong-limbed bodies of men cleave through the elements – earth, sea and wind – cutting a pathway forward. The women carry receptacles, the men carry knives, sticks, a rudder.

The parasitic tendrils of a rapidly expanding capitalist economy transform men into drudges, laboring day after day in vast complexes of machinery and earthworks. The villages are now the provenance of women and children, as families become scattered across space. Railway tracks and highways cut across the landscape while planes fly in and out of cities: the movement of goods and people, commodities all, seems endless. Our introduction to the market places and residences of the towns and cities is via an increasing number of angles – square fields, square houses – until at last the edifices of churches, office blocks and apartment buildings reach into the sky, the camera gazing upward in awe. The apartment houses are now so high they seem to loom, forcing the surrounding mountains to become a mere backdrop in comparison. The city lights up in neon as goods and people continue to flash across the screen. Within the city, advertisements crowd in, selling hair products and make-up; with the arrival of these First World icons natural sexuality gives way to artificial lust and longing. Individual movement is no longer a natural expression, but has become a regimented posture as bands of soldiers and young girls march through the streets.

Given this textual reading of the signifiers present in *Powaqqatsi*, how do we proceed to uncover and defuse the subtexts embedded here? To begin we might note that while the producers of the film have recognized and combated the 'commonsense' discourse that links the signifiers of capitalism, progress, equality, and beneficence, they have also *un*problematically incorporated various 'subtexts'. For example, no matter what area of the world is being displayed within *Powaqqatsi*, there is a continuing dichotomy between female and male spaces. Women work in the villages, the place of home and hearth, while men till the fields and navigate the rivers. Furthermore, through the association of the bodies of women with the hills and valleys of the countryside, the discourse by which women are portrayed as 'of nature', rather than 'civilization', is maintained (see AITKEN and ZONN 1993, for further explication of this forceful stereotype). One might argue that it is the blatant presence of these associations that give them power: presented as unproblematically 'natural' ways of thinking about the world, these associations are *sub*texts in the sense that they are almost, but not quite, beyond question. Indeed, it is only the expert reader who can locate and identify them as such.

While the impulse to open up commonsensical or naturally given meanings to critical scrutiny is a laudable one, from a poststructuralist viewpoint there are certain limitations within this text-centered approach. Within these analyses, meanings are taken as intrinsically fluid in the 'reel' world, the realm of the symbolic. There remains the presumption, however, that a fixed power relationship between dominant and subordinate subjects exists in the 'real' world. Intertextuality, or the deferral of an 'absolute' meaning, has been limited to the screen. The presumption of a stable, or *fixed*, power relationship between 'central' and 'othered' discourses, therefore, relies on a form of structuralism, whereby certain social relations of dominance and subordination 'fix' the subject position of individuals.

The ramifications of this structuralism become more apparent if we consider the conceptualization of the 'subject' that ensues from such a stance. In the work of some feminists, for example, the binary opposition of male-female is *the* focus of film research: the filmic privileging of the former is taken as a fixed, or determined, power relation that merely re-inscribes patriarchal relations in the real world (MULVEY 1975, 1981; KUHN 1982, 1985, 1990; DE LAURETIS 1984). As a result, the female viewer is forced into insubordinate, or surreptitious, glances that seek to avoid this patriarchal rendering of the feminine (GAINES 1988; GAMMAN and MARSHMENT 1989). The problem here is not that such a conceptualization of the subject is necessarily 'incorrect', but rather that the results of one's film analysis are wholly *expected*; that is, not only is the identification of subtexts a product of the researchers' own assessment of the present status of real world power relations, but also there is no room within this approach for representations to transform or challenge one's presumption of what those real world relations are. The dichotomy presumed by text-centered approaches between the 'real' and its mere 'representation' is one of causal connection: the real governs the non-real. From a poststructuralist viewpoint, this binary must itself be problematized.

One entry point by which this deconstruction can proceed is via the largely undertheorized concept of 'looking'. As CORRIGAN (1991) suggests, the relationship between viewer and image, the 'real' and the 'reel' world, is itself a socially mediated process, and as such is a product of diverse relations of domination and subordination. The privileged place of the 'expert' viewer, for example, is the product of a particular Western conflation of 'objective' observation with the role of the 'academic' (GREGORY 1994; JONES 1995) – a conflation that has legitimized, and thereby facilitated the maintenance of, a voyeuristic relationship between 'First' and 'Third' World. As SPIVAK (1988) notes, voyeurism is a power relation that constitutes, and is constituted by, the viewer and the viewed: while the latter are certainly rendered 'visible' by expert accounts such as film analyses, they are present *within* the expert's economies of signification. It is toward a theorization of the relation between viewer and viewed that the next section turns.

READER-CENTERED APPROACHES: LOCATING THE OTHER

A reader-centered approach focuses on the means by which meaning is perceived, or "poached" (DE CERTEAU 1984, 174), from the text. Within this mode of reading, viewing is conceived of as a fluid process of appropriation, resistance and selection of images – a process that allows the viewer to become their own authority (CORRIGAN 1991). Indeed, it is through this appropriation that the discursive power relations within which the viewer is embedded are re-negotiated. Rather than presume fixed dominant and subordinate subject positions, therefore, this mode of reading emphasizes the myriad discourses each 'subject' is engaged within (ECO 1979; CORRIGAN 1991). It is the *diversity* of audience reception that becomes the focus of inquiry.

While a reader-centered approach is usually associated with an idealist stance in regard to the essential uniqueness of individual world views, we argue that this mode of reading also incorporates those approaches that lay claim to 'decenter' the subject, an impulse drawn from poststructuralism. In following through the reader-centered mode of analysis – that is, an appreciation of the socially mediated reception of meaning – it is the production of subjectivity that becomes the locus for reconceptualization and analysis. We would agree that this task is indeed critical, for it raises an issue all too often taken for granted: that is, the means by which 'personality', 'behavior' and 'self' are constructed from social relations of power. As noted earlier in regard to both author- and text-centered approaches these concepts have generally been taken as the product of dominant ideologies, or hegemonies, wherein the individual's imagined relationship with society, or 'place in the world', is constituted from existent norms and mores. At the basis of this formulation is a commitment to real world structures, or conditions of existence, directing the formulation and implementation of such ideologies. Where a reader-centered approach breaches this formulation is in its emphasis on the multiplicity of discourses each individual is interpellated by, such that there is no one 'subject position' to be held by an individual, but rather multiple, and conflicting, positionalities. This multiplicity is furthered by the interposition of dominant discourses with the unconscious – an insight that has revived interest in geography's engagement with psychoanalysis (PILE 1993). In a reader-centered approach, then, it is the multitude, and intersection, of economies of signification that becomes the object of interest.

By way of exposition, the following is a reading of *Powaqqatsi* by a group of thirty university students in a junior-level environmental perception course. The students were given one week to complete the following: write a three to five page paper describing your images of the film, distinguish its basic themes, and identify what the title has to do with the film. The fact that the film consists of a collage-like series of images unlike most cinematic experiences was noted by almost all students. The perceived themes of the movie were quite varied. Certainly, everyone was cognizant of the fact that this was a film about the less developed world, but the similarities ended there. Most of the perceived themes, however, fell into one of the following categories, listed in order of the frequency with which they were cited:

(1) human-environment relations and the impact of technology,
(2) the nature of work and survival,
(3) movement,
(4) culture and values,
(5) children, gender and the nature of the family.

As can be seen from Table 1, the role of technology in transforming the human-environment relationship was a prominent theme, stated both in general terms and in regard to the technological superiority of the First World. Many students mentioned the fact that people could be seen walking throughout the film, while the scene that focussed for a full minute upon a train passing through the countryside was noted by several, particularly in terms of the symbolism of technology in a physical wasteland. The nature of family, especially children, was noted on occasion, while gender was infrequently noticed as an element of the less developed world. The role of women in society was specifically addressed by only one student. In regard to *powaqqatsi*, the entity that consumes all in order to further its own life, technology and change were the most often-cited culprits, while the role of individuals and groups as the cause of change were mentioned on occasion. A few were explicit in their characterization of the developed world as *powaqqatsi*.

Table 1. A Class Reading of Powaqqatsi *(Part 1)*

Format:

"In a way it reminds me of the movie *Lawnmower Man*, and the flashing images that teach you things at a faster rate."

"... the 'images' of the geographic 'places' replaced the dialogue and told their own story... The viewer must literally 'think' about the messages being portrayed as if they were reading a script instead of seeing the images."

Major Issues:

(1) Human-Environment Relations and the Impacts of Technology:

"By using silent images, the director allows the audience to obtain their own personal and unique perception of the relationship between technology and culture."

"... technology is miraculous all over the developed worlds, while the Third world is left in dust. It is like they are forgotten. They cannot hang with the rest of the powerful countries."

(2) The Nature of Work and Survival:

"One of the obvious images is that manual labor overwhelms the life of many in these less developed regions ... everyone in the family works, including the children."

"The movie ... is basically about the different ways of life on our planet ... about showing how hard the less fortunate people in this world work and that the people who are better off should be more grateful for what they have."

Table 1. A Class Reading of Powaqqatsi *(Part 2)*

---

(3) Movement:

"I was especially awe-struck by the overall continuance of movement of everything in the movie ... the people who were carrying things seemed to dance for the camera. The water scenes seemed to have rhythm. Even the aerial scenes had rhythm. Everything moved to ultimately keep your attention."

(4) Culture and Values:

"They have nothing, but they have so much inside. They are not trying to keep up with the Jones'."

"... it did not appear to be all that bad, there seemed to be some beauty within their environment and within the cultures itself. Even though they live in relative poverty they keep their culture ... The physical labor doesn't stop their work, as their cultural celebration is portrayed by dancing and chanting rituals."

(5) Children, Gender and the Nature of the Family:

"One of the main themes in this movie was the burden which is put on children in less developed regions of the world..."

"Families tend to stay together throughout their entire lives. They work, eat, sleep, and entertain each other day after day. Families of the Third World seem to have very strong morals and beliefs."

"Many times they showed young girls working much like their mothers... but on the other end of the spectrum, the boys were running around and having fun... This aspect of the movie confused me... Both the men and women worked as they were older but the boys got to play while the girls did the manual labor."

Defining *Powaqqatsi*:

"The essence of a people's culture and beliefs are being sacrificed for the spread of technology in lesser developed nations."

"A person cannot progress through technological advances, and at the same time totally keep the heritage."

"... we humans are the consumers of Mother Earth and all she has to offer. However, we as humans also consume each other, the poor people in a Third World country work for their overlords as human mules, which makes a twisted government or the few wealthy people even richer, who, in turn feed the fully developed countries that have an insatiable hunger for more."

"The definition ... I believe deals with the exploitation of the Third World by the wealthier nations of the world. The entity in this case would be the wealthier nations. The consumption would then be how those wealthier nations use the resources of the Third World for their benefit and prosperity. Although aid is given to the Third World by many countries the overall repression toward the Third World will always exist so that the rich can get richer, thus making themselves more powerful."

"The United States and other first world countries use these under developed countries as guinea pigs. Whether or not that is wrong depends on the individual and his / her feeling towards Third World cultures."

Granted that each student has 'poached' images from the film and re-presented meaning in their own 'individual' fashion, the question arises as to how we subsequently interpret and contextualize such readings? One reader-centered approach that explicitly critiques the modernist presumption of an integrated, conscious, rational self, or subject, has been articulated by AITKEN and ZONN (1993, 1994). As they explain their Lacanian approach, the self is fragmented at an early age as a sense of 'identity' emerges; this identity is not predicated, however, in the conscious realization of an inner being, but rather in the unconscious dependence on socially mediated symbols for the expression of that identity. While the conscious mind (the realm of the Imaginary) presumes a transparent reality, the unconscious desires to locate identity within the Symbolic order, which consists of modes of discourse such as language. Because symbols can never actually 'contain' meaning, this desire can never be fulfilled, but must always be deferred. In consequence, while the Symbolic order can provide a sense of self *awareness*, the self is constantly in search of new 'moments' within that order by which its identity can be fully expressed. The self is in search of the 'Other'; that is, those fragments of meaning that express the self, but are produced within the social realm. It is because films are purportedly representations of reality, or real modes of existence, that the viewer seeks within the reel world those lost fragments, selecting out image-events that heighten a sense of belonging to the real world. As the audience watches, such moments on screen the reel and the real worlds are combined. The reel / real world becomes an arena wherein the othered fragments of identity can be re-appropriated, at least while the lights are down. For AITKEN and ZONN (1993), textual analysis becomes a means of tracing the presence of those Other, socially produced, fragments, and noting the ways in which they are re-presented on the screen for audience consumption (see also ZONN and AITKEN 1994).

Within this theorization of the production of subjectivity there remains, however, more than a trace of structuralism. Importantly, for Lacan, the Other is signified by the female, in that the first instance of detachment or decentering occurs when the bond between mother and child is broken by the presence of the Father, who evokes the Symbolic order: the search for the Other, then, is a nostalgic desire for that intimate bond. Because this bond can never be re-attained, the feminine as a form of identity can also never be fully achieved. To put this another way, there is no essential identity that can be located and labelled 'feminine', but rather a continuous deferral of the feminine ideal. As feminist writers have pointed out, such a theorization may be poststructuralist in the sense that it is anti-essentialist; however, feminine identities are always considered the Other, or abnormal in some manner (see STACEY 1993, for a summary of this argument). Furthermore, male identities are considered as constituting the Symbolic order, wherein meaning is assessed, articulated and used in a 'rational' manner. Patriarchy, then, consists of much more than mere real world power relations between men and women; it is both a product of, and productive of, our conscious and unconscious notions of 'male' and 'female'. As such, patriarchy as a social structure not only operates across the boundary between 'psyche' and 'reality' – through its role in the production of identity patriarchy is necessary to the very notion of a boundary between 'self' and the world.

In sharp contrast to an idealist approach to reader responses, therefore, an approach that focuses attention on the decentering of the subject must take account of those *socially produced* symbols embedded within the text that evoke meaning for the reader. While the lost bond with the Mother cannot be attained, the self desires and seeks out substitutes for this identity. In semiotic terms, the Symbolic order becomes an endless chain of signifiers, each signifying both the lack of, and the possibility of, identity. These signifiers are, in turn, produced through socially mediated discourses (or, as PILE 1993, terms them, "semiotic laws") on the nature of race, class and, of course, patriarchy. There is no *one* determining hegemonic discourse fixing the subjectivity of individuals. Rather, each empirical instance is an exemplar of the intersection of these semiotic laws within which identities are fixed as either dominant or subordinate. As noted in the previous section, this theorization of the subject is not necessarily incorrect – rather, it is problematic in the sense that there are no surprises to be gained from this type of analysis. As with the expert reader of texts, the expert interpreter of readers must project broad-scale ideologies – 'objectivism', 'racism', 'scientism' and so on – into the analyses of their subjects. These analyses must then be conceived of as mere *responses* to the imposition of those broad-scale ideologies. In place of the one reader duped by capitalism, we have multiple subjects enmeshed in a complex web of semiotic laws.

Finally, in regard to studies that focus on the unique intersection of ideologies in the conscious / unconscious mind of individuals, we interject the cautionary note that the epistemological foundation for these ideologies, or 'shared' discourses, has been presumed rather than posited – an elision that by default invokes the specter of structuralism. The notion of broad-scale ideologies, or semiotic laws, necessitates the presumption of fixed power relations operating to produce dominant discourses. While the intent of such approaches may have been to undermine the determinism of ALTHUSSER's concept of ideology, such reader-centered approaches undermine the concept of center-margin, but only through the *multiplication* of center-margin relations throughout society. The presumption that a structural relation exists between centered and marginalized subject positions is actually retained.

CONCLUSION: A *POST*STRUCTURALIST RESEARCH AGENDA

It would seem from our reassessment of the major analytical stances toward a geography of film that, from a poststructuralist perspective, there is no easy or safe reading of this or indeed any textual form. This is because each of the readings we have illustrated rely on, and reinforce, certain structuralist presumptions concerning the character of social relations. More specifically, each mode of reading points toward a particular way in which power is deployed in a unidirectional manner within a social totality, such that one can assess how and why the roles of the dominant and the dominated are produced. To conceive of film as a mere ideological tool, for example, as do author-centered approaches, is to presume a society wherein power is a matter of coercion and persuasion between autonomous, or Cartesian, subjects, linked by their participation within a shared, hegemonic, discourse. Similarly, if we locate the various 'subtexts' within media, as do text-centered approaches, we must then assess not only the question of how such meanings are produced though a variety of shared discourses, but also of how 'real' world power relations govern those meanings considered 'given', or 'commonsense'. While reader-centered approaches decenter the notion of a Cartesian subject, the presumption concerning shared discourses is retained on the basis that such interactions are part and parcel of the Symbolic order to which all individuals must ascribe.

From a poststructuralist vantage point, the limitations established within these forms of analyses stem from the basic premise all make that there indeed exists a social 'totality'. Such approaches recognize that all meanings and identities are relational in the sense that there is no essential core to either: meanings and identities are symbols, located and defined according to their difference from other symbols. However, while the arbitrary character of all meanings and identities has been taken as a given, the presumption has then been made that the association between signifier and signified (in case of author-centered approaches) and signifier and signifier (in the case of text- and reader-centered approaches) is not only fixed, at least temporarily, but also communicated *in the same form to all members of society*. To put this another way, a social totality is actually the product *of* the effective transfer of these associations within symbolic modes of communication such as film. Critical analyses of symbolic texts must then revolve around the questions of which discourses are being deployed, how they are being effectively transferred, and to the benefit of whom?

We would suggest that the ontological presumptions underpinning these questions, while laudable in intent, have led to a theoretical and methodological cul de sac in regard to the critical analysis of 'representation' and 'power'. Within the methodologies discussed, the focus of inquiry always proceeds from an existing 'shared' discourse, that may be uncritically consumed, negotiated or transgressed by the everyday reader, or actively uncovered and defused by the expert reader. How, then, can we reach beyond this current conceptualization of a geography of film, locating new research thresholds? How can we proceed to a poststructuralist reading of film as well as other modes of commnication? At a theoretical level, we can problematize the notion of a shared discourse by pointing to the work of DERRIDA (1978a, 1978b), wherein the recognition of the relational character of all symbols leads him to argue that there is no 'center' and 'margin' within discourses, but rather a constantly shifting 'constitutive outside'. DERRIDA suggests that the 'difference' between meanings initially noted by SAUSSURE is not the creation of a 'space' in between things, for such a notion would retain the illusion that ideas and elements of the material world can be defined in relation only to themselves. Meanings can only be defined in relation to what they are not. Because this absence (what is not) is essential to the construction of meaning, it is present as a 'trace' within meaning, hidden by the seeming 'presence' of the thing or idea in question. This concept of the required presence and absence of the other is summed up in DERRIDA's use of the term "constitutive outside". For DERRIDA, it is only through this embeddedness, or incorporation of the other, that a communication system can actually operate, because it allows for the process of differentiation to take place between what would otherwise be wholly disparate elements. Given this constitutive outside to all signifiers, there can be no simply derived realtionship between central and marginal meanings (or as AITKEN 1993, would put it, 'text' and 'subtext'). As FOUCAULT (1980, 100) notes:

> ... we must not imagine a world of discourse divided between accepted discourse and excluded discourse, or between the dominant discourse and the dominated one; but as a multiplicity of discursive elements that can come into play in various strategies.

Furthermore, from this perspective, the temporary 'fixing' of signifiers in relation to each other is not only a losing battle, but merely one tactic possible in using signifiers to communicate meaning. Alternate strategies, such as allegory and irony, rely on the proliferation of meanings, as the possible associations between signifiers proceed toward infinity. For DIXON and JONES (1996, 769), the arbitrary character of the moments embedded in any system of thought can be exposed through the practice of allegory, which refuses to take any meaning as fixed or stable. Using a Derridean understanding of communication, they argue that:

> As the endless conveyance of meaning from one context to another, allegory generates an potentially infinite number of associations between narratives, thereby deliberately refusing the rigidification of categorical designations, fixed meanings, and literal truth. Thus, while any one narrative may presume to fix meaning as "literal" ... the practice of allegory disrupts these certainties by bringing the narrative into play with that of another. As a consequence, under allegory no narrative can retain its fixed and essential character, thus providing the allegoricist with insight into the construction of meaning and the oppositional traces it relies upon.

DERRIDA also provides the inspiration for DOEL (1993) and DOEL and CLARKE's (1996) ironic commentary on the nature of the 'real' and 'representation'. The impetus behind their deployment of irony is not critical detatchment, as SMITH (1996) has suggested, but a progressive politics wherein meaning is constantly unhinged from any and all fixed moorings. Within their work, irony is the vehicle by which a constant transfer of signifiers between localized discursive communities takes place. These communities are linked not by a 'shared' understanding of terms, but through the production and recognition of a proliferation of associations between signifiers and, thereby, meanings.

Both allegory and irony, therefore, are becoming legitimate research strategies, as well as objects of analysis, for academics. There remains, however, a strong prejudice against the using of these and similar forms of anlaysis – a prejudice based on the notion that the goal of academic research into 'representation' is the uncovering and re-presentation of 'shared' discourses. Dismissed as mere 'postmodern' forms of play, allegorical and ironic methodologies have been berated for their lack of an obvious (that is, fixed) meaning (see, for example, critiques launched by JAMESON 1981, 1992, 1993, 1995, and in Geography by BEAUREGARD 1988, and HARVEY 1989, 1992, 1993). As we have argued, this critique is unnecessarily dismissive, in that it is underpinned by a structuralist commitment to the notion of a social 'totality'. If research into representation and power is to reach new thresholds, the limitations established by structuralism must be problematized and overcome. In sum, there must be the recognition that the much heralded "crisis of representation" (see, for example, the debate by COSGROVE 1994, and DEAR

1994) bemoaned by those still adhering to the 'commonsense' status of structuralist research is no crisis at all, but rather an exploration of the diverse forms of inquiry and explanation available to researchers.

REFERENCES

AITKEN, S.C. (1991): A transactional geography of the image-event: the films of Scottish director, Bill Forsyth. *Transactions of the Institute of British Geographers*, N.S. 16, 105–118.
AITKEN, S.C. (1993): I'd Rather Watch the Movie than Read the Book. *Journal of Geography in Higher Education* 18 (3), 291–307.
AITKEN, S.C. and L.E. ZONN (1993): Wier(d) sex: representation of gender-environment relations in Peter Weir's Picnic at Hanging Rock and Gallipoli. *Environment and Planning D: Society and Space* 11 (2), 191–212.
AITKEN, S.C. and L.E. ZONN (1994): Re-Presenting the Place Pastiche. AITKEN, S.C. and L.E. ZONN (Eds.): *Place, Power, Situation and Spectacle*. Savage, Maryland, 3–25.
ALTHUSSER, L. (1971): Ideology and Ideological State Apparatuses'. *Lenin and Philosophy and other Essays*. London, 121–173.
BARNES, T. and J. DUNCAN (Eds.) (1992): *Writing Worlds: Discourse, Text and Metaphor in the Representation of Landscape*. New York.
BARTHES, R. (1985): Day by Day with Roland Barthes. BLONSKY, M. (Ed.): *On Signs*. London, 98–117.
BEAUREGARD, R.A. (1988): In the absence of practice: the locality research debate. *Antipode* 20 (1), 52–59.
BOWDEN, M.J. (1994): Jerusalem, Dover Beach, and King's Cross: Imagined Places as Metaphors of the British Class Struggle in Chariots of Fire and The Loneliness of the Long-Distance Runner. AITKEN, S.C. and L.E. ZONN (Eds.): *Place, Power, Situation and Spectacle*. Savage, Maryland, 69–100.
BURGESS, J. (1985): News From Nowhere: the press, the riots and the myth of the inner city. BURGESS, J. and J.R. GOLD (Eds.): *Geography, The Media and Popular Culture*. Kent, 192–228.
BURGESS, J. (1990): The production and consumption of environmental meanings in the mass media: a research agenda for the 1990s. *Transactions of the Institute of British Geographers* 15 (2), 139–161.
CORRIGAN, T. (1991): *A Cinema Without Walls: Movies and Culture After Vietnam*. New Brunswick.
COSGROVE, D. (1994): Postmodern Tremblings: A Reply to Michael Dear. *Annals of the Association of American Geographers* 84, 305–307.
DALBY, S. (1994): Gender and critical geopolitics: reading security discourse in the new world disorder. *Environment and Planning D: Society and Space* 12, 595–612.
DANIELS, S. (1989): Marxism, culture and the duplicity of landscape. PEET, R. and N. THRIFT (Eds.): *New Models in Geography*. London, 196–220.
DE CERTEAU, M. (1984): *The Practice of Everyday Life*. Berkeley.
DE LAURETIS, T. (1984): *Alice Doesn't: Feminism, Semiotics and Cinema*. Bloomington.
DEAR, M. (1994): Who's Afraid of Postmodernism?: Reflections on Symanski and Cosgrove. *Annals of the Association of American Geographers* 84, 295–300.
DEMPSEY, M. (1989): Quatsi Means Life: The Films of Godfrey Reggio. *Film Quarterly* 42, 2 12.
DER DERIAN, J. (1992): *Anti-Diplomacy: Spies, Terror, Speed and War*. Oxford.
DERRIDA, J. (1978a): *Positions*. London.
DERRIDA, J. (1978b): *Of Grammatology*. Baltimore.
DEUTSCHE, R. (1990): Men in Space. *Strategies* 3, 130–137.
DEUTSCHE, R. (1991): Boys Town. *Environment and Planning D: Society and Space* 9, 5–30.

DIXON, D. and J.P. JONES (1996): For a Supercalifragilisticexpialidocious Scientific Geography. *Annals of the Association of American Geographers* 86, 767–779.
DOEL, M. (1993): Proverbs for paranoids: writing geography on hollowed ground. *Transactions of the Institute of British Geographers* 18 (3), 377–394.
DOEL, M. and D. CLARKE (1996): *A night at the movies: the virtual, psychoanalysis, and everyday life*. Paper presented at the Institute of British Geographers Annual Conference, University of Strathclyde in Glasgow, January.
ECO, U. (1979): *The Role of the Reader: Explorations in the Semiotics of Texts*. Bloomington.
FOLCH-SERRA, M. (1990): Place, Voice and Space: Mikhail Bakhtin's Dialogical Landscape. *Environment and Planning D: Society and Space* 8, 255–274.
FOUCAULT, M. (1980): *Power / Knowledge*. New York.
GAINES, J. (1988): White Privilege and Looking Relations: Race and Gender in Feminist Film theory. *Screen* 29 (4), 12–27.
GAMMAN, L. and M. MARSHMENT (1989): *The Female Gaze: Women as Viewers of Popular Culture*. Seattle.
GODFREY, B.J. (1993): Regional Depiction in Contemporary Film. *The Geographical Review* 83 (4), 428–440.
GOLD, J.R. (1985): From Metropolis to The City: Film Visions of the Future City, 1919–39. BURGESS, J. and J.R. GOLD (Eds.): *Geography, The Media and Popular Culture*. Kent, 123–143.
GREGORY, D. (1994): *Geographical Imaginations*. London.
HANNA, S.P. (1996): Is it Roslyn or is it Cicely? Representation and the Ambiguity of Place. *Urban Geography* 17, 633–649.
HARVEY, D. (1989): *The Condition of Postmodernity*. London.
HARVEY, D. (1992): Postmodern morality plays. *Antipode* 24 (4), 300–326.
HARVEY, D. (1993): From space to place and back again: Reflections on the condition of postmodernity. BIRD, J et al. (Eds.): *Mapping the Futures: Local Cultures, Global Change*. London, New York, 2–29.
HORKHEIMER, M. and T.W. ADORNO (1973): *Dialectic of the Enlightenment*. London.
HOPKINS, J. (1994): Mapping of Cinematic Places: Icons, Ideology, and the Power of (Mis)representation. AITKEN, S.C. and L.E. ZONN (Eds.): *Place, Power, Situation and Spectacle*. Savage, Maryland, 47–65.
JAMESON, F.R. (1981): *The Political Unconscious: Narrative as a Socially Symbolic Act*. Ithaca.
JAMESON, F.R. (1992): *Signatures of the Visible*. New York.
JAMESON, F.R. (1993): Postmodernism, or the cultural logic of late capitalism. DOCHERTY, T. (Ed.): *Postmodernism: A Reader*. New York, 312–332.
JAMESON, F.R. (1995): *The GeoPolitical Aesthetic: Cinema and Space in the World System*. Indiana.
JONES, J.P. (1995): Making geography objectively: occularity, representation and The Nature of Geography. NATTER, W., T. SCHATZKI and J.P. JONES (Eds.): *Objectivity and its Other*. New York.
JONES, J.P., W. NATTER and T. SCHATZKI (Eds.) (1993): *Beyond Modernity? Postmodernism, Politics and Space*. New York.
KLAK, T. (1994): Havana and Kingston: mass media images and empirical observations of two Caribbean cities in crisis. *Urban Geography* 15 (4), 318–344.
KRIM, A. (1994): Filming Route 66: Documenting the Dust Bowl Highway. AITKEN, S.C. and L.E. ZONN (Eds.): *Place, Power, Situation and Spectacle*. Savage, Maryland.
KUHN, A. (1982): *Women's Pictures: Feminism and Cinema*. London.
KUHN, A. (1985): *Power of the Image: Essays on Representation and Sexuality*. New York.
KUHN, A. (Ed.) (1990): *Women in Film: an International Guide*. New York.
MACDONALD, G.M. (1994): Third Cinema and the Third World. AITKEN, S.C. and L.E. ZONN (Eds.): *Place, Power, Situation and Spectacle*. Savage, Maryland, 27–46.
MANVELL, R. (1956): Geography and the Documentary Film. *The Geographical Magazine* 29, 417–422.

Marcuse, H. (1972): *Counter-Revolution and Revolt*. Boston.
Massey, D. (1991): Flexible Sexism. *Environment and Planning D: Society and Space* 9, 31–57.
Mulvey, L. (1975): Visual Pleasure and Narrative Cinema. *Screen* 16 (3), 6–18.
Mulvey, L. (1981): Afterthoughts on 'Visual Pleasure and Narrative Cinema' inspired by Duel in the Sun. *Framework* 6, 12–15.
Natter, W. (1994): The City as Cinematic Space: Modernism and Place in Berlin, Symphony of a City. Aitken, S.C. and L.E. Zonn (Eds.): *Place, Power, Situation and Spectacle*. Boston, 203–228.
Natter, W. and J.P. Jones (1993): Pets or Meat: Class, Ideology and Space in Roger and Me. *Antipode* 25 (2), 140–158.
Nicholson, D. (1991): Images of Reality. *The Geographical Magazine* 63 (4), 28–32.
Ó'Tuathail, G. (1993): The Effacement of Place? US Foreign Policy and the Spatiality of the Gulf. *Antipode* 25, 4–31.
Ó'Tuathail, G. (1994): (Dis)placing geopolitics: writing on the maps of global politics. *Environment and Planning D: Society and Space* 12, 525–546.
Philo, C. (1992): Foucault's Geography. *Environment and Planning D: Society and Space* 10, 137–161.
Pile, S. (1993): Human Agency and Human Geography Revisited: A Critique of "New Models". *Transactions of the Institute of British Geographers* 18 (1), 122–139.
Rose, G. (1994): The Cultural Politics of Place: Local Representations and Oppositional Discourse in Two Films. *Transactions of the Institute of British Geographers* 19 (1), 46–60.
Shapiro, M.J. (1992): *Reading the postmodern polity: political theory as textual practice*. Minneapolis.
Sharpe, J.P. (1993): Publishing American Identity: popular geopolitics, myth and the Readers Digest. *Political Geography* 12, 491–503.
Smith, J. (1996): Geographical Rhetoric: Modes and Tropes of Appeal. *Annals of the Association of American Geographers* 86 (1), 1–23.
Soja, E. (1989): *Postmodern Geographies: The Reassertion of Space in the Social Sciences*. London.
Soja, E. (1991): Heterotopologies: A Remembrance of Other Spaces in the Citadel-LA. *Strategies* 3, 6–39.
Spivak, G. (1988): *In Other Worlds: Essays in Cultural Politics*. New York.
Stacey, J. (1993): Textual Obsessions: methodology, history and researching female spectatorship. *Screen* 34 (3): 260–274.
Stam, R. (1992): Mobilizing fictions: the Gulf War, the media and the recruitment of the spectator. *Public Culture* 4, 101–126.
Wright, B. (1956): Geography and the Documentary film: Britain, since 1945. *The Geographical Magazine* 29, 586–595.
Zonn, L.E. (1984): Images of Place: A Geography of the Media. *Proceedings of the Royal Geographical Society of Australia* 84, 35–45.
Zonn, L.E. and S.C. Aitken (1994): Of Pelicans and Men: Symbolic Landscapes, Gender, and Australia's Storm Boy. Aitken, S.C. and L.E. Zonn (Eds.): *Place, Power, Situation and Spectacle*. Boston, 137–159.

THE AUTHOR

Joseph Palis

AN UNMAPPED PEOPLE AND PLACES: CINEMA, NATION AND THE AESTHETICS OF AFFECTION

> *This is when cinema becomes interesting to me, when it stops being the representation of something and becomes the thing itself*
>
> (Walter SALLES 1998).

> *Nations, like narrative, lose their origins in the myths of time and only fully realize their horizons in the mind's eye*
>
> (Homi BHABHA, "Nation and Narration", 1990).

A ROAD MAP: INTRODUCTION

In 1990, President Fernando Collor de Mello suddenly suspended the finances of Brazil "with a stroke of his neo-liberal pen" (JOHNSON 2000, 1). Embrafilme, the state-owned production and distribution company, became one of the casualties of this decision and was promptly dismantled (NAGIB 2007; SHAW 2007). For the next few years after that, Brazilian cinema, which had alternately seen a cinematic plateau and resurgence in terms of production, suddenly hit what Lucia NAGIB calls a "cinema's real year zero" (2007, viii). In 1995, with the return of the democratic government and the institution of a nationally elected president, Fernando Henrique Cardoso, Brazil experienced a renewed vigor in filmic outputs. Although this renewal never fully developed nor fulfilled its early promise, it nevertheless provided new opportunities for filmmakers to engage in international collaboration. One successful film that benefited from this cinematic dialogue is *Central do Brasil* (*Central Station*, 1998) that was directed by Brazilian documentarist and filmmaker, Walter SALLES.

This paper aims to investigate and discuss two films in the cinematic oeuvre of SALLES: *Central do Brasil* and *Diarios de Motocicleta* (*The Motorcycle Diaries*, 2004), as a recuperation of the auteur in conjunction with transformative cinema. I argue that SALLES' brand of cinema verite filmmaking, 'miracles of improvisation' and 'aesthetics of affection' brand his films as reconfigured Cinema Novo with neo-realist registers. His distinctive filmic imprimatur both acknowledges a commitment to resistant cinema replete with un-rehearsed documentary-feel realism and an accessible populism. I contend that SALLES has created a distinctive film language that combines a rootedness to Latin American geographies, Cinema Novo aesthetics, and an unembarrassed appropriation of cinema with populist accessibilities. The paper outlines SALLES' background in documentary that emphasizes his imbrication of the film audience to the real-feel of the narrative. The road movie thematics of *Central do Brasil* and *Diarios de Motocicleta* highlights the various mobilities the films' characters have undertaken as well as life-changing encounters with the cinematically unmapped people and places. Finally, I will show how SALLES participates in the re-narration of national imaginaries through his films' explicit politics that cinema can, ultimately, transform people into action.

A DOCUMENTARY APPROACH TO FICTION: *CENTRAL DO BRASIL* AND THE MIRACLES OF IMPROVISATION

The critically-lauded *Central do Brasil* managed to ensnare state funding as well as foreign private sector investments. The film's commercial success and international circulation solidified its reputation as a Brazilian product, one that is rooted in local sensibilities but has an international appeal. *Central do Brasil* typifies a film practice that incorporates Cinema Novo-informed verisimilitude. Atypical of Cinema Novo, however, it offers no apologies for its visual splendor. In its insistence on showing the 'true face of Brazil,' *Central do Brasil* pays homage to the 'aesthetics of hunger' first introduced by Glauber Rocha and other Cinema Novo practitioners in the 1960s. It also, however, combines high production value and an engaging storyline (SHAW 2007). Julianne BURTON-CARVAJAL (2000) comments that the tendency of national and extra-national film observers to create easy binaries between visual splendor and social concern has led to the demonization of the former and its supposed propensity to undermine the realist registers of a film. *Central do Brasil* certainly benefited from the cinematographic flourishes of Walter Carvalho – especially in the depiction of the cinematically unmapped spaces of the *sertao* in the northeastern part of the country – but they ultimately do not bury or submerge the sociopolitical concerns under formal beauty.

Critics noted that the film somehow invited a touristic view of the folkloric landscapes of northeastern Brazil by indulging in what Ivana BENTES terms a 'cosmetics of hunger' (a reworking of Rocha's 'aesthetics of hunger') and the "aestheticized and clean images of poverty" (BENTES 2003; NAGIB 2007, 42; SHAW 2003). Despite these observations, the stark contrast between the dissonant and nightmarish *favela* in urban Rio de Janeiro and the placid *sertao* in the countryside, as glimpsed by the film's two protagonists, was intended by SALLES to metamorphose the image of the nation – whether resplendent or dull in its ordinariness. The *sertao*, in particular, as Flora SUSSEKIND insists in her dissection of Brazilian literary forms, "indicates dualities ... oppositions and mediations ... between universalization and themes of regional, coastal and interior character" (SUSSEKIND 2002, 14).

Walter SALLES directed and produced documentaries for ten years before he focused and trained his field of vision on fiction films. "I have always admired documentaries, because they open windows that can make you understand much better where you come from" (SALLES in G. ANDREW interview, 2004, 1). This early start in documentaries imbued his subsequent feature-length fiction films with a certain gravitas, grounded realism, and an imperfection that comes from the improvisatory techniques he employed and favored in his early career. These filmic practices seem to counter the critiques that his films privilege text and a self-conscious auteurism more than authenticity and emphasis on national and regional receptions.

SALLES confesses, "I'm a strong believer in the necessity of imperfection coming into film ... I also think that the more you reason collectively about what the project should be at the beginning of the process, the more you can improvise later." (SALLES in G. ANDREW interview, 2004, 1). In his 1998 interview with *Cineaste*, SALLES championed the so-called 'miracles of improvisation' as key to his films' realism. These on-the-spot improvisations allow his actors to inhabit their character roles in a naturalistic way and respond to "feelings aroused by the new surroundings" (SALLES in A. KAUFMAN interview, 1998, 21).

These geographical spaces where 'miracles of improvisation' take place elicited an instinctive response from his characters, particularly during the scene of the pilgrimage in *Central do Brasil*. This is also evident in *Diarios de Motocicleta* where encounters with what SALLES calls "new realities" profoundly affected the actors portraying Ernesto "Che" Guevara de la Serna and Alberto Granado. The characters' responses assume a quasi-documentary feel that is both spontaneous and un-rehearsed. The pilgrimage scene in *Central do Brasil* is based on the actual event that SALLES videotaped while scouting locations for the film. He re-staged the pilgrimage for inclusion in the actual film. Buoyed by the spiritual performativity of the ritual, however, the faux pilgrimage suddenly became real and followed its own internal logic. According to SALLES, the extras hired for the filming quickly stopped acting and followed the ritual's carnivalesque rhythm – thus turning the simulacra of the pilgrimage into a real event. SALLES states: "When you put the camera in an actual geography, small miracles sometimes occur" (SALLES in A. KAUFMAN interview 1998, 20).

EASY RIDERS IN BROKEN VEHICLES

A fascination with the themes of wandering, running, loss, the possibilities of finding people and of being transformed by change permeates *Central do Brasil*, *Diarios de Motocicleta* and SALLES' first feature film, *Terra Estrangeira* (*Foreign Land*, 1996). Not surprisingly, the road movie that has now entered the lexicon as a film genre became a natural vehicle for SALLES' explorations. Claire WILLIAMS (2007, 15) notes that road movies center on a character's escape and eventual discovery of new experiences in comparison to "home and past." In *Central do Brasil*, the transformative quality of the contact and encounter with hitherto unknown people engenders a correlative search for a country's national identity. Dora and Josue – the two main characters in *Central do Brasil* – travel from Rio de Janeiro in search of Josue's absent father. As imagined by SALLES, this journey is also a quest for a lost homeland that Brazil, as a country, is still searching for. The *sertao* that both characters glimpse in the long bus rides to Brazil's northeastern province of Pernambuco is a "paradigmatic image of Brazility" (SUSSEKIND 2002, 14). Similarly, the search of pre-revolutionary Ernesto "Che" Guevara for an idealized Latin America leads him and Alberto to meet strangers and common people along the way. These common people, whose concerns range from transitory labor employment to long-term land tenurial security, stand in stark contrast to the hedonism the two privileged Argentines are avidly pursuing. These encounters are said to have stimulated the young Che to chart his path toward advocating rights for the landless later on in life.

In *Central do Brasil* and *Diarios de Motocicleta*, the physical and human geographies encountered by the characters in their travels correspond to retrieving a homeland and national identity perceived as in danger of disappearing. Both films benefit from 'miracles of improvisation' that recall the cinéma vérité of filmmakers as different in styles from Vittorio de Sica to Mike Leigh. While the *sertao* seen by Dora and Josue is used to mark the passage of time and distance and is found on-location en route to Pernambuco, Ernesto and Alberto's Latin American travels were filmed chronologically for 84 days similar to the route taken 50 years earlier by the real-life Alberto Granado and Che Guevara. The curious passers-by featured in the film "add to the sense of authentic interaction between Ernesto and Alberto and the 'real' Latin America" (WILLIAMS 2007, 12). SALLES confesses that "[t]his is when they started to meet a lot of people that they are unaware of – the indigenous populations of Chile, in Peru ... They were much more in direct contact from that moment on with the social injustice than they were before, and they started slowly, little by little" (SALLES in J. RIVERA interview, 2004, 4). This so-called 'aesthetics of affection' that SALLES claims is ever-present in his films, serves as an allegory of the Brazilian nation where national belongingness can be achieved by familial connection and not by political action. Distrustful of the past leaders of the country, his recuperation of the cinematically unmapped northeast as the site for national regeneration rather than in the urban area, situates and emplaces Josue with his long-lost brothers.

The structure of road movies emanating from Hollywood to Bollywood is hinged on characters' self-discovery. SALLES' own road movies always establish the breaking down and non-functionality of technology-powered vehicles: a broken motorcycle in *Diarios de Motocicleta*, and the unavailability and unreliability of buses and trucks in *Central do Brasil*. SALLES admits that these breakdowns paradoxically signify the moment of change when characters improvise and continue their travels on foot resulting in significant and meaningful encounters with people whose own mobility is limited to walking. The break-down of motorcycles and other forms of transportation "completely transformed" the characters "not just by physical geography but by the people they started to encounter" (SALLES in G. ANDREW interview, 2004, 3). Just as the characters' transformation occurs because of these encounters with people and landscapes, SALLES argues that film is constantly transformed by its contact with reality (SALLES in J. RIVERA interview, 2004).

AN ALTERNATIVE FAMILY: A RE-NARRATION OF THE NATION

The roots of SALLES' cinematic oeuvre grow from the revolutionary Cinema Novo movement in terms of its desire to establish links with the radical aesthetics that defined its politics. Interestingly, Cinema Novo sought ways to break its own links with the previous filmmaking tradition, known as 'cinema du papa' in France or 'cinema Kino' in Germany (ARRIGUCCI 2007; NAGIB 2007). Cinema Novo, as practiced by its founder Glauber Rocha and others, severed ties to its filmic predecessor as a radical break to mark ideological differences.

The tropes of most SALLES' films, however, especially as portrayed in *Central do Brasil,* seek to re-establish links to a common father and brother as a way to forge and renew fraternal bonds. The failure of the political system that engendered the governments of Collor de Mello, and later Cardoso, help explain SALLES' refusal to acknowledge political action as a viable solution. Rather, SALLES' film sets its sights on the possibility of an alternative family for national reconstruction. In *Central do Brasil*, Josue is reunited with his Biblically named brothers Moises and Isaias in Pernambuco; although the father he is searching for remains absent towards the film's conclusion. It is this absence that marks the condition of possibility for an alternative family to happen because Moises, who is distrustful of their common father, nevertheless accepts Josue to join him and Isaias in their abode.

Lucia NAGIB (2007, 41) asserts, "The search for the father [in *Central do Brasil*] is equivalent, on a meta-linguistic level, to the search for a home country lost in the Cinema Novo past, where the filmmaker of the present hopes to find historical affiliation." Employing the raw and documentary styles used by Cinema Novo practitioners in the past by taking the camera out of the studio and taking it closer to the faces in the street, SALLES reinforces the connection between homeland and Brazilian-ness in *Central do Brasil*. "It's a film searching for a certain human and geographical territory. It's not only the Northeast of Brazil, it's a territory of solidarity, of a certain fraternity amongst equals" (SALLES in A. KAUFMAN interview, 1998, 20).

Deborah SHAW (2003) shows in her brilliant reading of *Central do Brasil* that despite the dichotomization of the rural and urban, the present and the future, between Old Brazil marked by cynicism and the New Brazil of renewed hope, the figure of Josue ultimately serves as the film's 'transforming angel' whose angelic innocence perfectly embodies the iconography of a new Brazil that emphasizes regeneration and confidence in the efficacy of fraternal relations for national reconstruction. Dora, not unlike Maria, in Fritz Lang's *Metropolis* (1930), must facilitate the coming together of the forces (in this case, Josue and his brothers who are builders and carpenters) that will rebuild a nation. "With *Central do Brasil*, the story was basically about the recuperation of one's identity and also, an investigation into the country's identity. In Portuguese, the words for father (*pai*) and country (*pais*) are almost the same. So the search for a father in *Central do Brasil* is also a search for a country. So the idea of recuperating one's identity is linked to the idea of having a more wide-ranging sensorial palette as well" (SALLES in G. ANDREW interview, 2004, 2).

ROADS AND MORE ROADS: CONCLUSION

Walter SALLES' cinematic truth is founded on the interplay of the real and the fictionalized account of the imagined. The creation of cinematic spaces for the unmapped ruralities of Brazil and Latin America in *Central do Brasil* and *Diarios de Motocicleta* alludes to SALLES' politics that pays homage to but goes beyond Cinema Novo and the radicalization of filmmaking practices. SALLES' character-driven films that are at once local in scope and international in appeal revisit key moments in his nation's history and suggest a populist stance that welcomes hybridities – no doubt fueled both by his international collaborations and the growing internationalization of the film industry that emphasizes cultural production. His occasional forays to Hollywood (i.e. *Dark Water*, 2005) continue to widen his palette due to his cinematic dialogues with American cinema. The precise nationality that informs his films, however, remains as distinctive as his auteurial preference for the underprivileged. While SALLES' filmic productions outside Latin America continue (*Paris, je t'aime*, 2006), the contexts remain rooted in ordinary people and their specific links to their nationality – echoing Craig CALHOUN's (2007, 1) claim that "nationalism helps locate an experience of belonging in a world of global flows and fears." The social solidarity and aesthetics of affection that inform the themes of his films appear prototypical of a nation still searching for its roots and historical affiliations. While he does not resist the temptation to approach his films with a cosmopolitanism that paves the way for post-nationalist politics, the materiality of national struggles in Brazil continue to provide rich material for SALLES to create more cinematic roads for the nation's continuous self discovery and surprising encounters with its own peoples in the course of the journey.

ACKNOWLEDGEMENTS

Special thanks to Negar Mottahedeh, Chris Lukinbeal, Tina Kennedy, Stefan Zimmermann, Susan Mains, Scott Kirsch & Alvira Galido.

REFERENCES

ANDREW, G. (2004): Interview with Walter Salles, *Guardian Unlimited*, August 26, 2004. http://film.guardian.co.uk/interview/interviewpages/0,,1291387,00.html (accessed November 13, 2007), 1–7.

ARRIGUCCI, D. Jr. (2007): Introduction. *Brazil on Screen: Cinema Novo, New Cinema, Utopia*. London, xvii–xxii.

BENTES, I. (2003): The *sertao* and the *favela* in Contemporary Brazilian Film. NAGIB, L. (Ed.): *The New Brazilian Cinema*. London, 121–137.

BURTON-CARVAJAL, J. (2000): "Araya" Across Time and Space: Competing Canons of National (Venezuelan) and International Film Histories. *Visible Nations: Latin American Cinema and Video*. Minneapolis, 51–81.

CALHOUN, C. (2007): *Nations Matter: Culture, History, and the Cosmopolitan Dream*, New York.

JOHNSON, R. (2000): Departing from Central Station: Notes on the Reemergence of Brazilian Cinema, *The Brazil e-journal*, Spring 2000. www.brasilemb.org/profile_brazil/brasil_ejournal_ randal.shtml (accessed September 16, 2007), 1–7.

KAUFMAN, A. (1998): Sentimental Journey as National Allegory: An Interview with Walter Salles. *Cineaste*, Winter 1998, 19–21.

NAGIB, L. (2007): *Brazil on Screen: Cinema Novo, New Cinema, Utopia*, London.

RIVERA, J. (2004): Then It Must Be True – Walter Salles, July 24, 2004, Los Angeles. http://www.thenitmustbetrue.com/salles/salles1.html (accessed November 13, 2007), 1–7.

SHAW, D. (2003): *Contemporary Cinema of Latin America*, New York.

SHAW, D. (2007): Latin American Cinema Today: A Qualified Success Story. *Contemporary Latin American Cinema: Breaking Into the Global Market*. Lanham, 1–10.

SUSSEKIND, F. (2002): Deterritorialization and Poetic Form – Brazilian Contemporary Poetry and Urban Experience. *Arachne@Rutgers: Journal of Iberian and Latin American Literary and Cultural Studies* 2 (1). http://arachne.rutgers.edu/vol2_1sussekind.htm.

WILLIAMS, C. (2007): *Los Diarios de Motocicleta* as Pan-American Travelogue. *Contemporary Latin American Cinema: Breaking Into Global Market*. Lanham, 11–28.

Gerd Becker

NOURI BOUZID'S *BEZNESS* AS A VISUAL STUDY ON THE GLANCE: REFLECTIONS ON EXPLORING THE SCIENTIFIC POTENTIAL OF NON-VERBAL CINEMA

For one and a half decades we have offered courses in Visual Anthropology to our students at the Institut für Ethnologie, University of Hamburg. Our lectures are not limited to the fields of history, theory and practice of ethnographic documentary, but also include a concern with non-western, fiction cinema. In a series of lectures and screenings called "Parallel Cinematic Worlds", we aim to communicate knowledge about other cultures by using the mirror of self-description that cinematic productions offer. Maghrebinean movies, Turkish cinema and Hindi films have all been on the agenda in different semesters. Indigenous films can give us ideas about cultural patterns in traditional narratives that are different from our own as well as views of cultures from the inside.

Films are "records of culture and records about culture" as Sol WORTH and John ADAIR (1972) stated. They describe culture and they are culture. While they intentionally tell stories, unintended subtexts may be read from them. Films describe what has been staged in front of the camera. From this, additional information of what happened behind the camera may be deciphered. Soundtracks and dialogues tell us a story. In addition, visual narratives show us aspects that may complement or deviate from the audible. Films provide dense descriptions of cultural patterns and the potential meanings they offer; they must; however, be decoded by the viewer.

A good example of a feature film from which we can learn about North African daily life and the relationship of western and non-western cultures is Nouri BOUZID's 1990 film *Bezness*. The Tunisian director, BOUZID, is known for his poetic films that, nevertheless, are strong due to precise observations and their documentary-like quality. *Bezness* is a film that communicates its story by both visual and auditory means, especially during dialogues about sex-tourism and jealousy.

The film is about a European photographer visiting Tunisia who feels challenged to photograph veiled Muslim women, thus unveiling them photographically. The beautiful girl, Khomsa, fascinates him. Khomsa's fiancée, Rufa, is working as a *bezness* (the Tunisian slang-word for men who make their money with female European tourists). On a visual level, an additional story is told – the story of how people look at each other.

Based on precise observation and experiences of a cultural insider, BOUZID's film can be considered a highly informative study on the glance. In many subjective, camera style takes, the film shows either the faces of protagonists while they look at 'others', or alternatively, what the protagonists see. The glance in the mirror, female eye from behind a veil, voyeuristic glances of the tourist's camera, and aggressive competition all play a central role in the movie. In Tunisia, the 'evil eye' is a synonym for envy. It is widely believed that the glance of an envious person will intentionally, or unintentionally, do harm in a magical way. Considerable effort is made, especially in Muslim societies, to seek protection from the 'evil eye'.

BOUZID's film does not verbally mention this central cultural concept. Nevertheless, the importance of this theme becomes quite clear through the film's visual narrative. BOUZID, who, although he does not intend or claim to make scientific statements, combines the knowledge of a cultural insider with the skills of a professional filmmaker. The resulting film is worthy of study by Visual Anthropology students seeking to express their own findings in visual form.

Observation, namely participant observation, is a key methodology in anthropological research. Finding modes of representation that correspond to this research method – visual forms of representing scientific insights – is desirable. Film may be the proper medium for this purpose. One of the hints we give our students when teaching them anthropological film-making is "Show it, don't tell it" to encourage them to put emphasis on visual expression.

Traditionally, science concentrates on *logos*, verbal expression. When we introduce film into science, we must try to make optimum use of the specific qualities of this medium. Doubtlessly, film can communicate scientific insights. Films can include any kind of text, written or spoken to fulfill this aim. The decisive question; however, is: can visuals alone be the means of rational argumentation?

Margaret MEAD (1975), one of the pioneers in applying visual methods to the study of culture, complained that "Anthropology is a discipline of words." Thousands of ethnographic films have been made since then. These films have been screened in numerous festivals and discussed in conferences. Images have gained weight in anthropology and neighboring disciplines. There have been developments and changes in the way images are used and considered. Early approaches stressed the importance of images as a loyal handmaiden to disciplines by producing measurements, mnemonics, and substitutes for first hand information. Visual Anthropology then moved toward holistic descriptions and didactic functions (see HEIDER 1976). Since, there has been a growing interest in experimentally addressing aspects of culture and the consciousness of specific social actors (MACDOUGALL 1998, 271).

Still one can observe an ongoing dominance of the word – even in the field of ethnographic film. Today, many documentary filmmakers refrain from a narrator's commentary. Instead, the protagonists' voices are heard – talking heads and heads talking – often in foreign languages. For translation, extensive use is made of subtitles. There are only a few examples of filmmakers showing trust in the communicative potential of the visual, independent from accompanying verbal statements; and, critics and audiences often discuss these examples as art rather than as science. Such has been the case with Robert GARDENER's film, *Forest of Bliss*, a visual portrait of the holy city of Benares (for extensive discussion of this film see ÖSTÖR 1990).

There is more trust in visual narratives in feature films than in documentaries. Before the invention of sound-films in the late 1920s, the cinematic art of expressing meaning with moving pictures was a *sine qua non* of cinema. It is in feature films that "visual language" and "film grammar" have been most refined (the linguistic metaphors "language" and "grammar" should be used skeptically for denoting nonverbal forms of expression). Therefore, it is a good idea to study professional fictional cinema in order to learn about the art of communicating meaning by managing light, conscious use of focus and image size, camera movement, and making sense by joining different takes in a meaningful way during editing. The development of film analysis theories is largely based on feature films. Most of the results; however, can be applied to documentary film as well and will be useful in the attempt to develop scientific film in accordance with the state of those theories.

In attempting to contribute to science through the medium of film, we are working within a triangle of a technology, an aesthetic form and a scientific intention. We first must master the devices for recording light and sound as well as for editing our footage. Second, we need a practical knowledge of the mechanisms and patterns of film perception to be able to communicate our message. Dealing with images and arranging filmed footage in a meaningful way also requires an understanding of aesthetic principles. Third, we have to use precise scientific methods and hold to the standards of our disciplines. Obviously these multiple hurdles are obstacles for the development of film as a scientific tool. Accepting film as an equivalent to texts requires developing criteria for judging film's quality analogous to criteria existing for written material. On the other hand, visual representation offers opportunities beyond verbal form. Visual representation need not compete with written texts, but rather, add its own specific qualities to deepen our insights.

One advantage of images is that they may facilitate cultural translation. They are not as exclusively comprehensible to defined groups of insiders as are languages. In Spring 2002, I came across a group of geography students from Johannes Gutenberg-Universität, Mainz. Under the guidance of Professor Anton Escher, they were doing field exercises in the Moroccan town of Essaouira. I stayed in Essaouira to continue my film-work on trance musicians and ritual healers of the Gnawa brotherhood. After being introduced to Cherif Regragui, the leader of Oulad Bombra music group, Escher asked the Gnawi to perform a *lila*, a trance night, for the students' last evening in town. Both the Germans and Moroccans expected me to document the encounter with my DV-cam. While editing the footage, I faced the problem of having to decide about the language version I would use: German, Arabic, French or English? Each of these choices would have privileged one group of viewers and excluded others. Because the participants of the *lila* had shared the same reality, I thought they should share also the same representation of this reality. I decided to make only one version of the documentary – independent from verbal expression.

Even when you reject words as the media of expression, there are still a large number of ways to create meaning in film. Mimic, gesture, sound, music, movement and light can create a dramatic narrative. Furthermore, cuts and transitions are genuine filmic means for inducing sense into a visual narrative. I screened the resulting film, *Gutenberg trifft Sidi Bilal (Gutenberg meets Sidi Bilal)* [1], for different audiences to test their reactions and understanding. The Moroccan and German protagonists, primarily for whom the film was made, had no problem understanding the film and enjoyed the 'reflection' of the night's event. Ethnomusicologists who had been present at other screenings were especially happy to be allowed to listen to a musical performance without the usual interruption of commentary or voice-over. Anthropologists from Mali and Niger were able to compare and find close similarities of the Gnawa-performance with cults known to them in their home countries. People with some professional or academic background regarding the cognitive structures of film had no difficulty understanding the message. Audiences without previous education in the practice or theory of film; however, tended to show some irritation because their expectation of being guided verbally through a film was not fulfilled. This experiment encouraged me to look for further experience with nonverbal film.

The chance for a follow up project occurred Spring 2003, when the artist and anthropologist, Nana VOSSEN, asked me to film the production of oil from the fruit of the argan-tree in Morocco, a topic she had researched. Editing the film, we found that it worked quite well without spoken commentary. This was due to the fact that argan oil production is an example of a process that can be well understood by simply watching it. This process is an aspect of material culture adequately described by simple glances of the camera – quite different from the topic I was still working on: trance and spirit possession.

I kept feeling unsatisfied with my visual representation of trance. Images of ecstatically dancing persons who were said to be under the control of *djnun* (spirits, demons) did not seem an adequate description of what happened to those in a trance. Their wild movements and shouts can not communicate their inner state of mind to a cultural outsider to whom such an experience is strange. Even if the images are accompanied by explanatory words, there is a high risk of producing 'exotism' and misunderstanding. In 1954, when the French anthropologist-filmmaker, Jean ROUCH, brought from West Africa his sensational film material on the Haukapossesion rites, he faced the problem that his film on the *maîtres fous* was both misunderstood widely and criticized forcefully – despite the extensive explanations ROUCH gave on the soundtrack. Spirit possession seems to be a phenomenon beyond the limits of rational mind and therefore, hard to describe properly in terms of rational science. Applying our rational concepts to such experiences, rooted in cultures both foreign to us and different from ours, may leave us unsatisfied. It may even imply imposing western concepts on non-western ideas with a claim of saying: "we know it better" – a questionable practice in postcolonial times.

In our own societies, expressing experiences beyond rationality is often considered to be the domain of arts, so I was very pleased when, in Summer 2003,

---

1. The title refers to the encounter of students from Johannes Gutenberg-Universität and the followers of Sidi Bilal, the mythic ancestor of all Gnawa – as much as to the encounter of scriptural culture and trance culture.

I was asked to collaborate with the Marrakech based artist, Hans-Werner Geerdts. Although born in Germany, Geerdts has lived in Morocco for more than 40 years. His oeuvre is influenced by the colourful life of *jema el-fna*, the central place in the Medina of Marrakech near Geerdts' home. Every night, acrobats and storytellers entertain people from near and far. Trance-musicians and Gnawa groups gather their adepts around them in *halqa*-circles. The melodies of *guembri*-lutes fill the air, accompanied by the beat of *tbal*-drums and the hypnotic rhythms of metal *qarqaba*-castangnettes. The sounds of this trance-music inspired Geerdts in most of his creative periods during which he tried to find visual expression for it in his paintings.

I had been asking myself if perhaps the synthesizing mind of an artist might have better ways of expressing the non-rational psychic of trance than that of an analyzing scientist and whether or not anthropological theory and practice could thus profit from applying the theory and practice of art in research. I very much enjoyed working with the artist, Geerdts. It was challenging to attempt fulfilling his wish of extending his art into the dimension of movement and sound by producing an animation film from the raw material of his paintings. The cooperation convinced me that genuine artists master modes of expression that go beyond the possibilities of sciences. Furthermore, during this work, it became clear to me that the artistic approach is substantially different from the scientific one.

Knowledge and skills in the field of arts are very useful when a filmmaker seeks to master the aesthetic problems of cinema. Cinema, in itself, may be considered an art. If a filmmaker fails to find the right answers to the aesthetic questions his work asks, he will face serious difficulties communicating his message. On the other hand, scientific questions deserve scientific answers. There is no doubt that art as well as science offers ways of enlarging human insight; but these ways may not necessarily be compatible with science. Artists are free to define the relationship of their products with reality. Modern art needs not even refer to a defined 'outer' reality – unlike science. Science is indivisibly linked to certain rules and standards. Despite what we learned from three decades of 'positivism-bashing' and post-modern critique; we must still insist on principles of rationality, on precise methods of research and on exact proofs for our results.

Instead of hoping for help from art theory, I find it more promising to work on building independent scientific theories of the visuals. Scientific approaches to 'visuals' date back to Socrates, who discussed the relationship of representation and the represented in his dialogues (asking Kratylos: "Or don't you see that the images by far do not have the same content, than that of what they are images of?"). George BERKELEY (1884, 286), working on a theory of visual language in the early 19th century, hoped that "When we have well understood and considered the nature of vision, we may by reasoning from thence, be better able to collect some knowledge of the external unseen cause of our ideas."

Geography is a science in which visuals occupy a central position: drawing and reading maps has been a standard method of this discipline. Maps are useful to such a high degree that it has become common, even for layman, to acquire the basic knowledge enabling him to read and understand maps as models of geographic realities. Maps can be seen as an analogous to film. Hence, films also may be considered models of reality. Films are not as commonly understood to be models of reality, or, realities of a second order. Viewers are thus tempted to accept them as reality itself. Films create the illusion of realty. The filmmakers' art is to form their product in such a way that a film's reception is similar to the reception of reality in decisive respects. Film offers, in fact, a sensual experience as remote from reality as a map. The experience of film is that of a two-dimensional representation with limited angles, cut off from smells, tastes, and tactile experience and with its own carefully constructed flow of time. Still, the experience of watching films seems so natural that few care to teach a conscious reception and analysis of film in schools – similar to the manner in which reading and understanding texts is taught. This failure in education is the reason most laypersons are still unable to read the visual after 110 years of cinema.

If we were able to prove that films are as useful in science as are maps, more scientists and students should be willing to systematically study the understanding, as well as conscious critical and analytic reception, of films. The guidelines for making films will then no longer need to be those of TV and Hollywood, but can shift to scientific standards. A science of images, based on the existing fundamental visual principles mentioned earlier, that would enhance disciplines for those wishing to work with visuals in their disparate fields, is still to be built. Currently, the question of whether or not visuals should be mere illustrative additives to words remains. If we can dare to think of non-verbal science, the question awaits future answers.

REFERENCES

BECKER, G. (2004): "Transes Sahariennes – Transsahariens": une contribution ciné-ethnographique à propos des cultes d'obsession des Gnawa du Maroc. MARFAING, L. and S. WIPPEL (Eds.): *Les Relations Transsahariennes à l'Époque Contemporaine*. Paris, 379–401.
BERKELEY, G. (1884): The Theory of Visual Language. Selections from George Berkeley. By A. C. FRASER (Ed.). Oxford.
HEIDER, K. (1976): *Ethnographic Film*. Austin.
MEAD, M. (1975): Visual Anthropology in a Discipline of Word. HOCKINGS, P. (Ed.): *Principles of Visual Anthropology*. Chicago, 3–10.
MACDOUGALL, D. (1998): *Transcultural Cinema*. Princeton.
ÖSTÖR, A. (1990): Wither Ethnographic Film? *American Anthropologist* 92, 715–722.
WORTH, S. and J. ADAIR (1972): *Through Navajo Eyes*. Albuquerque.

FILMOGRAPHY

BECKER, G. (2002): *Gutenberg trifft Sidi Bilal*. Morocco / Germany.
BECKER, G. and N. VOSSEN (2003): *Argania Spinosa*. Morocco / Germany.
BECKER, G. (2003): *Marrakshi Trance*. Morocco.
BOUZID, N. (1990): *Bezness*. Tunesia.
GARDENER, R. (1985): *Forest of Bliss*. India / USA.
ROUCH, J. (1954): *Les Maîtres Fous*. Ghana / France.

Deborah Dixon

'INDEPENDENT' DOCUMENTARY IN THE U.S.: THE POLITICS OF PERSONAL PASSIONS

INTRODUCTION

This chapter addresses documentary film, a genre that has been the subject of intense debate as to its form and function. It has been lauded as an ethical and worthy form of commentary on the social and natural world that is capable, in a more pointed political sense, of exposing and critiquing the causes of inequity and exploitation. Documentary film has also been condemned, however, as a bourgeois, aesthetically driven medium that plays with the idea of protest, but serves merely to bolster the status quo. In this sense of the term, documentary allows for the spectator to indulge in middle-class guilt as a substitute for actively working to change society. This paper takes a rather different approach to the subject. Rather than adhere to a particular definition of documentary film, I deploy a constructivist perspective, wherein it is *the process by which this set of filmmaking practices is defined*, as well as the question of to *whose benefit* that becomes of interest.

It is important to point out that a constructivist analysis does not conform to the modernist, mainstream, academic notion of a theoretical framework as providing an 'explanation' of the cause-effect relations between things; instead, emphasis is placed on how the objects of analysis we deal with have come to be defined in very particular ways; such as, for example, 'radical,' 'ethical,' and 'worthy' as well as 'independent,' 'experimental' and 'innovative.' The characteristics and qualities of an object such as cinema, then, are not assumed to be pre-given, but are embedded in a host of meanings and practices that are differentiated through time and across space. And yet, it is not enough simply to point to the often controversial etymology of an object; for, as HACKING (1999) points out, all of our objects of analysis are socially constructed in this manner. The questions become, rather, what are the power relations that allow for particular definitions to become naturalized and how is contestation expressed within what can be termed a 'hegemonic' state of affairs?

Specifically, this chapter addresses the construction of 'independent' documentary filmmaking in the U.S. Accordingly, it focuses on the various academic debates concerning the defining characteristics of the genre, as well as comments from celebrated documentary filmmakers themselves as to their understanding of cinema. While these and other contributions have allowed for the notion of a distinct 'genre' to emerge, I argue that, in very practical terms, key discourses concerning the form and function of documentary have been provided by the *state* which, in the U.S., has become the primary source of funding and distribution for filmmakers working outside of the Hollywood system. I intend to show that through a variety of state-initiated and funded agencies, a neoliberal discourse on the rights and responsibilities of the individual has emerged which favors 'personal viewpoints' over, and against, more structural accounts of social life. This discursive framing of the subject serves to reiterate an idealized notion of American nationhood, wherein the land of the free is seen to be constituted from a hard-working, worthy citizenry unified by shared 'human' values.

The ensuing production of agency-orientated documentary is illustrated via reference to the work of filmmaker Eren MCGUINESS, who, alongside Christine FUGATE, has produced rural documentary as part of Café Sisters Productions; and to Dos Vatos Productions, with Ari PALOS. Café Sisters produced *Tobacco Blues* (1998) that addressed the struggle of Kentucky tobacco farmers in the face of global shifts in capital investment and changing public tastes. Dos Vatos more recently produced *Beyond the Border* (2003) that follows the migrant experience of four Mexican brothers as they try to make a living in the thoroughbred horseracing industry of Kentucky. In both films, the individualized 'human face' of social inequity is valorized as the protagonists provide their own, passionately felt, stories of life in the U.S. Although both films point up the failure of American society to deal with exploitation and discrimination, there is no doubting the underlying presumption that this failure is of concern precisely because the U.S. was founded upon a particular, political ideal of 'freedom for all,' that is inextricably linked to a strong sense of individuality. As I note below, a neoliberal discourse on individualism praises hard work and effort, but also can be used to lay blame for social ills firmly at the feet of those individuals deemed unworthy of citizenship in what President Johnson called the 'Great Society.'

WHAT IS 'DOCUMENTARY'?

For Basil WRIGHT, writing in 1947, the defining characteristics of the documentary were manifold but uncontroversial. Indeed, these diverse frames of reference ensued simply from an appreciation of the many groups (including film exhibitors, teachers, academics and filmmakers) involved in debating and working with the genre: "A documentary would be variously defined as a short film before the feature, as a travelogue, as a description of how films are made, as an instructional film, as an aid in teaching, as an artistic interpretation of reality and, by some theoreticians in the documentary field, as a film made by themselves." Each group appreciated a different aspect of the documentary; but, its fundamental status as a mode of representation that captured actualité,[1] or reality, was not in question. At most, a distinction could be made regarding the diverse realities captured. The genre was seen as constituted of both sociological documentaries dealing "with industrial man, urban or machine-minding man," and naturalistic documentaries focused on "man in a state of nature-primitive, unaffected by machinery" (SMITH 2003). For many commentators, these two lifestyles not only had much to tell us of the

---

1. The term actualité dates back to 1896 and the short films of everyday life produced by the Lumière Brothers. The term documentary ensues form the French for travelogue, documetaire.

diversity of Mankind and the landscapes he [sic] inhabited in the 20th century, but also of the ever increasing levels of economic, political and economic contact that threatened this same diversity (see, for example, ROTHA 1936).

Of course, even in the years before WRIGHT's (1947) review of the genre, documentary's status as a form of filmmaking that could and should 'capture' real world experiences and situations had come under scrutiny (CORNER 1996). For the most part, debate centered on how film, as a deliberate and skilled form of image-making, could be used to express a 'truth' that was not necessarily visible to the naked eye. To the great Soviet filmmaker, Dziga VERTOV, for example, continuous screen shots of everyday people in place did not necessarily succeed in expressing the 'essence' of a given situation. Using fast-cut editing and special effects, including reverse action and slow motion, VERTOV sought to evoke in films such as Kino Eye (VERTOV and MICHELSON 1995): *Life Caught Unawares* (1924) and *The Man With the Movie Camera* (1929) the social ethos underlying life's seeming chaos.[2] Social realist documentaries of the 1930s also used experimental filmmaking techniques in an effort to reach an otherwise elusive profundity. According to Dutch filmmaker Joris IVENS (1969, 137), a committed Communist, documentary was akin to a form of testimony, and, as such, required concentration and effort to compose a balanced picture of society:

> I was surprised to find that many people automatically assumed that any documentary film would inevitably be objective. Perhaps the term is unsatisfactory, but for me the distinction between the words document and documentary is quite clear. Do we demand objectivity in the evidence presented at a trial? No, the only demand is that each piece of evidence be as full a subjective, truthful, honest presentation of the witness's attitude as an oath on the Bible can produce from him.

Often labeled the 'father of the documentary' because of his efforts to establish state-sponsorship of this genre in England and Canada, John Grierson chose a poetic style to drive his politically charged documentary form. As he explained in 1943, "We thought that even so complex a world as ours could be patterned for all to appreciate if we only got away from the servile accumulation of fact and struck for the story which held the facts in living organic relationship together" (cited in FULFORD 2000).

Underpinning this interest in the manipulation of the filmic image, then, is a desire to use cinema as a means to expose otherwise hidden truths and, moreover, to intervene in the everyday lives of people – or, as ROTHA (1936) termed it – to educate, agitate and inform, as well as entertain. Propelled, in part, by a wide-spread dissatisfaction with the emergent European and Hollywood fictive filmmaking genres, the documentation of the 'real' world came to be read as a political strategy – one which relied on its own compendium of cinematic techniques to uncover and

---

2. For VERTOV, "Kino-eye plunges into the seeming chaos of life to find in itself the response to an assigned theme. To find the resultant force amongst the million phenomena related to the given theme. To edit; to wrest, through the camera, whatever is most typical, most useful, from life; to organize the film pieces wrested from life into a meaningful rhythmic visual order, a meaningful visual phrase, an essence of 'I see.'" (From Kino-Eye to Radio-Eye, 1929 [repr. 1995]).

illuminate capitalism at work (NICHOLS 2001). It is in this regard that documentary came to be synonymous with the term 'Second Cinema'.

Second Cinema was defined as a serious alternative to 'First Cinema,' namely mass-produced Hollywood film and its imitators. Variously known as *auteur* cinema, art cinema, or, in a later phase, new wave cinema and independent cinema, Second Cinema was considered distinct by virtue of the lack of commodification involved in its production, as well as the provision of experimental and, it was hoped, enlightening, modes of spectatorship. Yet, as the century wore on, Second Cinema lost its status as 'radical' critique of, or alternative to, First Cinema. Indeed, for some, it had become a bourgeois institution in its own right. As CHANAN (1997, 375–376) argues, Second Cinema was,

> a misplaced ambition to develop a film industry to compete with First Cinema, and this could only lead to its own institutionalisation within the system, which was more than ready to use Second Cinema to demonstrate the democratic plurality of its cultural milieu. These groups were politically reformist – for example in opposing censorship – but incapable of achieving any profound change. They were especially impotent in the face of the kind of repression unleashed by the victory of reactionary, proto-fascist forces.

The term 'Third Cinema' was coined by Argentinean filmmakers Fernando SOLANAS and Octavia GETINO in 1969. Invoking the Cuban Revolution of 1959, as well as a post-1968 European and American avant-garde film school, SOLANAS and GETINO extolled Third Cinema as an artistic and social movement hostile to the dominance of an industrialized, ideologically corrupt Hollywood, as well as a politically inept Second Cinema located in the First and Third World. For Teshome GABRIEL (1982, 2):

> The principal characteristic of Third Cinema is really not so much where it is made, or even who makes it, but, rather, the ideology it espouses and the consciousness it displays. The Third Cinema is that cinema of the Third World which stands opposed to imperialism and class oppression in all their ramifications and manifestations.

Key targets of Third Cinema's provocative stance were the state-sponsored documentaries developed in the U.K. and the U.S. Although these documentaries worked to draw the public's attention to 'social issues,' they were, by default, implicated in a liberal agenda.[3] During the second half of the 1930s, for example, Roosevelt's administration, under the auspices of the U.S. Department of Agriculture's Resettlement Program, funded two major works by filmmaker Pare Lorentz. *The Plow that Broke the Plains* (1936) dealt with the problems of wheat production and cattle ranching in the Great Plains, and, in particular, the record drought that culminated in the Dust Bowl. *The River* (1938) focused on the environmental management work of the Tennessee Valley Authority (TVA), emphasizing the majesty of the American landscape but also the need for large-scale, technocratic mastery of Nature. Using stunning photo work and stirring musical scores, both films served to underpin the New Deal philosophy regarding the necessity for state control of the economy so that capital could be invested in the working classes.

---

3. Even committed leftist Joris IVENS worked for the USDA Resettlement Program. His *Power and the Land* (1940) lauded the benefits of rural electrification.

Also targeted were urban-based documentaries of the 1960s and 1970s that embraced a more polemic approach to filmmaking. Civil rights, anti-war movements and the women's movement provided the impetus for much of this cinematic activism. Inspired by student protests in 1968 independent film collectives with the aim of producing cinema that would document and contribute to political protest emerged in cities across the country, from New York to San Francisco. Although these films served to highlight exploitation and social discord engineered under capitalism, they also, it was argued, tended to work within the same capitalist mode of production as mainstream Hollywood. The latter drew upon Second Cinema's various auteur techniques for its own ends, while political content became subsumed into a generalized 'counter-culture' attitude that could be sold to youth audiences.

The documentary as 'genre', then, is a complex subject. It emerged as a form of representation that sought to capture something profound and interesting about the way we live – from the inner city to the furthermost wilderness. As a counterpoint to mass-produced fiction film, the documentary offered an alternate perspective on the world, one that could even serve to challenge hegemonic attitudes and prejudices. Although some of the early, classic documentary filmmakers ascribed to the revolutionary potential of the medium, many later commentators, however, pointed to the fact that predominant examples of the genre were politically passive – serving to remind spectators of the wonderful diversity of the world or, at best, their responsibility to those less fortunate.

It is not surprising, therefore, that the documentary defies easy categorization. For those, such as WRIGHT (1947), who valorizes the human agency involved in making, showing and looking at film, documentary is distinct by virtue of the *individual's* attempt to highlight something 'truthful' about the world. By contrast, for those such as SOLANAS and GETINO (1976) who look to the social conditions within which these films exist, documentary is, by and large, a *class-ridden*, bourgeois product that serves only to maintain the status quo. Rather than become mired in this agency versus structure debate, however, it is possible to step back from the theoretical battleground and, instead, consider film as a *social construct*. That is, labels such as 'independent,' 'alternative,' 'radical' and 'critical' – all of which have been used to define documentary – can be considered means by which the identity, and in turn efficacy, of this 'object' is actively constructed over time and across space. Rather than accept these labels as given, then, it is possible to inquire into the means by which they have become attached to film as an object of interest and, moreover, to whose benefit.

Importantly, within this understanding of film, such labels are not considered to be the product of a class-based ideology, nor the original expression of individual subjects. Instead, these and other labels are part and parcel of broader-scale discourses[4] concerning the nature of the filmmaking enterprise that circulate

---

4. In this sense of the term, discourse refers not to a way of speaking, but a comprehensive and complex view of the world that is manifest in how an object such as film is discussed, as well as the day to day practices within which that object is dealt with and experienced.

through society; mutating and transposing in the process as they interconnect with *other* discourses pertaining to, for example, progress, the responsibility of government, social welfare and nationhood. As such, the question of whether or not a film is 'independent' is redundant; instead, the question becomes, 'who has used such as designation in reference to a particular form of filmmaking, and, for what purpose?'

In the following section, I undertake a partial constructivist analysis of one particular kind of documentary filmmaking, namely U.S. independent cinema. As noted above, the label 'independent' was traditionally associated with the genre because of many filmmakers' distrust and dislike of mainstream Hollywood filmmaking, which relies on formulaic storylines that offer escapism and / or voyeurism. Moreover, Hollywood cinema is considered the mass product of a 'system' that works to subsume individual talent and vision. In this sense of the term independent has come to mean outside of the capitalist mode of production and reproduction. And yet, many independent documentaries are funded by the state, which, almost without exception, is in place to maintain a capitalist economy. The competitive character of this funding process means that such films not only must adhere to funding guidelines that dictate content and perspective, but also must offer exhibition opportunities to particular audiences. In this sense of the term, independent is a label that signifies the adoption of a non-mainstream 'voice' that is, nevertheless, deemed of worth to society at large. How, then, has this framing of the term 'independent' come into place? And, who has benefited from this particular construction of the practice of filmmaking?

CREATING 'SPACE' FOR U.S. INDEPENDENT DOCUMENTARIES

In the wake of President Kennedy's assassination in 1963, a wave of sympathy and public support enabled his successor, Lyndon B. Johnson, to pass a number of Kennedy Administration proposals including the Civil Rights Act of 1964. In what ANDREW (1998) calls, "a liberal interlude unmatched in the twentieth century," Johnson introduced his own vision for America. Within what he called the Great Society, the state would push to end poverty, promote equality, improve education, rejuvenate cities, and protect the environment.[5] Significantly, while the Great Society was to be orchestrated under state control, it would facilitate *opportunity* for

---

5. The *Civil Rights Act* of 1964 and the *Voting Rights Act* of 1965 outlawed racial discrimination in public accommodations and schools and removed obstacles to voting. As part of the Civil Rights Act, the federal government would withhold funds from any state that did not desegregate. The introduction of Medicare brought quality health care to senior citizens. The *Economic Opportunity Act* 1964 created a Job Corps similar to the New Deal Civilian Conservation Corps; a domestic peace corps; a system for vocational training; and Head Start, a pre-school program designed to prepare children for success in public school. The bill also funded community action programs and extended loans to small businessmen and farmers. The *Elementary and Secondary Education Act* of 1965 redefined the federal role in education and targeted funding to poor students. The *Housing and Urban Development Act* of 1965 established the Department of Housing and Urban Development (HUD) and expanded funding for public housing.

individuals, rather than provide automatic welfare entitlements for social groups. According to DAVIES (1999), the Great Society was very much couched within accepted, American ideals: "When Lyndon Johnson declared a 'War on Poverty,' he took great care to align his ambitious program with national attitudes toward work, worthiness, and dependency."

Between 1964 and 1967, the President submitted, and Congress enacted, more than 100 major proposals in each of the 89th and 90th Congresses (CALIFANO 1999). Part and parcel of this effort was the *Public Broadcasting Act* of 1967. Concerned that radio and television would be used solely for lowbrow, commercial purposes, the Federal Communications Commission had already reserved both radio and TV channels for noncommercial stations. In 1967, the U.S. Congress established and funded the Public Broadcasting Service (PBS) with the aim of creating programs that had, "...instructional, educational, and cultural purposes...." (Figure 1); these programs would be 'independent,' then, in the sense that they were to be free from Hollywood commercialism.

Figure 1. Public Broadcasting Act: Subpart D – Corporation for Public Broadcasting. Sec. 396. [47 U.S.C. 396]

The Congress hereby finds and declares that:
(1) it is in the public interest to encourage the growth and development of public radio and television broadcasting, including the use of such media for instructional, educational, and cultural purposes;
(2) it is in the public interest to encourage the growth and development of nonbroadcast telecommunications technologies for the delivery of public telecommunications services;
(3) expansion and development of public telecommunications and of diversity of its programming depend on freedom, imagination, and initiative on both local and national levels;
(4) the encouragement and support of public telecommunications, while matters of importance for private and local development, are also of appropriate and important concern to the Federal Government;
(5) it furthers the general welfare to encourage public telecommunications services which will be responsive to the interests of people both in particular localities and throughout the United States, which will constitute an expression of diversity and excellence, and which will constitute a source of alternative telecommunications services for all the citizens of the Nation;
(6) it is in the public interest to encourage the development of programming that involves creative risks and that addresses the needs of unserved and underserved audiences, particularly children and minorities;
(7) it is necessary and appropriate for the Federal Government to complement, assist, and support a national policy that will most effectively make public telecommunications services available to all citizens of the United States;
(8) public television and radio stations and public telecommunications services constitute valuable local community resources for utilizing electronic media to address national concerns and solve local problems through community programs and outreach programs;
(9) it is in the public interest for the Federal Government to ensure that all citizens of the United States have access to public telecommunications services through all appropriate available telecommunications distribution technologies; and
(10) a private corporation should be created to facilitate the development of public telecommunications and to afford maximum protection from extraneous interference and control.

Source: http://www.cpb.org/about/history/

Even at the height of Johnson's missionary effort, however, dissent emerged over the appropriate form and function of a 'public' media. Appalshop, intended to train disadvantaged Appalachian young people for jobs in the media, was established in 1969 as part of Johnson's War on Poverty program. Rather than relocate to urban locations and take part in the dissemination of an urban-based 'high' culture, trainees incorporated as a not-for-profit organization, based in Whitesburg, Kentucky, dedicated to creating opportunities for 'regional self-expression.' According to HANNA (2000), Appalshop sought to counter over a century of mass media representations of rural Appalachia as a region apart from modern America. The clichéd use of mountains, poverty, and violence as symbols of Appalachia, it was felt, had served to erase heterogeneity and difference within the region from the public imagination. Rather than become part of the public broadcasting system, founders of Appalshop looked for ways to reanimate, as well as preserve, diverse, Appalachian-based folk traditions through radio, film and TV (compare with Kentucky Educational Television, below, founded a year earlier).

Under the terms of the 1967 legislation, Public Broadcasting was to be overseen by a state-sponsored organization, the Corporation for Public Broadcasting (CPB). Under the auspices of the CPB, over 1,000 public television and radio stations were developed nationwide. As a medium between Congress and media producers, the CPB was intended to be 'independent' of partisan political interests. A crucial clause expressly forbade government "direction, supervision, or control" of public broadcasting. Accordingly, composition of the CPB is delimited; although the President appoints CPB Board of Directors, the White House can put appointees of one political party in no more than five of the nine CPB Board seats. This does allow for a controlling majority, however, and is an issue that has been raised time and again in regard to the 'loading' up of Republican committee members.[6]

More controversially, while the CPB receives about 15 percent of its revenues from Congress and disperses it to noncommercial stations for the production of radio and television programming, it also receives numerous grants from foundations, such as the Ford Foundation, universities, company 'underwriting' and individual subscribers (see Figure 2 for a breakdown of financial contributors). The business 'underwriting' of CPB programs has long been an issue, with the obvious comparison made to advertising. As the advocacy group, Citizens for Independent Broadcasting (CIPB), argues, PBS has been "privatized within an inch of its life" (see http://www.cipbonline.org/) as companies gain a particular veneer of social respectability through their association with this 'worthy' form of media representation.

More controversy ensued from the CPB's perceived failure to support truly non-'independent' filmmaking. As can be seen in Figure 3, the CPB's mission statement is very much in line with Johnson's vision of a Great Society; note the emphasis on the provision of 'high' culture, alongside cultural diversity and local

---

6. Currently, the CPB Board consists of five Republicans, two Democrats and one independent. The most recent Republican appointees are also massive donors to the Republican party (£491,699 and £324,420 respectively).

Figure 2. Breakdown of Financial Contributors to the Corporation for Public Broadcasting, FYI 2001.

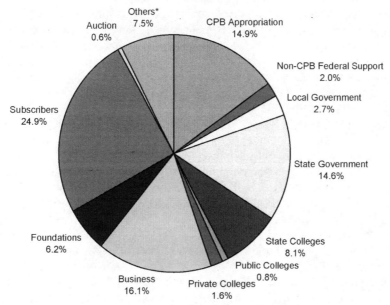

Source: http://www.cpb.org/about/funding/whopays.html

Figure 3. Mission Statement for the Corporation for Public Broadcasting.

> The fundamental purpose of public telecommunications is to provide programs and services which inform, enlighten and enrich the public. While these programs and services are provided to enhance the knowledge, and citizenship, and inspire the imagination of all Americans, the Corporation has particular responsibility to encourage the development of programming that involves creative risks and that addresses the needs of unserved and underserved audiences, particularly children and minorities.
>
> The Corporation is accountable to the public for investing its funds in programs and services which are educational, innovative, locally relevant, and reflective of America's common values and cultural diversity. The Corporation serves as a catalyst for innovation in the public broadcasting industry, and acts as a guardian of the mission and purposes for which public broadcasting was established.

Source: http://www.cpb.org/about/corp/mission.html

activism. The ideal is a nation that, although culturally diverse, is united through the shared values and concerted efforts of an informed and worthy citizenry. Accordingly, the rhetoric is one of inclusion, wherein all Americans, regardless of ethnicity or age, can see something that pertains to their interests and needs This desire to promote a multicultural vision of the U.S. can be seen in the CPB's support of organizations such as Latino Public Broadcasting (LPB), which, in line with other members of the National Minority Consortia, "celebrates and highlights the cultural heritage of America's diverse populations" (see http://www.lpbp.org/background.htm).

Wide-spread dissatisfaction with the CPB's interpretation of its mission emerged in the 1980s. Under the 1978 *Telecommunications Act*, the CPB was obliged to allocate a 'substantial' amount of their programming funds to 'independent producers.' A committee report eventually defined 'substantial' as no fewer than fifty percent. But, the CPB counted anyone not salaried by a Public Broadcasting Station as an independent; a definition that includes, somewhat ironically, those affiliated with the Hollywood system. Many documentary filmmakers preferred to define themselves as producers of their own 'standalone' films, as opposed to programs where final creative authority rested with a staff producer who made the production fit within a tight framework and 'identity' of an established series of productions. Throughout the decade, this self proclaimed 'independent' production community rallied advocates to convince Congress that funds for producers working outside of public TV stations were significantly fewer than the fifty percent or so of the programming funds claimed by CPB. From this struggle, Congress, in 1988, created the Independent Television Service (ITVS), as a separate organization to ensure that CPB would indeed financially support this group and give them the access to the public television system.

Since its foundation in 1991, ITVS has put over $58 million into U.S. films produced by its 'independent' members. ITVS provides, in addition: creative development, feedback during production, and a public television launch that includes marketing, publicity, station relations and outreach support. In contrast to the CPB, the ITVS Board is elected by its affiliates. And, one can see in its statement of values (Figure 4) a much more explicit acknowledgement of social inequity and conflict as well as a commitment to diversity. Reference to the provision of 'high culture' items is noticeably absent. What is also noticeable, however, is that this particular rhetoric has been tied to the rights and responsibilities of the *individual*; more of these individual voices are to be heard, telling their *own* stories and providing their *own* opinions.[7] The 'head'line devised by ITVS to present itself online (Figure 5) is symbolic of this attention to the individual. It is composed from

---

7. It is fascinating to find individual ITVS Board members questioning this same emphasis on the individual. According to ITVS board member Larry DERESSA (1995), the mission of documentary should be the presentation and dissemination of what might be termed a 'critically aware' form of knowledge: "... these more interactive environments (like democracy itself) can never eliminate the 'problem' of voice, the responsibility for developing a point of view, but only generalize it. The most self-effacing and guilt-ridden post-modern ethnographer, the most self-absorbed and candid personal filmmaker, cannot escape the responsibility of shaping a 'voice.' Anyone with a degree of self-awareness knows that how we describe others and even ourselves results from deeply embedded psychological influences and cultural norms; authenticity, even our own, is an illusion. We cannot represent our selves or our communities because there is no essential self there to represent, as a result absolute transparency is unachievable and, ultimately, absurd. We are, in a sense, only points of view, or more precisely the continual search for new, more fulfilling, points of view. Thus the role of the teleplex, indeed, of any critical discourse, is to scrutinize received points of view, old ways of 'speaking' ourselves, and to develop new more empowering ones."

Figure 4. Independent Television Service's Statement of Values

> In an era that encompasses both the explosion of commercial information enterprises and a consolidation of media empires, the role of public sector media becomes critical to a free, open, and informed society. ITVS holds the following values as essential to carrying out the organization's work: Freedom of expression is a human right. A free press and public access to information are foundations of democracy. An open society allows unpopular and minority views to be publicly aired. A civilized society seeks economic and social justice. A just society seeks participation from those without power, prominence, or wealth. A free nation allows all citizens forums in which they can tell their own stories and express their own opinions.

Source: http://www.itvs.org/about/

Figure 5. Independent Television Service's 'Head'line.

Source: http://www.itvs.org/about/

a series of facial close-ups; these are differentiated not only by gender, age, ethnicity and occupation, but also angle – the faces are turned in different directions. Despite this variety, however, the faces invoke a sense of common humanity, for, in each close-up, the eyes draw our attention – invoking a sense of interpersonal connection. The close-up draws us into the personal space of the subject being represented. We may all be unique by virtue of our differences; but this visual connection serves to remind us of our shared ability to think, feel and express (KRESS and VAN LEEUWEN 1998).

Such an appeal can simply be read as a paean to tolerance. In the context of state-sponsored broadcasting, though, a link can also be made to the ideal of American nationhood; wherein, a country built on colonization and wave upon wave of migration is seen to be united under the rubric of 'freedom and equality for all.' Indeed, for ITVS this is a crucial point; for, it is only through the inclusion of all, however unpopular or marginal, that a true 'democracy' can come into being.

ITVS funds a series of filmmaking units, including PBS' most visible venue for independent documentary, the P.O.V. (Point of View) series. P.O.V. is a division of American Documentary Inc, a non-profit agency founded in 1987 and based in New York. Funding for P.O.V. is provided by the ITVS, but also, by the MacArthur Foundation, National Endowment for the Arts, and, Open Society Institute amongst others. Given their reliance on ITVS for capital, it is not surprising to find a similar invocation of neoliberalism. As Figure 6 makes clear, narratives are fundamentally 'personal'; moreover, it is the voice of the individual that allows for an 'unvarnished' representation of social life – not because they have insight into some kind of fundamental ethos, but because they express passion and poignancy. In other words, P.O.V. documentaries aim to capture and express what it is to be human, in all its manifold variety. Less overtly political than ITVS, P.O.V. has, nevertheless, retained a claim to local activism; in this case, viewers are encouraged to 'talk back' via email as well as through community group meetings, thereby achieving some form of interactive media. In an interesting update of Johnson's Great Society, P.O.V. has showcased the voice of the Other as educational and worthy, with the added implication that viewer response to this can be taken as a sign of good citizenship.

P.O.V. in turn works with PBS affiliates, such as Kentucky Educational Television (KET), which is, perhaps surprisingly,[8] the country's largest single PBS station. Based in Lexington KY, KET began life in 1968 as part and parcel of President Johnson's attempt to use TV media as a means of social inclusion. Their mission statement (Figure 7) uses several metaphors to emphasize this sense of connection, defining the station as a window on the world, pipeline for ideas, and even, magic carpet for the imagination. The statement also is couched within the rhetoric of the Great Society as family members, students and workers are all encouraged to take charge and empower themselves. As the founders of Appalshop noted, however, this homage to the individual is largely predicated on the disadvantaged, rural subject; since regions, such as Appalachia, are targeted as being in need of transformation by an urban-based media provider. KET still identifies itself primarily as an educational provider that can and should cross socio-geographic divides.

Having outlined the legislative and institutional context within these agencies operate, I now turn to examples of the kinds of films successful in gaining funding. *Tobacco Blues* (1998), produced by Café Sisters, was sponsored by P.O.V., ITVS and KET. As the website for *Beyond the Border* (2003) indicates (Figure 8), this Dos Vatos production gained sponsorship from KET, ITVS and the Latino Broadcasting Service. These agencies sponsoring the two films in turn rely on the CPB for the majority of their finances. What I hope to make clear is that these films work within some well-established discourses on the character of the rural that also invoke the individual as a site for concern and approbation. Both *Tobacco Blues* and *Beyond the Border* work within a discourse on social justice that positions rural America as a place of diversity, injustice, and inequality. Within an overarching context of 'globalization,' variously defined as big business – or, simply, the manifest flows of capital, people and products – some will win at the expense of others. To care for the fate of each individual is to acknowledge this fundamental humanity.

---

8. Perhaps even more surprisingly, KET was also the first station to support local documentary filmmaking using funds specially allocated by the Kentucky General Assembly as opposed to federal funding. The KET Fund for Independent Production has been awarding grants to Kentucky-based film and video makers each biennium since 1990.

Figure 6. Company Profile for P.O.V., a division of American Documentary Inc.

> P.O.V. (a cinema term for 'point of view') is public television's annual award-winning showcase for independent non-fiction films. Passionate, powerful and poignant, P.O.V. films – regardless of their subjects – are ultimately personal and unvarnished reportage on our lives. The series continues to challenge the notion of television as a one-way medium by creating pioneering models and innovative broadcast-related projects designed to maximize television's potential – talk back component. Comments from viewers are recorded at regional station sites, or via home video letter, phone, e-mail, web site or regular mail.
>
> The films on P.O.V.'s broadcast list reflect all styles of non-fiction film: personal, investigative, cinema verité, traditional documentary, as well as experimental approaches. Please note that you do not have to be in your P.O.V. film-we are looking for films that express an opinion, which can be done in a variety of ways.

Source: http://www.pbs.org/pov/utils/aboutpov.html

Figure 7. Mission Statement for Kentucky Educational Television.

> To serve the unmet needs of:
> The home / family
> The institution / students
> The workforce.
>
> KET is a resource for lifelong learning ... a window, a pipeline, and a magic carpet carrying students of all ages to places they've never been, introducing them to people they've never seen, and giving them experiences they otherwise would never have-thereby helping to raise the educational level of all Kentuckians and to empower them to take control of their lives.

Source: http://www.ket.org/agency/about/mission.htm

Figure 8. PBS Web-Site for Beyond the Border.

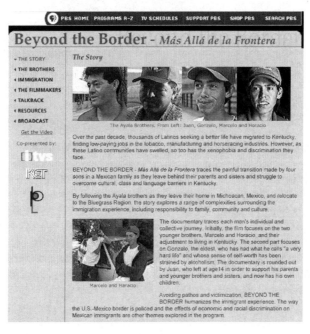

DOCUMENTING THE RURAL

The films outlined below form an interesting pair. While the first to be produced, *Tobacco Blues*, presents a sense of anxiety around the issue of globalization, and, in particular, the fate of 'rooted' communities, as capital continues to flow in and out of place; the second, *Beyond the Border*, takes on the trials and tribulations of migrant workers, who travel hundreds of miles and spend years away from their 'home' communities to make a living. What I suggest, though, is that despite these distinct foci, both films highlight discrimination and its effects, while, at the same time, working to an idealized notion of American society as inclusive. It is the country's failure to achieve a particular ideal – the Great Society, as Johnson termed it – that preoccupies both and gives shape and direction to their critique.

Tobacco Blues

Tobacco Blues (1998) was produced by Café Sisters Productions, a non-profit, woman-operated film company, formed in 1987 by Christine FUGATE and Eren MCGUINESS. It addresses the fate of the small-scale, family farmer in Kentucky as tobacco companies increasingly disinvest in favor of cheap produce from foreign sources. As such, it can largely be seen as a 'dissonant' perspective on the rural because of its strong anti-globalization stance. As WOODS (2005) has observed, the predominant discourse pertaining to the U.S. countryside used by the state was, and is, resource capitalism, which constructs the rural as a space of resource extraction and production – as an export economy needing to be supported by infrastructure developments (e.g. railroads) and by social policies that facilitate capitalist accumulation. In its southern manifestation, resource capitalism was a product of the deal that ended the Reconstruction era and cemented the South's status as a 'resource colony' for the industrial northeast; one supplying cotton, sugar, tobacco and other commodities from plantations owned by a plutocratic elite. The western manifestation of resource capitalism, in contrast, was entrepreneurial – constructing the rural west as a 'virgin territory' to be exploited for its resources of minerals, oil, timber and agricultural produce.

There was yet another discourse the state tapped into at particular times and in particular places, namely agrarianism. Farmers are represented in this discourse as 'pioneers,' at once taming the wilderness and building a unique nation-state. The yeoman farmer was a central figure in the ideology of Jeffersonian democracy, "an independent spirit free from the corrupting influence of the city, who would work hard, take responsible care of the land, and uphold the values of liberty and individualism cherished by the new nation" (WOODS 2005). Populist movements made much of this valorization of the family farm as the moral and economic fulcrum around which American society was organized. And, on occasion, state policy (ironically, including some otherwise extreme Republican administrations) was seen as being driven by the desire to maintain this group over and against the interests of a free market economy (DIXON and HAPKE 2003).

Tobacco Blues taps into this discourse. In the proposal written for the project (MCGUINESS and FUGATE 1996), much is made of the 'family farmers' who lie at the heart of the film. The tag-line is: "KENTUCKY'S FORGOTTEN SMALL FAMILY FARMERS GRAPPLE WITH THE BURNING QUESTION: CAN A GOOD PERSON GROW TOBACCO?" The film proposal argues that, caught between increasing restrictions against smoking on one hand, and footloose, multinational tobacco companies on the other, the fate of the small, family farm is of greatest significance; not only because their voice is rarely heard at the level of policy making, but also because they are the 'backbone' of the economy. Tobacco farming is not about making a profit, but preserving a 'lifestyle.' The film will accordingly follow the lives of some of these farmers – "each dealing with these pressures in their own way" – and put, "a human face on the men and women who make their living raising the state's most profitable legal crop." According to Director Christine FUGATE, the intent is to educate and inform the wider public about the virtues of agrarianism, and specifically, the worthiness of tobacco farmers. She suggests that the group is stigmatized largely due to their association with the crop: "The troubles facing the farmers in *Tobacco Blues* are really troubles facing farmers all over America ... Small farmers are gone in other states – the reason they still exist in Kentucky is because of tobacco. My hope is that people who see the film will begin to look at small farmers in general as the valuable resources that they are" (P.O.V. Press Release, 1998, http://www.pbs.org/pov/pov1998/ tobaccoblues/index.html#pressroom).

With voice-over provided by actor and Kentucky-native Harry Dean Stanton and backdrop of Blue Grass music, *Tobacco Blues* follows the year-long cycle of tobacco growing, emphasizing the traditional, communal character of this activity. As one protagonist interviewed in the film observes,

> Critics of tobacco don't bother to look at our heritage or our culture ... Tobacco is one of those rare crops that brings people together. It's a handmade crop. Every step of the way, it involves a lot of people. It strengthens the bonds of kinship and friendship. It is an opportunity for people to help each other. The best people I know are tobacco farmers.

What we do not see in *Tobacco Blues* are the people behind the multinational corporations, or the seasonal labor used in tobacco harvesting. Arguably, this dulls the edge of the film's critique of large-scale agribusiness in general, as it becomes a mere backdrop to events beyond the transformative power of human agency. And, it presents a somewhat insular view of rural Kentucky farming communities as hardworking but ineffective. The film, however, is not intended to be an objective account, but stands by its evocative portrayal of a way of life under threat. As such, it is a 'passionate' presentation that lauds those same virtues of hard work and individual effort that Johnson so admired. As shown below, the follow-up, *Beyond the Border*, builds on precisely this rhetoric.

Beyond the Border

Beyond the Border (2003) was made by Dos Vatos Productions, a company founded by director Ari Luis PALOS as a means of "bringing the voice of Mexicanos to a nationwide audience" (http://www.pbs.org/itvs/beyondtheborder/filmmakers.html). The film is produced by Eren McGuinness, also of Café Sisters Production. The film's website, hosted by PBS, provides a broad overview of the narrative (see Figure 8). The film follows four brothers as they travel from Michoacan, Mexico to Kentucky, USA. It is their individual experiences of the complexities of immigration, including xenophobia and discrimination, as well as cultural linguistic barriers, that constitute the heart of the story.

Given the U.S.' turbulent history of immigration policy, and racism in general, this project is arguably much more contentious than that on tobacco farming. Its stance also is much more transgressive, particularly as the people portrayed have entered the U.S. illegally. Yet, although it does not partake of the agrarian discourse noted above, the film does tap into a recognized body of thought and practice – that of 'social justice' – which, as WOODS (2005) points out, has constructed the rural as a space of systematic exploitation based on racism. Indeed, *Beyond the Border* has a predecessor in the film *Harvest of Shame* (1961), narrated by journalist Edward R. Murrow, which documented exploitation of the Black migrant worker in rural America. According to 'Time' (1961, March 31, see http:// www.vcdh.virginia.edu/HIUS316/mbase/docs/harvest.html),

> Deliberately scheduled for the day after Thanksgiving, the documentary drew for turkey-stuffed Americans a stark picture of the field hands who rove about the country, living in makeshift squalor, and selling their labor for an average of $900 a year. Moving in shirtsleeves among the film's subjects, Narrator Murrow reached heights of personal indignation, as when he quoted one migrant-hiring Southern farmer: 'We used to own our slaves; now we just rent them.'... because of its overstatement, Harvest drew howls, especially from Florida's U.S. Senator Spessard L. Holland, whose state was the one visited by Murrow. *Harvest of Shame*, said Holland, contained at least seven distortions and errors of fact. Holland cited, among others, the example of the 29-year-old Negro woman who told Murrow that she was the mother of 14 and had earned $1 for a full day's work in the fields. The facts were, said Holland, that seven of her children were dead and that her meager wage was a measure of her own indolence.[9]

What is interesting about attitudes invoked by *Harvest of Shame* (1961) is that they *also* tap into a neoliberal discourse on the virtues of hard work and effort; in this case, the argument made is that some individuals are naturally more 'indolent' than others. We can read this as a racist framing of the issue because those individuals deemed to be indolent all happen to be African American.

Beyond the Border seems to make a direct effort to counter precisely this kind of racist stereotyping. Time and again throughout the narrative, the individual worth of the Mexican protagonists is stressed. As most of the e-mail responses to the showing of the film on PBS indicate, this tactic appears to have been generally

---

9. Murrow later attempted to halt the showing of the documentary in the U.K. because, in his new job as Director of the U.S. Information Agency, he deemed it to portray the U.S. in a bad light.

successful. According to those viewers who saw the show, had access to e-mail and bothered to send in a comment, *Beyond the Border* did indeed 'educate and inform,' in that it both revealed to them the 'human face' of immigration and bolstered their sense of immigration as an integral part of the American nation-building rather than a problem to be overcome (see http://www.pbs.org/itvs/beyondtheborder/talkback.html). As one viewer wrote:

> I am the son of Mexican immigrants. I worked in the fields starting at age five. 39 years later I am in Clinical research for a good medical school. The depictions of this family are a good example of what contributions immigrants give to our wonderful country. My Parents always encouraged education, to pursue a better life and how working hard to study and learn is nothing compared to working in the fields or other hard labor. This beuatiful family in your film is doing the same thing but at a more basic level. Most hard working people like this come from strong religious morals and stay honest. We are all Humans in the end and should love and support one another like this family does. God Bless them (spelling as in original).

Key to this realization is an emphasis on the fundamental humanity of immigrants, despite their apparent cultural and ethnic differences.

> I just finished watching this wonderful and poignant film. My emotions ran the gamut, along with the emotions of those on the screen. An interesting realization is that although this family was from a different culture than mine, their experiences and processes were likely as diverse as those of any 4 brothers and their families from America, or from any other country. I'm again reminded of the adage: It's not about content; It's about process. While our individual experiences may differ, we all laugh, hurt, cry, bleed, and above all, love.

Such comments also make clear the fact that this realization is strongly against the grain of accepted opinion[10]:

> I saw the documentary about a month ago on Public Television and was very moved. As a Californian, it is rare to hear about the humanity behind Mexican immigration, and the basic struggle of people for survival.

Another wrote:

> An extraordinary film that put a human face on the people who are contributing to the making of America. Just imagine America without Latinos for one day. What will it be?

This effort to place a 'face' on the immigrant experience is manifest not only in the narrative structure, as the brothers take turns at center stage, but also in the film's web-site presentation (Figure 8). Echoing the 'head'liner provided by ITVS, the *Beyond the Border* imagery relies on facial close-ups of each protagonist. Again, they differ in age and in dress, as well as facial angle and expression; but it is the use of the close-up itself that draws us into their personal 'space.'

---

10. Very few comments speak to this more mainstream framing of Mexican immigration. One of the exceptions is the following (spelling in original): "Trouble is , you cannot trust, or respect illigals, 1) because, they may be sleeper cells, and since 9–11 why should we trust anyone. 2) they are bleeding us of our tax dollars, especially since so many american children go without adaquate nutrition. 3) taking jobs from americans, on & on." Such sentiments present a very different picture of the U.S., one that must become insular if it is to be 'safe'.

CONCLUSIONS

Both documentaries, then, draw on existing discourses concerning the rural. *Tobacco Blues* taps into an agrarian framing of farmers and farming, wherein both are lauded as the backbone of American democracy. *Beyond the Border* taps into a more controversial discourse – on the need for American society to overcome exploitation and discrimination, as manifest in the suffering experienced by migrant laborers. Underpinning both is an idealized notion of the U.S. as a unique nation-state that, by virtue of its history of immigration, is ethnically and culturally diverse, but, nevertheless, is united by shared political values. These films play a significant role in the process of state-building as their narratives are rife with rhetoric pertaining to inclusion, tolerance and individual worth.

Rather than question the 'accuracy,' or lack thereof, of this representation of rural life, I have attempted to show that this framing of the rural is strongly in accord with President Johnson's notion of a Great Society, wherein an informed and active citizenry, composed of hard working individuals, can and should be produced under the aegis of state intervention. This ideal lies at the heart of the Public Broadcasting Service and must be taken into account if applications for funding are to be successful. Furthermore, I argue it is the predominance of the state as a source of sponsorship that has significantly shaped the form and function of 'independent' documentary in the U.S. This result is because although documentary, as a genre, emerged as a form of filmmaking made distinct by its ability to 'capture' a profound truth about the world – in contrast to mainstream Hollywood, it was argued – it has since come to be associated with the representation of highly personal, emotion-filled, narratives from those deemed to be marginalized. Therefore, it is no surprise to find that, for many, documentary has lost its 'radical' edge as more structuralist accounts of social life have been effectively displaced.

Although I do not suggest that a more structuralist account is 'correct,' what I wish to point out is that the range of attitudes and opinions driving independent filmmaking and that can be represented through this medium, is effectively curtailed by its current form of competitive funding. Ironically, mission statements promising to look favorably on diverse narratives, particularly those of marginalized groups, do so only on the basis that each narrative be a uniquely *personal* one emphasizing individual passions and emotions. This means that publicly funded commentaries on the inequities of life in the U.S. must portray these issues as significant only in relation to particular protagonists and must, moreover, emphasize the ability of the individual, rather than organized group, to overcome adversity. While such representations may well educate and inform about the suffering of others and our need to be tolerant and respectful of each other, they simultaneously cast American society, the Land of the Free, within a neoliberal discourse. As was seen with the documentary *Harvest of Shame*, the downside of this discourse is that responsibility for failure can also be laid at the feet of the individual on the grounds that they have not been sufficiently hard-working, and, hence, is undeserving of our help or support. President Johnson's vision of a Great Society, of which Public Broadcasting is such an integral part, promises much for those who are seen to adhere to its principles, but provides no comfort for those who do not 'fit' its associated picture of a truly American citizen.

REFERENCES

ANDREW, J. (1998): *Lyndon Johnson and the Great Society*. New York.

CALIFANO, J. (1999): What Was Really Great About The Great Society: The truth behind the conservative myths. *The Washington Monthly Online*, accessed at http://www.washingtonmonthly.com/features/1999/9910.califano.html.

CHANAN, M. (1997): The Changing Geography of Third Cinema. *Screen: Special Latin American Issue* 38 (4, Winter), 372–388.

CORNER, J. (1996): *The Art of Record: Critical Introduction to Documentary*. Manchester.

DAVIES, G. (1999): *From Opportunity to Entitlement: The Transformation and Decline of Great Society Liberalism*. Kansas.

DERESSA, L. (1995): Reflections on ITVS. *California Newsreel*, accessed at http://www.newsreel.org/articles/goodbye.htm.

DIXON, D. P. and H. M. HAPKE (2003): Cultivating discourse: the social construction of agricultural legislation. *Annals of the Association of American Geographers* 93 (1), 142–64.

FULFORD, R. (2000): Review of Harvest of Shame. *The National Post*, October 3rd, accessed at http://www.robertfulford.com/JohnGrierson.html.

GABRIEL, T. (1982): *Third Cinema in the Third World: An Aesthetic of Liberation*. Ann Arbor, Michigan.

HACKING, I. (1999): *The Social Construction of What*. Cambridge, Massachusetts.

HANNA, S. (2000): Representation and the Reproduction of Appalachian Space: A History of Contested Signs and Meanings. *Historical Geography* 28, 171–199.

IVENS, J. (1969): *The Camera and I*. Berlin.

KRESS, G. and T. VAN LEEUWEN (1998): *Reading Images. The Grammar of Visual Design*. New York.

MCGUINESS, E. and C. FUGATE (1996): *A Funding Proposal for Tobacco Blues*. Accessed with kind permission from Café Sisters Productions.

NICHOLS, B. (2001): *Introduction to Documentary*. Bloomington, Indiana.

ROTHA, P. (1952): *Documentary Film* [first published in 1936]. London.

SMITH, L. (2003): Chips off the Old Ice Block: Nanook of the North and the Relocation of Identity. CRESSWELL, T. and D. DIXON (Eds.): *Engaging Film: Geographies of Mobility and Identity*. Lanham, Maryland, 94–122.

SOLANAS, F. and O. GETINO (1976): Towards a Third Cinema. NICHOLS, B. (Ed.): *Movies and Methods: An Anthology*. Berkeley, 44–64.

VERTOV, D. and A. MICHELSON (1995) [first published in 1929]: *Kino-Eye: The writings of Dziga Vetov*. University of California Press, Los Angeles.

WOODS, Mike. (2005): *Rural Geography: Process, Responses and Experience in Rural Restructuring*. London.

WRIGHT, B. (1947): Documentary Today, The Penguin Film Review 2 (January 1947); reprinted in: AITKEN, I. (Ed.): *The Documentary Film Movement: An Anthology*. Edinburgh, 237–243.

THE TEXT

Marcus A. Doel

FROM ANIMATED PHOTOGRAPHY TO FILM: THE FORMATION OF VERNACULAR RELATIVITY IN EARLY ENGLISH FILMS (1895–1908)

> *The essence of a thing
> never appears at the outset,
> but in the middle...*
> (DELEUZE 1986, 3).

INTRODUCTION

> *[E]arly cinema –
> an all but lost continent
> of invention and discovery*
> (CHRISTIE 1994, 8).

The relationship between geography and film is gradually becoming an established area of research (e.g. AITKEN and ZONN 1994; CRESSWELL and DIXON 2002; LUKINBEAL and ZONN 2004). While this research embraces a very wide range of interests (social, cultural, economic, political, ecological, etc.), special emphasis has been placed on understanding how fiction and nonfiction films have represented different kinds of places, and in so doing fostered certain senses of place and particular kinds of identities (local, regional, and national; individual, inter-subjective, and collective; gendered, racialized, and sexualized; etc). Work on the 'cinematic city' is exemplary in this regard (e.g. BARBER 2002; BRUNO 1993; CHARNEY and SCHWARTZ 1995; CLARKE 1997; SHIEL and FITZMAURICE 2003). Although there has been burgeoning research into the geographical *content* of films, much less attention has been paid by Geographers to the *medium* of film itself (although, see CLARKE and DOEL 2005; DOEL 1999; DOEL and CLARKE 2002). This is a significant omission for three reasons. First, form structures content (DELEUZE 2004). Second, form always has a particular spatiality and temporality. Finally, researchers need to appreciate the specificity of film as a socio-technical medium. It has an historical geography that is distinct from the historical geographies of other media (cf. LATOUR and WEIBEL 2002).

Accordingly, this chapter is concerned with film *qua* film. It engages with the form rather than the content of film, and, in particular, those crucially important formative years at the end of the nineteenth century and start of the twentieth (c. 1895 to 1908) when 'animated photography' underwent a profound transformation, into what we would recognize as 'film.' What became of animated photography, however, was not inevitable. The transformation was subject to contingency rather than necessity; a result of aleatory encounters rather than teleological determination (cf. DOEL 2004). This has led some film historians to suggest that there is a fundamental difference in kind, rather than a mere difference of degree, between the earliest films and those that came later (e.g. BURCH 1990; ELSAESSER and BARKER 1999; EZRA 2000). Here, I want to account for this difference using the case of early English film.[1] England was especially important in the early years of animated photography because it had a sophisticated visual culture that was exceedingly well catered for by photographic equipment manufacturers, accomplished photographers and magic-lanternists, film pioneers, and trade journals.[2] Primary research for this chapter was undertaken at the British Film Institute and the National Film and Television Archive in London, and the Library of Congress in Washington D.C.

From the outset, it is worth underscoring the specificity of the very earliest films (c. 1895 to 1901). They were all extremely short (a minute or so) because of the unavailability of long lengths of film. With rare exceptions, staged films consisted of a tightly framed shot of a single scene using an immobile camera, frontal presentation, and histrionic acting. Effectively, filmmakers filmed a continuous take of a theatrical scene staged for the benefit of the camera – usually outdoors for maximum daylight. (As late as 1906, journals such as the *PLC* advertised cinematograph cameras as a "seasonal speciality." English filmmaking was concentrated in spring and summer, while exhibition accorded with the 'lantern season' of October to March.) The rare exceptions included 'panoramic films' taken from moving vehicles, usually trains, and the 'trick films' exemplified by Georges Méliès, which often used techniques drawn from stage magic, still photography, and lanternism (e.g. Pepper's Ghost, multiple exposure, and dissolves), although he is personally credited with inventing many cinematic techniques (e.g. substitution splicing and the close-up). One should think of early films as if they were music-hall turns, although their tight framing and two-dimensional composition tended to make them appear to be little more than self-contained, animated photographs. If the essence of film is to be found in the editing which is to say in the spatial and temporal relationship between that which is 'framed' and that which is 'out-of-field' (DELEUZE 1986; DELEUZE 1989), then the earliest results of animated photography were something other than film. The distinction between an animated *photograph* and an edited *film* is well illustrated by Mike FIGGIS in *Timecode* (2000): the screen is divided into four sections, each of which presents one of four continuous 93-minute takes filmed simultaneously.

1. USAI (1994) provides a helpful introduction to the difficulties involved in researching early film.
2. The following abbreviations for trade journals have been employed:
   CBM = Cinematograph and Bioscope Magazine.
   KLW = The Kinematograph and Lantern Weekly.
   OLCJ = The Optical Lantern and Cinematograph Journal.
   OLKJ = The Optical Lantern and Kinematograph Journal.
   OMLJPE = The Optical Magic Lantern Journal and Photographic Enlarger.
   OPTR = The Optician and Photographic Trades Review.
   PLC = Projection, Lantern and Cinematograph.
   WB = The Westminster Budget.

ANIMATED PHOTOGRAPHY: FILM BEFORE FILM

> *[W]hat can be done to stem the already ebbing tide of popular favour[?]*
>
> (OMLPE, Vol. 8, No. 97, June 1897, 103).

It is often thought that the public début of the Lumière Cinématographe in 1895 in Paris, and 1896 in London, introduced audiences to an *absolute novelty*: 'living pictures.' Since time immemorial, virtually all forms of visual representation have been associated with unprecedented realism: paintings, camera obscuras, dioramas, panoramas, photographs, stereoscopes, etc. For example, an article in *Photographic Art Journal*, August 1853, characterized photography as a "solar pencil" able to "transcribe *exactly*." Animated photography reputedly offered something more than ultra-realism, however. For the images projected onto the screen were not simply *life-like*. They actually seemed to *be alive*. Little wonder, then, that contemporary trade journals, exhibitors, and the public referred to animated photography as 'living pictures;' although, once again, this phrase was widely associated with the camera obscura, the magic lantern, and photography (e.g. *The New Yorker*, 13th and 20th April 1839), and commentators were acutely aware of the fact that photographers needed technical competence, artistic skill, and an empathetic 'soul' to "give the semblance of *life*, instead of a mere *shadow* of life" (Photographic Art Journal, August 1853). The same distinction was applied to animated photographs (BURCH 1990). It is a distinction that subtends the *entire* history of Western representation's skiamachy.

The prefix 'bio-' (signifying life) was just as prevalent in the early years as that of 'ciné-' or 'kino-' (signifying movement). In the U.S. the Bioscope was the major competitor of the Lumière Cinématographe, and both came in the wake of the commercial success of Edison's peepshow Kinetoscope.[3] Only gradually did the less emotive word 'film' come to supplant 'bio,' 'ciné,' and 'kino' as the preferred name for the medium as a whole. The word 'film' was initially reserved for the light-sensitive strip of material upon which the images were fixed; although, it quickly became synonymous with the images themselves and the medium in its totality. This conflation resulted in confusion about the object of early 'film' criticism. When the *OMLJPE* (Vol. 8, No. 97, June 1897, 105) stated that "good films ... have been ... few and far between," Eastman Kodak insisted that its films were always of excellent quality.

The sense of absolute novelty occasioned by the advent of animated photography is best illustrated by what CHRISTIE (1994, 15) calls "*the* founding myth of cinema." This refers to reports of audiences panicking when they saw the

---

3. 'Bioscope' was originally a Registered Trade Mark for cinematographs manufactured by the Warwick Trading Co. The protection was subsequently withdrawn, however, when the High Court determined that the word was "more or less descriptive." The company lamented the fact that competitors rapidly appropriated the name: "Rotomotoscope, Vitaflashograph, Flickerlessoscope, Vivascope, and other words with the suffixes 'graph' and 'scope' were immediately changed to 'Bioscope'" (*CBM*, No. 4, July-September 1906, 63).

LUMIÈRES' *Arrivée d'un train en gare à La Ciotat*, which seemed "to dart out of the screen like an arrow," according to Maxime Gorki. Unfortunately, this affect is not borne out by documentary evidence (BOTTOMORE 1999). The mythical status of the panicking audience is well illustrated by the fact that it was parodied in films such as Robert W. PAUL's *The Countryman and the Cinematograph* (1901). One should also recall that roller-coasters and phantasmagoria had already made fear an amusing thrill long before the advent of film (CASTLE 1988; GUNNING 1995). Indeed, films found an early home in fairgrounds; and, one of the most commercially successful outlets for film before the U.S. nickelodeon boom of the late 1900s was the so-called "Hale's Tours" (a.k.a. 'phantom rides') of 1904–1907, which screened films taken from moving trains in a mocked-up railway carriage (FIELDING 1984; RABINOVITZ 1998). Hale's Tours came to England in 1906, and received great acclaim (*OLKJ*, Vol. 3, No. 3, January 1907, 78; *KLW*, Vol. 1, No. 3, 30 May 1907, 44).

The longevity of claims to ultra-realism and the mythical status of the 'train effect' suggest that the novelty of animated photography lay elsewhere. What appears to have amazed audiences was movement within the *detail* of the image (especially water, leaves, dust, and smoke), rather that the movement of the image per se, which was already an accomplished fact by the 1890s (see HECHT 1993). Yet again, it is worth noting that earlier visual technologies were associated with this quality. For example, in his diary entry for the 4th December 1839, Philip Hone described the Daguerreotype (the prototypical form of photography) thus: "Every object, however minute, is a perfect transcript of the thing itself; the hair of the human head, the gravel on the roadside, the texture of a silk curtain, or the shadow of the smaller leaf reflected upon the wall."[4]

Coming in the wake of a vast amount of experimentation that tried to perfect the reproduction of a moving image, what was being sought in the 1890s was an apparatus capable of recording and projecting a *continuous* strip of instantaneously exposed photographic images. While Louis Le Prince, William Friese Greene, Wordsworth Donisthorpe, and the Skladanowsky brothers all attempted to answer this call (in 1888, 1889, 1890, and 1892/4, respectively), the Lumière brothers' success in projecting their results – to critical acclaim in 1895 – appeared to assure them of the accolade. Such an accolade was far from assured, however, not least because of the tendency for critics to be incredulous about optical 'novelties.' This tendency is well illustrated by the derision heaped upon Thomas Edison's Kinetoscope when it was exhibited in London in 1894. One commentator suggested that it should "only be regarded as an amusing toy" owing to "the smallness of the pictures and the want of clearly defined light and shade, as well as by the inconvenience of looking down into the instrument" (*WB*, Vol. 4, No. 91, 26th October 1894, 754). Similarly, while the *KLW* recalled that in 1896, "people flocked in crowds" to the Empire Theatre, London, to see Lumière films, it remarks that the Alhambra Theatre, London, was also offered the Lumière show but "threw a cold blanket on the proposed enterprise" (*KLW*, No. 8, 4th July 1907, 125). In short, late nineteenth-century visual culture was not waiting expectantly for cinema to be born.

4. http://www.iath.virginia.edu/fdw/volume3/werner/contexts4.html. Accessed: 29.07.04.

Even though the Cinématographe managed to establish itself as an optical novelty suitable for a paying public (especially as part of music-hall variety programs), few imagined that animated photography would remain a popular attraction for long (the downfall of once incredibly popular visual attractions such as the stereoscope, Panorama, Praxinoscope, and X-rays provides an apt illustration of the fate that seemed to await even the most startling of optical novelties). Many feared that the medium would not survive the waning public interest in seeing yet another form of living pictures. BOTTOMORE (1996) reports evidence that in the first few years of the twentieth century film slipped down the order of attractions and disappeared entirely in some places. This fact is supported by contemporary trade journals. The *OMLPE* began to worry about waning public interest in film as early as 1897, just one year after the public début of the Cinématographe in England. "During the past year or so no novelty connected with optical projection has secured so much of the attention of the public as what are known as animated photographs. This attention has been due in no small measure to curiosity, and signs are not wanting that it has already begun to flag" (*OMLPE*, Vol. 8, No. 97, June 1897, 103). The article lists many failings of animated photography, including poor equipment, bad films, and incompetent exhibition. Indeed, as late as 1908, the *KLW* felt moved to promote cinematography by publishing a bumper international edition of the journal at the end of the lantern / film season. It called the issue its "Propaganda Summer Number" (*KLW*, Vol. 3, No. 60, 2nd July 1908).

AN UNTIMELY PROBLEM: 'TRUE MOTION'

Realism is the cry, and realism they must have

(OMLPE, Vol. 11, No. 131, April 1900, 48).

From the outset, then, the principle attraction of animated photography was tautological. The public wanted *animated* photography. Accordingly, one of the pioneers of early English film noted, "The films consisted in the old days of pictures of railway trains in cuttings and of omnibuses in Piccadilly – any little thing which tended to movement. ... Any form of movement satisfied us, because it was a miracle to see moving photographs, and that was what people were asking for" (HEPWORTH 1917, quoted in HERBERT 2000, xii). While many craved animation, those who were enamored by the tradition of landscape idealization and Romanticism deplored film's aesthetic consequences. For example, the Showman insisted, "[T]here is a want of beauty in animated photographs from the fact that they depend on the reproduction of street scenes and others in which moving objects predominate – simple landscape subjects being quite out of the question" (*OMLJPE*, Vol. 8, No. 97, June 1897, 105).

What mattered to early film-makers, exhibitors, and audiences was the animation of animated photography. This fixation is starkly illustrated by the fallout from the 1906 decision of Pathé Frères to charge 4d. per foot for its films. Until then, films were typically priced according to the costs incurred (The global dominance of Pathé Frères was such that all other producers did likewise). Once they began to pay for film by length, exhibitors became concerned that some footage did not contain suitably animated photographs. In particular, the *KLW* highlighted concerns about what it ironically called 'non-animated film.' Tellingly, "Chas. Lewis complains that in some films, after the action of handing a letter (in the scene) a great number of feet of film are used containing nothing but the repetition of this letter, the object being to enable the audience to read it. The part he objects to is that all this measurement is charged to him as so many feet, yet there is no action shown" (*KLW*, Vol. 3, No. 84, 17th December 1908, 823). The complainant suggests that rather than be charged for a contradiction in terms (non-animated film), the exhibitor should be supplied with a magic-lantern slide – the cost of which would be much cheaper. While this aversion to static images might seem like an overly literal concern, it is worth remembering that late nineteenth-century and early twentieth-century visual culture had no shortage of devices for reproducing static and moving images, especially the well-established, and increasingly sophisticated, magic lantern (BARBER 1993; COOK 1963). What everyone wanted from the Cinématographe was truly animated pictures. One of the most telling sales-pitches, in this regard, is the claim made by the Charles Urban Trading Co. that "all 'padding' is eliminated" from its films (Catalogue, February 1905, 6).

With the accent placed firmly on the animation of animated photography, trade journals focused their attention squarely on refining the moving image. Over and over again, advertisements for early films emphasized their animation (e.g. an 1897 advertisement for Robert W. Paul's "Animated photograph films" lists dozens of animated subjects, while an 1897 advertisement for Rigg's "Kinematograph" includes images of roundabouts, railway stations, tram termini, and children leaving school). And, what did the Lumière brothers' film in 1895/6? They filmed action: the *demolition* of a wall, workers *leaving* a factory, the *fluttering* of leaves, the *disembarking* of passengers, Jerusalem from a *moving* train, and, most famously of all, the *arrival* of a train.

Far from solving the problem of recording and projecting ultra-realistic and life-like animated photographs, however, the Cinématographe gave rise to all manner of optical oddities and technical difficulties. First and foremost, hand-cranking during filming and projection meant, that "[U]nless the projecting of the subject upon the lantern screen is conducted precisely at a speed corresponding to that at which the negative picture was taken, false representations of nature will result. Our beloved art becomes a cause for laughter when men march at a running speed; when artillery guns skate over the ground on carriages with stationary wheels; and when the wheels on the Royal carriage revolve backwards" (*OLCJ*, Vol. 1, November 1904, 11). Indeed, trade journals tried in vain for more than a decade to convince the film industry to adopt the more costly but 'flickerfree' rate of 24 frames per second as its standard, rather than the customary (but cost-effective) rate of 12 to 16 frames per second.

As well as fretting about flicker and the misrepresentation of natural movement, English trade journals were especially scathing of that "class of trickery" in which "the laws of nature are assumed to be set at variance" (e.g. unnatural camera angles, as in W. R. BOOTH's 1899 film *Upside Down*; or, *the Human Flies*; the splitting of the screen, as in James WILLIAMSON's 1901 film *Are You There?*; speed magnification, as in Robert W. PAUL's 1906 film *How To Make Time Fly*); and, they deplored the use of lenses whose focal length gave "false perspective" and therefore "false motion" (*KLW*, Vol. 2, No. 35, 9th January 1908, 141–143). Consequently, journals declared that "the various illusions to which the art is subject" means that "it becomes a problem taxing the greatest genius, how best to avoid giving false effect upon the screen" (*OLCJ*, Vol. 1, November 1904, 11). As late as 1908, journals, such as the *KLW*, could still bemoan the fact that film-makers had only managed to effect a "continuity of impression," not "true motion" (*KLW*, Vol. 2, No. 37, 23rd January 1908, 179; cf. BERGSON's [1907] condemnation of the cinematic granulation of duration: time dried up as space). "[A]lmost every scene we witness furnishes subject matter for adverse criticism, insomuch as either optical or motional defects are sure to crop up" (*KLW*, Vol. 2, No. 35, 9th January 1908, 141).

The obsession with perfecting the reproduction of 'true motion' was unlikely to combat waning public interest in film during the 1900s. What ensured its continuing success after the initial novelty of animation wore off was arguably the public's appetite for comic subjects (which was begrudgingly acknowledged by most of the trade journals; although, that did not stop them from promoting more edifying, educational, and bourgeois subjects). This appetite was well catered for by filmmakers. Before the onset of news-reels and full-blown narrative films in the 1910s, the earliest films (c. 1895 to 1906) are best thought of as constituting a 'cinema of attractions' that gave audiences a form of visceral pleasure (BURCH 1990). Only very gradually did films depart from the structure of an animated *photograph*, a living *picture* or a moving *tableaux* (this is not to say that they were atemporal, only that time tended to be inscribed synchronically *within* the scene, rather than being fashioned diachronically *between* scenes through editing). As I noted at the outset of this paper, before 1903, nearly all of the 'fiction' films were very short (less than a minute or so) and consisted of a tightly framed shot of a planar scene using an immobile camera, frontal presentation, and histrionic acting. This is why they could be used interchangeably with other music-hall turns, since their staging accorded with the prevailing theatrical conventions. Indeed, such turns were frequently the subject of early films. The excavation of depth, formation of perspective, use of off-screen space, and linking of scenes were things that took years to develop. Contrary to what one might expect, these aspects were absolutely not inherent features of the medium (ABEL 1996; BOWSER 1990; BREWSTER and JACOBS 1997; BURCH 1990; ELSAESSER and BARKER 1990; LANT 1995; PEARSON 1992). It took decades for film-makers to fashion the kind of 'narrative space' governed by 'continuity editing' that became the bedrock of classic Hollywood cinema and so familiar to twentieth-century audiences (HEATH 1981).

The fixation of the trade journals on the need to refine a moving image was already anachronistic in the 1890s. Why? Because animated photography was not only widely anticipated, but effectively accomplished by the end of the 1880s. The sticking point was not animated pictures per se, but the difficulty of emancipating the moving images from the small loops, slide-sequences, and peep-boxes within which it had been ensnared, and projecting them onto a screen.

The nineteenth century gave rise to innumerable devices dedicated to the reproduction of moving images. The Thaumatrope, Phenakistiscope, Zoëtrope, and Praxinoscope are widely regarded as the most important precursors of film. For centuries, people had been aware that the images on either side of a spinning coin seemed to fuse into a single image. The spinning coin, or Thaumatrope ('wonder-turner'), was first commercialized as a visual attraction by John Paris in 1825. This was soon followed by the Phenakistiscope ('deceptive view') or stroboscope; invented independently in 1832 by Joseph Plateau and Simon Ritter von Stampfer. It consisted of a disc upon which a series of pictures representing the consecutive positions of a moving body were arranged radially. When the disc was spun, and the pictures viewed through a fixed slit, the images blended into continuous movement. The Zoëtrope ('wheel of life') or Daedelum, patented by William Horner in 1834, employed the same principle; although, the images were arranged on a paper band inside a slotted drum. In 1877, Emile Reynaud adapted the Zoëtrope by mounting mirrors on a central polygonal drum to produce his Praxinoscope ('action view'), thus dispensing with the need for slots, increasing the clarity of the image, and achieving 'optical stationarity' of the image (The absence of flicker led at least one commentator to suggest using cinematographic prints in a Praxinoscope: OPTR, 29th March 1901, 71). In 1882, Gaston Tissandier described, in *La nature*, a projection Praxinoscope, produced by Reynaud as a domestic entertainment. Reynaud belatedly developed a theatrical version – the *Théâtre Optique* – in 1889, and showed his first three strips in 1892, at the Musée Grévin in Paris. Although a great success, production of the strips was laborious: each image was a separate drawing that was transferred to gelatin and hand colored. Also in 1892, J. A. R. Rudge, the 'Wizard of the Magic Lantern,' experimented with various lantern adjuncts to create an impression of continuous and naturalistic movement using rotating galleries of photographic slides (e.g. facial grimaces). Other significant devices included the peep-box Filoscope, Kinora, and Mutoscope – each of which showed a sequence of photographic prints in rapid succession to cinematic effect (*OPTR*, 29th March 1901, 7172). However, perhaps the most accomplished apparatus for presenting a moving image was the theatrical stage set known as the 'Diorama' (not to be confused with the 'Panorama'). Dioramas positioned the spectator on a viewing platform at the centre of a 360° circular painting (of a landscape, battlefield, cityscape, etc.) that was housed in a purpose-built rotunda with false terrain and an interior roof – thus giving the spectator an impression of being totally immersed in a complete illusion (COMMENT 1999; OETTERMANN 1997; SCHIVELBUSCH 1988). BENJAMIN (1999, 529) described the Diorama as "a sportive precursor of fast-motion cinematography – a witty and somewhat malicious, 'dancing' acceleration of time."

The enormous Diorama stage sets were most famous for their transformation of day into night by the application of lighting effects onto a scene such as a landscape rendered in two different forms on either side of a translucent canvas. "Only two effects were actually painted on – day on the front of the canvas, night on the back, and one could only shift from one to the other by means of a series of complicated combinations of media the light had to pass through. But these produced an infinite number of additional effects similar to those Nature offers in its course from morning to night and vice versa" (Daguerre, quoted in VIRILIO 1994, 41). This lighting technique was based on Jean Servandoni's *Spectacles de decoration* (c. 1738), Philippe-Jacques Loutherbourg's Eidophusikon (c. 1781), Franz König's Diaphanorama (c. 1811), and the well established tradition of light-boxes, peep-shows, and magic-lanterns.

Given the sophistication of nineteenth-century visual culture, animated photographs and living pictures were not actually that novel; and, they were certainly not startling enough to precipitate audience panic. The Cinématographe did not appear out of the blue. It brought together and refined a whole series of previous inventions, and was commercialized with reference to a paying public already well versed in the pleasures of disenchanted night (from light-boxes and peep-shows to phantasmagoria and roller-coasters). Likewise, as attractions, films were not necessarily that attractive. As late as 1907, the *KLW* was still lamenting the fact that "In the music hall programme the kinematograph is merely regarded as a turn instead of a separate entertainment.... 'American Bioscope' ranks on the equal to 'So and so, the comedian'" (*KLW*, No. 4, 6th June 1907, 59), while the *OLKJ* once again labored the virtues of those few music-hall managers who were "awakening to the fact that the kinematograph should be regarded as something more than a stop gap" between other entertainments (*OLKJ*, Vol. III, No. 5, March 1907, 115).

A TIMELY PROBLEM: VERNACULAR RELATIVITY

The photograph ...
has a completely different ambition
than representing, illustrating, or narrating

(DELEUZE 2003, 8–9).

Late nineteenth-century visual culture had little use for yet another form of 'moving picture.' Likewise, the trade journals' obsession with perfecting the ability of animated photography to represent 'true motion' rather than a mere 'continuity of impression' appeared at best anachronistic and at worst entirely misplaced. From the 1820s and 1830s, vision was de-naturalized and thoroughly grounded in artifice (CRARY 1990; STAFFORD 1994). Fortunately, something entirely unexpected was happening to animated photography that carried it away from the false problem of perfecting true motion: the advent of editing techniques. These were a radical departure from the techniques associated with other nineteenth-century optical devices (e.g. the ghostly multiple exposures of still photography, and the animation techniques of magic-lantern slides). For example, Georges Méliès claimed to have inadvertently invented stop-motion cinematography (*arrêt de caméra* or substitution splicing) when his camera jammed outside the Paris Opéra. The visual effect of stopping and then restarting his camera was to transform an omnibus into a hearse, and men into women. While stop-motion was especially associated with phantasmagoric effects of appearance, transformation, and vanishing – which EZRA (2000) dubs 'fantastic realism' – it also gave rise to time-lapse cinematography. This method was famously employed in the 1902 Biograph film of the demolition of New York's Star Theatre, where so-called "speed magnification" seemed to make the building melt into the ground in a matter of minutes. Time-lapse was used as early as 1897, when Birt Acres filmed clouds at about a frame per second, "thus exaggerating the movement but retaining the form" (Birt Acres 1897; quoted in BARNES 1983, 21).

'Stop-motion,' 'speed magnification,' and a host of other editing techniques suggested an alternative future for animated photography. Hereinafter, editing would enable the Cinématographe to stop slavishly re-presenting an actual or staged instant, and to start functioning as an apparatus that could both manipulate and manufacture space and time. In so doing, animated photography ceased being a *referential* medium, bound to the Real, to become a *simulacral* medium, free to fabricate a reality-effect (BAUDRILLARD 1994; DELEUZE 1994). The word that captured the new potential of film was 'montage' a word drawn from the surreal world of paper-play. Modernity had set the "laws of nature at variance;" and, through editing, film became the quintessential medium for making this variance visible. Each frame (image) refers to that which is out-of-frame; but, this latter is necessarily two-fold. On the one hand, the frame refers to what is around the frame – a spatially and temporally contiguous 'unseen' that may, in its turn, subsequently enter the frame and so become actualized as a seen / scene. On the other hand, the frame also refers to the absolute proximity of non-contiguous spaces and times – a manifold 'unseen' that can never be actualized as a framed seen / scene, but which nevertheless is pullulated and ramified to infinity (DELEUZE 1986; cf. the two-fold cinematic 'gesture' in AGAMBEN 2000). The essential thing about film, then, is not the framed image, but that which comes *between* the frames: *the cut* (cf. DELEUZE 1990; DELEUZE 1994). In the first two decades of film exhibition, the main scourge of animated photography, according to trade journals, was neither the failure to render 'true motion' nor waning public interest in 'living pictures.' The main scourge was *flicker* – the trace of the cut par excellence. The war against flicker was won when filmmakers eventually adopted the rate of 24 frames per second in the late 1900s. It was only with the advent of continuity editing and narrative cinema, however, that the out-of-frame was finally tamed. Thereafter, the explosive potential of the out-of-frame is barely felt beyond the narrow confines of avant-garde filmmaking.

Editing enabled film to express what CHRISTIE (1994, 33) aptly calls "vernacular relativity." Yet, given the initial fixation of the medium on animating a *still* photograph and reproducing *true* motion, it should be clear why it was not certain that film would come to reproduce the "mechanization, jerkiness, and rush of modern times," or, that it would end up heightening the "public consciousness of differential speed" (KERN 1983, 117 and 130, respectively). Similarly, it was not inevitable that "The compacting of events in time was best suited for the new art form of the period – the cinema" (KERN 1983, 279). Nor was it self-evident that film would expand "the sense of the present" by allowing one "to splice open a moment and insert a number of simultaneous activities" (KERN 1983, 70 and 71, respectively); and, in so doing, become a critical, explosive, and potentially revolutionary medium that would need to be muffled by the formation of continuity editing and narrative space (MCCOLE 1993).[5] Indeed, rather than acknowledge this explosive potential, trade journals preferred to advocate the pulling power of so-called "local" or "see yourselves" films, which accords with the enthusiasm in the 1890s for the novelty of full-length "look at-yourself" mirrors in department stores.

Let me end with a powerful example of the wide-spread inability of contemporary commentators to conceive of animated photography as a space and time machine. In February 1897, the *OMLJPE* (Vol. 8, No. 93, February 1897, 39) published a reader's letter and its own humorous reply.

> DEAR SIR, – Might it not be of interest to the temperance cause, by means of quick exposures and the cinematograph, to publish a roll of pictures showing the effect of alcohol upon the system by starting with a person perfectly sober, and plying him with drink until he becomes incapable, meantime taking pictures all the time so as to show the results until the patient, in common parlance, 'falls under the table.' ... If you know of any such set of slides, will you kindly let me know where I can obtain such, as I would then at once purchase one of the cinematographic apparatus, and include this subject in a series of lectures. Yours, etc., BARTOS.
>
> Seeing that many exposures are made per second, and that the effects of which 'Bartos' speaks would take some considerable time, it is likely that a film to embrace this subject would have to be several miles long. As a film about 70 feet long costs a few pounds, we wonder if 'Bartos' would have sufficient ready cash to purchase one of the desired length, say twenty miles for £7,000 pounds. – ED.

Two months later, the journal republished a rejoinder that appeared in the Alliance News: "The editor is too humorous in his reply, and Bartos too wholesale in his suggestion to be practical. Photographs of a tippler gradually 'getting forrarder' taken at quarter hour intervals, would answer every purpose of instructive illustration" (*OMLJPE*, Vol. 8, No. 95, April 1897, 62). What is striking is that none of those involved in this exchange could envisage anything other than the continuity of real-time and the reciprocity of still photography and animated photography. The late nineteenth century witnessed the advent of film but not in the *form* that we have come to know it. Only the *flikker* testified to the cuts that were coming.

ACKNOWLEDGEMENTS

The research was undertaken in conjunction with Dr David CLARKE. The paper was presented to The Geography of Cinema: A Cinematic World symposium held at Johannes Gutenberg-University, Mainz, Germany, June 2004. I am grateful to Prof. Dr Anton Escher and Stefan Zimmermann for organizing this event, and to the

---

5. To the consternation of countless critics, one of the pioneers of continuity editing, Cecil HEPWORTH, famously renounced it: "Only the direst need will form an excuse for lifting an audience up by the scruff of the neck and carrying it round to the other side, just because you suddenly want to photograph something from the south when the previous scene has been taken from the north" (HEPWORTH 1951, 139).

participants for their comments. I would also like to thank the British Film Institute, the National Film & Television Archive, the Library of Congress, and the Arts & Humanities Research Board (Award No. B/SG/AN2054/APN10258).

REFERENCES

ABEL, R. (Ed.) (1996): *Silent Film*. London.
AGAMBEN, G. (2000): *Means Without End: Notes on Politics*. London.
AITKEN, S. and L. ZONN (Eds.) (1994): *Place, Power, Situation and Spectacle: A Geography of Film*. Totowa.
BARBER, S. (2002): *Projected Cities*. London.
BARBER, X. T. (1993): The roots of travel cinema: John L. Stoddard, E. Burton Holmes and the nineteenth-century illustrated travel lecture. *Film History* 5 (1), 68–84.
BARNES, J. (1983): *The Rise of the Cinema in Gt. Britain: The Beginnings of the Cinema in England 1894–1901. Volume 2: Jubilee Year 1897*. London.
BAUDRILLARD, J. (1994): *Simulacra and Simulation*. Ann Arbor.
BENJAMIN, W. (1999): *The Arcades Project*. Cambridge.
BERGSON, H. (1907): *L'Evolution créatrice*. Paris.
BOTTOMORE, S. (1996): "Nine days' wonder": early cinema and its sceptics. WILLIAMS, C. (Ed.): *Cinema. The Beginnings and the Future: Essays Marking the Centenary of the First Film Show Projected to a Paying Audience in Britain*. London, 135–149.
BOTTOMORE, S. (1999): The panicking audience? Early cinema and the 'train effect'. *Historical Journal of Film, Radio & Television* 19, 177–216.
BOWSER, E. (1990): *The Transformation of Cinema, 1907–1915*. Berkeley.
BREWSTER, B. and L. JACOBS (1997): *Theatre to Cinema: Stage Pictorialism and the Early Feature Film*. Oxford.
BRUNO, G. (1993): *Streetwalking on a Ruined Map: Cultural Theory and the City Films of Elvira Notari*. Princeton.
BURCH, N. (1990): *Life to those Shadows*. London.
CASTLE, T. (1988): Phantasmagoria: spectral technology and the metaphorics of modern reverie. *Critical Inquiry* 15, 26–61.
CHARNEY, L. and V. SCHWARTZ (Eds.) (1995): *Cinema and the Invention of Modern Life*. Berkeley.
CHRISTIE, I. (1994): *The Last Machine: Early Cinema and the Birth of the Modern World*. London.
CLARKE, D. B. (Ed.) (1997): *The Cinematic City*. London.
CLARKE, D. B. and M. A. DOEL (2005): Engineering space and time: moving pictures and motionless trips. *Journal of Historical Geography* 31 (1), 41–60.
COMMENT, B. (1999): *The Panorama*. London.
COOK, O. (1963): *Movement in Two Dimensions: A Study of the Animated and Projected Pictures Which Preceded the Invention of Cinematography*. London.
CRARY, J. (1990): *Techniques of the Observer: On Vision and Modernity in the Nineteenth Century*. Cambridge.
CRESSWELL, T. and D. DIXON (Eds.) (2002): *Engaging Film: Geographies of Mobility and Identity*. Lanham.
DELEUZE, G. (1986): *Cinema 1: The Movement-image*. London.
DELEUZE, G. (1989): *Cinema 2: The Time-image*. London.
DELEUZE, G. (1990): *The Logic of Sense*. London.
DELEUZE, G. (1994): *Difference and Repetition*. London.
DELEUZE, G. (2003): *Francis Bacon: The Logic of Sensation*. London.
DELEUZE, G. (2004): *Desert Islands and Other Texts: 1953–1974*. New York.

DOEL, M. A. (1999): Occult Hollywood: unfolding the Americanization of world cinema. SLATER, D. and P. J. TAYLOR (Eds.): *The American Century: Consensus and Coercion in the Projection of American Power.* London, 243–260.

DOEL, M. A. (2004): Poststructuralist geographies: the essential selection. CLOKE, P., P. CRANG and M. GOODWIN (Eds.): *Envisioning Human Geography.* London, 146–177.

DOEL, M. A. and D. B. CLARKE (2002): An invention without a future, a solution without a problem: motor pirates, time machines, and drunkenness on the screen. KITCHIN, R. and KNEALE, J. (Eds.): *Lost in Space: Geographies of Science Fiction.* London, 136–155.

ELSAESSER, T. and A. BARKER (Eds.) (1990): *Early Cinema: Space, Frame, Narrative.* London.

EZRA, E. (2000): *Georges Méliès: The Birth of the Auteur.* Manchester.

FIELDING, R. (1984): Hale's Tours: ultrarealism in the pre-1910 motion picture. FELL, J. (Ed.): *Film Before Griffith.* Berkeley, 116–130.

GUNNING, T. (1995): An aesthetic of astonishment: early film and the (in)credulous spectator. WILLIAMS, L. (Ed.): *Viewing Positions: Ways of Seeing Film.* Piscataway, New Jersey.

HEATH, S. (1981): *Questions of Cinema.* Bloomington.

HECHT, H. (1993): *Pre-Cinema History: An Encyclopaedia and Annotated Bibliography of the Moving Image Before 1896*, ed. A. HECHT. London.

HEPWORTH, C. M. (1951): *Came the Dawn.* London.

HERBERT, S. (Ed.) (2000): *A History of Early Film.* 3 Volumes. London.

KERN, S. (1983): *The Culture of Time and Space: 1880–1918.* Cambridge.

LANT, A. (1995): Haptical cinema. *October* 74, 45–73.

LATOUR, B. and P. WEIBEL (Eds.) (2002): *Iconoclash: Beyond the Image Wars in Science, Religion, and Art.* Cambridge.

LUKINBEAL, C. and L. ZONN (Eds.) (2004): Theme issue: cinematic geographies. *GeoJournal* 59 (4), 247–333.

MCCOLE, J. (1993): *Walter Benjamin and the Antinomies of Tradition.* London.

OETTERMANN, S. (1997): *The Panorama: History of a Mass Medium.* New York.

PEARSON, R. E. (1992): *Eloquent Gestures: The Transformation of Performance Style in the Griffith and Biograph Films.* Berkeley.

RABINOVITZ, L. (1998): From Hale's Tours to Star Tours: virtual voyages and the delirium of the hyperreal. *Iris* 25, 133–152.

SCHIVELBUSCH, W. (1988): *Disenchanted Night: The Industrialisation of Light in the Nineteenth Century.* Oxford.

SHIEL, M. and T. FITZMAURICE (Eds.) (2003): *Screening the City.* London.

STAFFORD, B. M. (1994): *Artful Science: Enlightenment Entertainment and the Eclipse of Visual Education.* Cambridge.

USAI, P. (1994): *Burning Passions: An Introduction to the Study of Silent Cinema.* London.

VIRILIO, P. (1994): *The Vision Machine.* London.

David B. Clarke

SPACES OF ANONYMITY

People come and go. Nothing changes
(*Grand Hotel*, d. Edmund GOULDING 1932).

INTRODUCTION

*The earth turned, but all other
things stayed in their proper place*
(SVEVO 2002, 157).

I suspect that I am not alone in finding some amusement in the following passage from LUHMANN (1998, 85): "We know that telecommunication tends to push the meaning of space towards zero (nevertheless, the earth still has simultaneous night and day, and depending on one's location an inconsiderate phone call can still get people out of bed)." One senses a certain irritation, no doubt deriving from personal experience, in the parenthetical aside. In the same way that the more mundane aspects of 'time-space compression' (HARVEY 1989) have tended to draw little comment, the increasing emphasis on *mobility* in social thought also seems to gloss over some of its subtleties. The fact that the world is increasingly on the move is indisputable (URRY 2000). Yet the well-documented acceleration of our globalizing world simultaneously increases the significance of the network of 'stopping places,' such as hotels and motels, where this unprecedented circulation pauses to recharge itself (MORRIS 1988). The still points around which the world circulates – both stopping places and points of transit like airports, railway stations, and bus terminals – have been assigned to the general category of 'non-places' by AUGÉ (1995).[1] While it is not difficult to understand why, this characterization arguably restricts a fuller appreciation of their qualities as places in their own right (CRANG 2002; CRESSWELL 2001). The thesis to be explored here is that film has consistently acknowledged the significance and, indeed, peculiarity of hotels and motels, and that a host of insights into their properties can be gleaned from considering their frequent cinematic appearances. If this recognition is evident within film itself, it has rarely extended into the film-studies literature. While road movies have become a staple of Hollywood production, for instance, attracting a growing body of popular

---

1. In The Terminal (d. Steven SPIELBERG, 2004), a point of transit becomes a permanent stopping place for Viktor Novorski (Tom Hanks), as geopolitical changes render this non-place his only home.

and academic analysis in their wake (COHAN and HARK 1997; SARGEANT and WATSON 1999; WILLIAMS 1982), the attention given to stopping places has been minimal. This situation deserves remedying.

From the so-called 'Hotelfilms', turned out by German studios (notably UFA) in the 1920s, to classic Hollywood, to virtually any contemporary national cinema – Korean, Hong Kong, Bollywood, etc. – the pervasive and diverse filmic presence of hotels and motels suggests the intrinsic significance they hold. The next section considers some of these cameos, as a basis for scrutinizing the way that qualities of such places have manifested themselves in recent fiction film. Two principal ideas are developed. The first centers on the space of the hotel lobby, exploring Siegfried KRACAUER's (c. 1922) seminal essay on this topic and its (unwitting?) dramatization in the COEN brothers' (1991) film, Barton Fink. The second, to which a separate section is devoted, extends this analysis by considering its implications in terms of memory, drawing on Christopher NOLAN's (2000) film, *Memento*. Finally, the concluding section discusses some of the broader consequences of the kind of social relations promoted by hotels and motels, discussing the possibility of another kind of togetherness with reference to Hayao MIYAZAKI's (2001) animated film, *Sen to Chihiro no kamikakushi* (*Spirited Away*). This assessment of stopping places in film is a preview of a topic that is ripe for wider exploration (CLARKE et al. forthcoming). The purpose of such work, moreover, takes us to the heart of the significance of recent cinematic geographies.

Engaging film is arguably one of the most profitable ways of enhancing our understanding of space, place, and social relations (cf. AITKEN and ZONN 1993; CLARKE 1997; CRESSWELL and DIXON 2002). Fiction film, in particular, typically expresses the sociospatial imaginary with an intensity that is absent from other forms of discourse. As cultural documents that can be subjected to a range of theoretical readings, film permits an exemplary understanding of the way that society speaks to itself about its spatial constitution.

LOST IN AESTHETIC SPACE

A Day or a Lifetime

(Motto of the Hotel Earle in *Barton Fink*, d. Joel COEN 1991).

"Togetherness," observes BAUMAN (1995, 44), "comes in many kinds." The kind of togetherness exemplified by those occupying, temporarily or more permanently, the spaces of hotels and motels reflects the extreme contingency of a "gathering of strangers who know that they will soon go, each one's own way, never to meet again – but before that happens ... are bound to share this space here and now" (BAUMAN 1995, 45). Being in the company of strangers, that most modern of experiences, is particularly well exemplified by the hotel: "Hotels house communities of strangers who gather outside their normal environments for brief periods," writes ALBRECHT (2002, 29). Little wonder, therefore, that, for many modern writers, the grand metropolitan hotel encapsulated the modern city in microcosm (DENBY 1998;

TALLACK 1998); or that KRACAUER (1922) should have devoted one of his Weimar-era feuilletons to the hotel lobby.

More recently, the confidence of modern society in its own self-assessment has been thrown into doubt. Much of this uncertainty has supposedly translated into a new, postmodern experience of space and time (HARVEY 1989). Yet the hotel remains very much in evidence. In a celebrated example, JAMESON (1992) proposes the Bonaventure Hotel in Los Angeles as a paradigmatic postmodern space. A massive structure with a mirrored façade, it seems to repel the surrounding downtown area, as if to dissociate itself from its own location. Yet this is nothing compared to "the experience of space you undergo when you step into the lobby or atrium. ... It is an element within which you yourself are immersed, without any of the distance that formerly enabled the perception of perspective" (JAMESON 1992, 42–3). The same theme of spatial dislocation that AUGÉ proposes in conceiving of 'non-places' is evident here. But, while technological developments such as cyberspace epitomize a kind of liminal communication, "so peculiar that it often puts the individual in contact only with another image of himself" (AUGÉ 1995, 79), it is difficult to discern a sense of radical rupture in such experiences. The aestheticization of space prompting JAMESON's account of the Bonaventure atrium, for example, is entirely of a piece with KRACAUER's (1922) description of the modern metropolitan hotel lobby. KATZ (1999, 150) is surely right, therefore, to diagnose conceptions such as JAMESON's as attempts to "reconstitute modernist historicism (and its rhetoric of breakthrough) via the back door, by spatializing it."

> Instead of a historical master narrative, we are given a master itinerary, with Los Angeles as its epoch-making capital. The thing about such mappings is that they are inevitably laid out in contrast to a nostalgically evoked, early-twentieth-century 'classic' metropolitan moment of the kind frequently represented by Weimar-era Berlin. But this is where KRACAUER may get the last word (KATZ 1999, 150).

No reading of KRACAUER's (1922) 'hotel lobby' essay could fail to confirm the reservations KATZ registers.

"The typical characteristics of the hotel lobby," KRACAUER (1922, 175–6) wrote, "indicate that it is conceived as the inverted image of the house of God... a negative church.... It is the setting for those who neither seek nor find the one who is always sought, and who are therefore guests in space as such – a space that encompasses them and has no function other than to encompass them." In a religious assembly, a form of communion is achieved in relation to a higher power that dissolves individual distinctions; "the differences between people disappear... when the congregation relates itself to that which no scale can measure" (KRACAUER 1922, 178). In the hotel lobby, however, the very conditions of possibility of this form of collectivity are extinguished entirely. The space of the lobby encompasses scattered individuals; it is a "space of unrelatedness" (KRACAUER 1922, 179). KRACAUER's analysis both directly and obliquely confirms FREUD's (1921, 61) description of Christianity as representing a situation in which "a number of individuals ... have put the same object in the place of their ego ideal and have consequently identified themselves with one another in their ego".[2] As KRACAUER (1922, 182) put it,

> Those who stand before God are sufficiently estranged from one another to discover they are brothers.... This limit case 'we' of those who have dispossessed themselves of themselves ... is transformed in the hotel lobby into the isolation of anonymous atoms.

The hotel lobby thus promotes a radical atomization over any image of collective endeavor:

> it does not foster the solidarity of those liberated from the name; instead, it deprives those encountering one another of the possibility of association that the name could have offered them (KRACAUER 1922, 183).

This atomization simultaneously translates into an *aestheticization* of space. The aesthetic gaze, as EASTHOPE (1993, 49) proposes, "treats something as an object for pleasure and contemplation." Aesthetic *space* thus centers squarely on the individual; "it does not choose as its points of reference and orientation the traits and qualities possessed by or ascribed to the objects of spacing, but the attributes of the spacing subject (like interest, excitement, satisfaction or pleasure)" (BAUMAN 1996, 33). As with BENJAMIN's (1999) flâneur, the aestheticized world is tailor-made to the measure of the individual. For example, the aesthetic proximity of the flâneur and those caught within his gaze "does not interfere with social distance; the city stroller can go on drawing the strangers around him into his private theatre without fear that those drawn inside will claim the rights of ... insiders" (BAUMAN 1993, 172). This is precisely the situation experienced in the hotel lobby. The loss of critical distance that JAMESON attributes to the Bonaventure Hotel is, then, already amply evident in Weimar-era Berlin. Indeed, it amounts to a definitive hallmark of modern space (CLARKE 2003).

The COEN brothers' (1991) film, *Barton Fink*, offers an almost literal dramatization of KRACAUER's image of the hotel as negative church. The film's eponymous protagonist (played by John Turturro) is a writer, an intellectual – hot from a successful Broadway run and transposed to Hollywood to work on the script of a wrestling 'B-movie.' He chooses to board in the distinctly run-down Hotel Earle, to both emphasize and cultivate his empathy for the 'common man.' But, Barton does not empathize with the common man. Rather, it is his own narcissistic identification as a 'lover of humanity' that manifests itself in his less-than-salubrious choice of residence. Crucial to the narrative of Barton Fink is the severe bout of writer's block Barton experiences in the isolation of his hotel room. He initially complains about the noise from the adjacent room that turns out to be occupied by an insurance salesman, Charlie Meadows (John Goodman) – whose alter ego, Karl 'Madman' Mundt, a murderer who decapitates his victims – turns out to be central to the plot. As the narrative proceeds, effects of LA summertime's soaring heat (such as loosening wallpaper and oozing wallpaper paste in Barton's room) give way, by the dénouement of the film, to a virtual descent into hell with flames ferociously pouring from the gas-fittings lining the walls of the hotel corridor. But the clues are there right from the start: in the desk clerks's ascent from the depths; in the incantation of '666' in Barton's and the elevator operator's

---

2. GILES (2000) questions the compatibility of FREUD and KRACAUER but, as HANSEN (1991) demonstrates, there are numerous points of contact.

exchange as Barton heads for his sixth-floor room; and, in the most innocuous of dialogue.

Barton: I'm a playwright. My shows've only played New York. Last one got a hell of a write-up in the *Herald*. I guess that's why they wanted me here.

Charlie: Hell, why not? Everyone wants quality

(COEN and COEN 2002, 423).

A full consideration of the film is clearly beyond the scope of a short paper, but a number of pertinent points can be developed.

The similarities of the plot of *Barton Fink* to the short story by Jorge Luis BORGES, *A Theologian in Death* (itself based on the writings of Emanuel Swedenborg), is worth noting. In BORGES' tale, the theologian, Melancthon, is unknowingly transported to Hell, his surroundings initially remaining familiar and unchanged. He seats himself at his desk, where he continues to write "on the subject of justification by faith alone ... writing nothing whatsoever concerning charity" (BORGES 1998, 65). His arrogance causes the angels to withdraw, and the "last word we have of Melancthon" sees him "carried out to the sand dunes, where he is now a servant to devils" (BORGES 1998, 67). The last image we see of Barton Fink shows him transported to a paradisiacal shoreline, lapped by waves, where a solitary woman sits on the sand to gaze out to sea – completing the picture-postcard image that has hung in Barton's hotel room for the duration of his stay (and which, presumably, he continues to endure). For HAINGE (forthcoming), "this scene would appear to have all the necessary ingredients to bring about an Adornian state of noetic anaesthesia and the ability to forget about everyday suffering."

Barton's predicament ultimately derives from his attempt to bear an identity that transcends any reliance on the Other. Yet, what the narcissistic subject misrecognizes as an inner sense of self necessarily derives from the outside, from the Other (LACAN 1977; FRIEDBERG 1990). "Make me your wrestler. Then you'll lick that story of yours," offers Charlie at one point, endeavoring to help Barton overcome his writer's block. But, faced with the thought of bodily contact – as opposed to an intellectualized, mental engagement with the idea of the common man – Barton squirms. This objectification is constitutive of Barton's attempt to substitute an aesthetic, personal narrative for a collective, social one; a maneuver that finds its origins in the eighteenth-century, when identity first took on an 'inner-directed' form (BELSEY 1986). The aesthetic self sustains the fiction of a complete identity by fantasizing an immediate correspondence between subject and object: "if the Other can be stripped of its alterity, if the object can appear to reflect the subject," all reliance on the Other can seem to be overcome (EASTHOPE 1993, 44). The effacement of the Other, however, is what ensures Barton's descent into 'The Hell of the Same' (BAUDRILLARD 1993).

The aesthetic self, on EASTHOPE's (1993, 33) suggestion, works by relocating "the transcendent from faith in a transcendent object to faith itself, to subjective experience as a domain of transcendence." But, the transcendent subject is a myth. In Ovid's *Metamorphoses*, as punishment for refusing the love of others, Narcissus is made to fall in love with his own reflection. He initially mistakes it for someone else, later recognizing the reflection as his own image and learning to his peril that one cannot love oneself. While it imagines itself complete, the subject can only ever attain a sense of identity from the Other, from the symbolic register, in terms that are necessarily shared by others. Its representation by a signifier is inadequate to the subject's being; and, a number of effects inevitably arise from the subject's narcissistic attempt to sustain its imaginary completion. The blurring of the distinction between perception and fantasy that FREUD (1936) termed 'derealization' [*Entfremdungsgefühl*] (more precisely, the effect of regarding the perceived as fantasy) grants an overpowering sense of subject-object unity; as FREUD learned from his own personal experience of such a disturbing effect on the Acropolis. Despite the evidence of the senses, reality undergoes a psychic transformation, bringing it into line with the subject's desires. The unrelentingly surreal cinematography of *Barton Fink* powerfully suggests this effect, as Barton struggles to maintain a sense of dyadic completeness, untrammeled by the presence of the Other. Could this film have been shot anywhere other than a hotel? Its diegesis is surely more than incidental. The anonymity of the hotel "deprives those encountering one another the possibility of association" (KRACAUER 1922, 183), arguably more so than any other space, rendering it the perfect setting for Barton Fink's obsessively individualistic existence.

A DISTURBANCE OF MEMORY IN THE METROPOLIS

Just some anonymous motel room.
Won't tell you anything

(*Memento*, d. Christopher NOLAN 2000).

The property of 'deferred interpretation' [*Nachträglichkeit*] that FREUD attributes to memory refers to the way in which memory is narrated retrospectively, typically in narcissistic confirmation of the self-identity of the ego. For LOCKE (1975, 336), memory was fully constitutive of personal identity; "as far as any intelligent Being can repeat the Idea of any past Action with the same consciousness it had of it at first, and with the same consciousness it has on any present Action; so far it is the same personal self." For BERGSON (1911, 6), however, "consciousness cannot go through the same state twice. The circumstances may be the same, but they will no longer act on the same person, since they find him at a new moment of his history" (One cannot help thinking of Phil Conners [Bill Murray] in *Groundhog Day* [d. Harold RAMIS, 1993], repeatedly waking up in his guesthouse bedroom to discover it is Groundhog Day all over again). The point on which FREUD and BERGSON concur has had particular significance ever since subjective experience itself came to figure as the foremost domain of transcendence. While the division between the Cartesian subject's inner self and its outward social role first solidified into an opposition in the seventeenth century (LACAN 1979), with the birth of the aesthetic self, "the opposition between self and world tends to become absolute, the I seeking full speech for itself, a personal narrative transforming contingencies into a necessity by re-imagining the traces of memories as a pre-given structure" (EASTHOPE 1993, 89).

The sense in which there can be a firm opposition between memory and fantasy is dramatically undercut by FREUD's sense of deferred interpretation. The distinction might seem clear-cut. Memories relate to the past, fantasies refer to the future. The former have a connection with reality that is absent in the latter. Yet recalling memories retrospectively changes them, altering the self in the process. In referring to 'screen memories' [*Deckerinnerungen*] – vivid but seemingly inconsequential memories deriving from early childhood – FREUD (1899, 322) suggests that; "a number of motives, with no concern for historical accuracy, had a part in forming them, as well as in the selection of the memories themselves." Memory traces invariably distort the past: "[I]nstead of the mnemic image which would have been justified by the original event, another is produced which has been to some degree associatively *displaced* from the former one" (FREUD 1899, 307). Screen memories, FREUD suggests, work like dreams, disguising their true content, and thereby indicating their proximity to repressed material. This is hardly a passing childhood phase, however. The perpetual reworking of memories is their most consistent feature. In his essay on derealization, for instance, FREUD (1936, 244) recounts his "momentary feeling" of being unable to accept the evidence of his senses when he finally found himself standing on the Acropolis: "*'What I see here is not real.'*" Attempting to overcome this dis-quieting sensation, FREUD (1936, 244) erroneously supposed he must have doubted the existence of the Acropolis all along: "I made an attempt to ward that feeling off, and I succeeded, at the cost of making a false pronouncement about the past." The experience "culminated in a disturbance of memory and a falsification of the past" as FREUD (1936, 246) attempted to realign the past to fit with his present feelings. This arose; he suggests, in an attempt "to keep something away from the ego" (FREUD 1936, 245), specifically, "something to do with a child's criticism of his father ... as though to excel one's father was still something forbidden" (FREUD 1936, 247). Memory, in other words, is deployed in the defensive armory of the narcissistic ego – motivated, in this instance, by a sense of filial piety and Oedipal guilt.

Leonard Shelby (Guy Pearce), the protagonist of Christopher NOLAN's (2000) *Memento*, suffers from severe anterograde memory dysfunction. His short-term memory has been decimated, we learn, by the head injuries he received from an intruder who raped and murdered his wife several years earlier. Drawing on his former experience as an insurance investigator, he attempts to track down his wife's killer, depending on notes jotted on scraps of paper; mnemonic Polaroids of people, locations, and cars; and – most dramatically of all – a list of the principal clues that he has tattooed onto his own body. In a way that recalls FREUD's deferred interpretation, NOLAN virtuosically constructs the narrative retrospectively, in five- to ten-minute sequences, such that, like BENJAMIN's (1992) Angel of History, we are propelled forwards with our backs turned. Only at the end can we understand the beginning, when we finally learn that Shelby's 'screen memories,' like FREUD's, are unconcerned with historical accuracy. Indeed, roaming the metropolis to avenge his wife's murder has become a serial task for Shelby; his amnesia prevents him from recalling that he has already avenged her death, and he is condemned to endlessly re-enacting the scenario. Despite overtones of manipulation by the usual noir suspects – the 'corrupt cop,' Teddy; the *'femme fatale,'* Natalie – there is an overriding impression that Shelby remains in control. "The notion of aggressivity as a correlative tension of the narcissistic structure" (LACAN 1977, 22) reveals itself in the ease with which Shelby takes to killing – though perhaps this should be understood in the context of its traumatic trigger. As the title of the short story – 'Memento Mori,' by the director's brother – on which the film is based suggests, Shelby's violence issues from "an identification of the ego with the abandoned object" (FREUD 1917, 249). The acts of violence in which he engages are those of an ego desperate to retain its connection to a lost other. Indeed, given that the blurring of the distinction between memory and fantasy has reached pathological proportions, there is always the possibility that Leonard's memory of his wife's murder is a fantasy, perhaps an effect of the remorse he feels at her accidental death by his own hand.

> *Leonard*: What the fuck are you talking about?
> T*eddy*: I dunno… your wife surviving the assault… her not believing your condition…the doubt tearing her up inside…, [*sic.*] the insulin.
> *Leonard*: That's Sammy, not me! I told you about Sammy

(NOLAN n. d., 111–112).

Leonard's repeated reminiscences of a 'parallel case' from his days as an insurance investigator – the accidental death of the wife of Sammy Jankis, who left her insulin injection in his hands to test the veracity of his memory disorder – suggest as much. If it is undecidable whether the violent murder of Shelby's wife is memory or fantasy, the character of his ego is ineluctably "a precipitate of abandoned object-cathexes" (FREUD 1923, 29).

Shelby's memory condition has a number of objective correlates in the film. Photographs that serve as surrogates for short-term memories he is unable to retain are a prime example. Memories are not really like snapshots, however.[3] The view that they are finds its most famous precursor in William Wordsworth (*The Prelude*, Book XII, lines 208–210):

> There are in our existence spots of time
> That with distinct pre-eminence retain
> A renovating virtue…

However, *pace* ELLIS (1985), such a conception goes against FREUD's notion of memory as subject to deferred interpretation, a clear intimation of which is seen in Shelby's repeatedly amending his annotations of what his Polaroids represent. The 'snapshot' view of memory mistakenly rests on a linear, spatialized conception of time, such that memories, like photographs, can be looked at repeatedly in confirmation of self-identity; "the I in the present can see them as objects, and so …

---

3. BARTHES (1981, 76) says, "There is a superimposition here: of reality and of the past."

can see itself reflected in these memories of itself" (EASTHOPE 1993, 61). With the advent of photography, such a conception is substantially reinforced; "The world itself has taken on a 'photographic face;' it can be photographed because it strives to be absorbed into the spatial continuum which yields to snapshots" (KRACAUER 1927, 59). Yet the fiction of the ego as a self-sufficient entity denies the "interminable dialectic in which each memory is rewritten ... on every occasion it is remembered," and hence the unavoidable condition that "it is only the inter-subjective Other of social life which can confer stable identity on the self (and a provisional stability at that)" (EASTHOPE 1993, 61). If the equation of snapshots as memories is familiar from other films, such as *Blade Runner* (d. Ridley SCOTT 1992; cf. SILVERMAN 1991), a less familiar correlate of Shelby's subjective condition is the motel room he occupies. As the repeated references to its anonymity make clear, the mise-en-scène is hardly incidental. A transcendental homelessness accompanies the transcendental subject.

Unlike a home, a hotel or motel room erases all traces of its previous occupants, paralleling Shelby's memory dysfunction. It is characteristically unhomely, *Unheimlich* – with all the implications this carries, in the German, of the *uncanny*. "An uncanny effect," says FREUD (1919, 244), arises "when the distinction between imagination and reality is effaced, as when something that we have hitherto regarded as imaginary appears before us in reality." Unlike derealization, where sense perception is misrecognized as fantasy in order to defend the unity of the ego, uncanny sensations effectively reverse this process, relating to "something which is secretly familiar [*heimlich-heimisch*], which has undergone repression and then returned from it" (FREUD 1919, 245). If the surprise appearance of something thought of as alien to our beliefs seems strangely familiar, this is because it relates to the "primary narcissism which dominates the mind of the child" (FREUD 1919, 235), when repressed thoughts are projected onto the primitive image of a double (RANK 1971). The double (or multiple) personalities the child constructs, FREUD suggests, initially serve as an assurance against its extinction. "But when this stage has been surmounted, the 'double' reverses its aspect. From having been an assurance of immortality, it becomes the uncanny harbinger of death" (FREUD 1919, 235). Shelby's obsession with Sammy Jankis suggests something like a regression to a state of 'primitive narcissism.' Tellingly, he occupies not one but two motel rooms at the Discount Inn, the desk clerk having taken advantage of his memory dysfunction (as he is forced to admit to Shelby at one point). The overriding sense of the anonymity of place pervading the film is also metonymically displaced onto a powerful sense of *contingency*. Despite his desire to be in control, Shelby's bid for mastery cannot ultimately be seen as anything other than a random killing spree, dictated by forces operating beyond his control. In this, it echoes any number of other Hollywood films from *Psycho* (d. Alfred HITCHCOCK 1960) to *Identity* (d. James MANGOLD 2003) – that render motels as scenes of violent murder perpetrated as a result of multiple personality disorders. The fact that Marion Craine's (Janet Leigh) fate was not necessarily her destiny is, moreover, underscored by its setting. "Marion's story has no necessary connection with her death; it is pure chance she stayed at the Bates Motel" (EASTHOPE 1999, 131).[4] Despite an often marked difference in the appearance of hotels and motels in Hollywood cinema, therefore, there is a strong similarity in the chance encounters they permit, the kind of subjectivity they promote, and the effects to which this gives rise.

CONCLUSION

> *A calling into question*
> *of the same – which cannot occur*
> *within the egoist spontaneity of the same –*
> *is brought about by the other*
>
> (LÉVINAS 1979, 43).

If the stopping places of Hollywood films typically replay the kind of situations we have analyzed, does this exhaust the topic? I want to conclude by briefly referring to another kind of togetherness than that of the 'being-with' that represented our point of departure. Hotels and motels are, *prima facie*, inhospitable to any other form of being. They are spaces designed to permit, as well as deriving their character from, an episodic and inconsequential form of togetherness. Yet, there is always the possibility of a different relation to the other. Insofar as "the one-for-the other exists before the one *and* the other exist for themselves" (BAUDRILLARD 1981, 75), *being-for* amounts to the pristine relation that is "banalized and dimmed in a simple exchange of courtesies which became established as an 'interpersonal commerce' of customs" (LÉVINAS 1991, cited in BAUMAN 1995, 56). Prior to the spoken demand of the other, there is the unconditional, unspoken demand of the Other – unspoken insofar as it issues directly from the strangeness of the Other as such. For BAUMAN (1995, 59)

> The 'unspokenness' means simply that the actor is now on his / her own, plotting his / her itinerary without assistance, groping in the dark and never quite sure that the road chosen is the right road. ... The 'unspokenness' means ... that the authority of command *has not been sought*, that the actor acts without command and acts as if command was not needed.

Being-for entails an ethic of responsibility, which includes being responsible for that responsibility, for determining the character of that responsibility without recourse to a higher authority.

In Hayao MIYAZAKI's (2001) animated film, *Sen to Chihiro no kamikakushi* (*Spirited Away*), we encounter something very much like this situation; in a very different kind of stopping place to those considered thus far – a bath-house for spirits, normally imperceptible to the human world. The story centers on a young girl, Chihiro, who finds herself abandoned when her parents are turned into pigs for consuming, excessively and without permission, food reserved for the spirits. As the

---

4. The different locations of the two murders in Psycho, according to ŽIŽEK (1992, 231), relate to "the way in which Norman is divided between two locales ... the first takes place in a motel which epitomizes anonymous American modernity, whereas the second takes place in a Gothic house which epitomizes American tradition." As EASTHOPE (1999, 133, citing FREUD 1919) notes, "The house is uncanny, a place which makes 'old discarded beliefs' believable alongside the 'common reality' of the motel."

spirit world begins to become perceptible to Chihiro, she finds herself beginning to disappear. A little boy, Haku, who also manifests himself as a dragon, comes to her aid; helping her to get a job in the bathhouse. There she is forced to give her name to Yubaba, the witch in charge of the place, in exchange for the name 'Sen.' Haku warns her to remember her real name if she is ever to return to her world. This she finds increasingly difficult, as her stay in the spirit world grows more protracted. To a far more extraordinary degree than *Barton Fink*, and not only because of the use of digital animation, the strangeness of the world in which Chihiro finds herself suffuses the entire character of the film. The almost unbearable ambivalence with which Chihiro is obliged to deal precludes any simple recuperation of the story in terms of Good versus Evil. Instead, a pervasive ethic of being-for lends the film its consistency. It is a fairy story, of course, and must have a happy ending. Chihiro realizes she has had a hidden bond with Haku all along. Unbeknownst to him (he has forgotten his real name) he is a river god, the spirit of the river in which Chihiro once almost drowned, and who came to her rescue then. Chihiro is able to give him back his name. If being-with entails a strategy of objectifying the other, therefore, this rendition of being-for seems to open up to the alterity of the Other. Chihiro's increasing attunement to the spirit world, which this openness has served to nurture, also allows her to get her parents back and to finally return to the human world.

One should, self-evidently, see this fairy story as a fantasy. Yet, if the ethic it dramatizes were itself a fantasy, it would preclude the possibility of a different relation to the Other. "For Lacan," EASTHOPE (2002, 146) insists, "there can be no relation to the other except on the prior basis of the Other, no relation which is not an effect of the order of the signifier, so that any venturing forth towards the other – my other – is fundamentally narcissistic and replete with fantasy and misrecognition." Or again:

> Lacan's position is that speaking subjects are separated from each other by 'the wall of language' (LACAN 1988, 244). What the Other, the big Other, of the symbolic order, excites in us – all it can do for us – does not come in any form of duty or imperative. Rather, it leads to uncertainty, to the 'Che vuoi?', the radical question, 'What do you want?'. But we cannot know what the Other wants of us because it constitutes our own desire (EASTHOPE 2002, 156).

The loss of proper names in *Spirited Away*, however, presents us with the possibility of the becoming-Other of the subject. The proper name, says KRACAUER (1922, 182), "reveals its bearer," but simultaneously "separates him from those whose names have been called; it simultaneously discloses and obscures, and it is with good reason that lovers want to destroy it, as if it were the final wall separating them." By relinquishing the name, as Chihiro is forced to do, the possibility of a different form of togetherness is opened up, and with it a different relation to the Other. Both the hotel lobby and the house of God are spaces of anonymity, with radically different implications in terms of togetherness. Other spaces, with other implications, remain to be created; in film and in life.

ACKNOWLEDGEMENTS

This paper was first presented to the 'Geography of Cinema: A Cinematic World' symposium at the Johannes Gutenberg-Universität, Mainz, June 2004. I would like to thank Professor Dr. Anton Escher and Stefan Zimmermann for their organizational prowess; their colleagues and students for their unfailing practical assistance; and the audience and other participants for their perceptive questions and comments.

REFERENCES

AITKEN, S. C. and L. E. ZONN (Eds.) (1993): *Place, Power, Situation and Spectacle: A Geography of Film*. Lanham.
ALBRECHT, D. (2002): 'Here you meet everybody and everybody meets you.' ALBRECHT, D. with E. JOHNSON (Eds.) (2002): *New Hotels for Global Nomads*. New York, 9–36.
AUGÉ, M. (1995): *Non-places: Introduction to an Anthropology of Supermodernity*. London.
BARTHES, R. (1981): *Camera Lucida: Reflections on Photography*. New York.
BAUDRILLARD, J. (1981): *For a Critique of the Political Economy of the Sign*. St. Louis.
BAUDRILLARD, J. (1993): *The Transparency of Evil: Essays on Extreme Phenomena*. London.
BAUMAN, Z. (1993): *Postmodern Ethics*. Oxford.
BAUMAN, Z. (1995): *Life in Fragments: Essays in Postmodern Morality*. Oxford.
BAUMAN, Z. (1996): From pilgrim to tourist-or a short history of identity. HALL, S. and P. DU GAY (Eds.) (1996): *Questions of Cultural Identity*. London, 18–36.
BELSEY, C. (1986): The Romantic construction of the unconscious. In: BARKER, F., P. HULME, M. IVERSEN and D. LOXLEY (Eds.) (1986): *Literature, Politics and Theory: Papers from the Essex Conference, 1976–84*. London, 57–76.
BENJAMIN, W. (1992): *Illuminations*. London.
BENJAMIN, W. (1999): *The Arcades Project*. Cambridge.
BERGSON, H. (1911): *Creative Evolution*. London.
BORGES, J. L. (1998): *A Universal History of Iniquity*. Harmondsworth.
CLARKE, D. B. (Ed.) (1997): *The Cinematic City*. London.
CLARKE, D. B. (2003): *The Consumer Society and the Postmodern City*. London.
CLARKE, D. B., V. CRAWFORD PFANNHAUSER and M. A. DOEL (Eds.) (forthcoming): *Moving Pictures / Stopping Places*. Minneapolis.
COEN, J. and E. COEN (2002): *Collected Screenplays*, Volume 1 (Blood Simple, Raising Arizona, Miller's Crossing, Barton Fink). London.
COHAN, S. and I. R. HARK (Eds.) (1997): *The Road Movie Book*. London.
CRANG, M. (2002): Between places: producing hubs, flows and networks. *Environment and Planning A* 34, 569–574.
CRESSWELL, T. (2001): The production of mobilities. *New Formations* 43, 11–25.
CRESSWELL, T. and D. DIXON (Eds.) (2002): *Engaging Film: Geographies of Mobility and Identity*. Lanham.
DENBY, E. (1998): *Grand Hotels: Reality and Illusion*. London.
EASTHOPE, A. (1993): *Wordsworth Now and Then*. Milton Keynes.
EASTHOPE, A. (1999): *The Unconscious*. London.
EASTHOPE, A. (2002): *Privileging Difference*. Basingstoke.
ELLIS, D. (1985): *Wordsworth, Freud and the spots of time: Interpretation in The Prelude*. Cambridge.
FREUD, S. (1899): Screen memories. STRACHEY, J. (Ed.) (1953–1974): *The Standard Edition of the Complete Works of Sigmund Freud*, Volume III. London, 303–322.
FREUD, S. (1917): Mourning and melancholia. STRACHEY, J. (Ed.) (1953–1974): *The Standard Edition of the Complete Works of Sigmund Freud*, Volume XIV. London, 243–258.

FREUD, S. (1919): The Uncanny. STRACHEY, J. (Ed.) (19531974): *The Standard Edition of the Complete Works of Sigmund Freud*, Volume XVII. London, 219–252.
FREUD, S. (1921): Group psychology and the analysis of the ego. STRACHEY, J. (Ed.) (1953–1974): *The Standard Edition of the Complete Works of Sigmund Freud*, Volume XVIII. London, 67–143.
FREUD, S. (1923): The ego and the id. STRACHEY, J. (Ed.) (1953–1974): *The Standard Edition of the Complete Works of Sigmund Freud*, Volume XIX. London, 12–66.
FREUD, S. (1936): A disturbance of memory on the Acropolis. STRACHEY, J. (Ed.) (1953–1974): *The Standard Edition of the Complete Works of Sigmund Freud*, Volume XXII. London, 238–248.
FRIEDBERG, A. (1990): A denial of difference: theories of cinematic identification. KAPLAN, E. A. (Ed.) (1990): *Psychoanalysis and Cinema*. New York, 36–45.
GILES, S. (2000): Cracking the cultural code: methodological reflections on Kracauer's 'The Mass Ornament'. *Radical Philosophy* 99, 31–39.
HAINGE, G. (forthcoming): No sympathy for the devil, or lobby music: spaces of disjunction in Barton Fink and The Shining. CLARKE, D. B., V. CRAWFORD PFANNHAUSER and M. A. DOEL (Eds.) (forthcoming): *Moving Pictures / Stopping Places*. Minneapolis.
HANSEN, M. (1991): Decentric perspectives: Kracauer's early writings on film and mass culture. In: New German Critique 54, 47–76.
HARVEY, D. (1989): *The Condition of Postmodernity: An Enquiry into the Origins of Cultural Change*. Oxford.
JAMESON, F. (1992): *The Geopolitical Aesthetic: Cinema and Space in the World System*. Bloomington.
KATZ, M. (1999): The Hotel Kracauer. *Differences* 11 (2), 134–152.
KRACAUER, S. (1922): The hotel lobby. LEVIN, T. Y. (Ed.) (1995): *The Mass Ornament: Weimar Essays*. Cambridge, 173–185.
KRACAUER, S. (1927): Photography. LEVIN, T. Y. (Ed.) (1995): *The Mass Ornament: Weimar Essays*. Cambridge, 47–63.
LACAN, J. (1977): *...crits: A Selection*. London.
LACAN, J. (1979): *The Four Fundamental Concepts of Psychoanalysis*. Harmondsworth.
LACAN, J. (1988): *The Seminar of Jacques Lacan: Book I*. Cambridge.
LÉVINAS, E. (1979): *Totality and Infinity*. The Hague.
LÉVINAS, E. (1991): *Entre-nous: Essais sur le penser-à-l'autre*. Paris.
LOCKE, J. (1975): *An Essay Concerning Human Understanding*. Oxford.
LUHMANN, N. (1998): *Obervations on Modernity*. Stanford.
MORRIS, M. (1988): At Henry Parkes Motel. *Cultural Studies* 2, 1–47.
NOLAN, C. (n. d.): *Memento Final Shooting Script*. http://www.christophernolan.net/files/memento-script.txt, accessed: 6/10/2004.
RANK, O. (1971): *The Double*. Chapel Hill.
SARGEANT, J. and S. WATSON (Eds.) (1999): *Lost Highways: An Illustrated History of Road Movies*. London.
SILVERMAN, K. (1991): Back to the future.*Camera Obscura* 27, 108–133.
SVEVO, I. (2002): *Zeno's Conscience*. Harmondsworth.
TALLACK, D. (1998): *'Waiting, waiting:' the hotel lobby*. http://www.nottingham.ac.uk/3cities/tallack1.htm, accessed: 06/06/2004.
URRY, J. (2000): *Sociology beyond Societies: Mobilities for the Twenty-first Century*. London.
WILLIAMS, M. (1982): *Road Movies*. London.
ŽIŽEK, S. (1992): 'In his bold gaze my ruin is writ large.' ŽIŽEK, S. (Ed.) (1992): *Everything You Always Wanted to Know about Lacan (But Were Afraid to Ask Hitchcock)*. London, 211–272.

Christopher M. Moreno / Stuart Aitken

SPACE OPERAS AND CULTURES OF ADDICTION: THE ANIMATED TALE OF PHILIP K. DICK'S *A SCANNER DARKLY*

> *The most dangerous kind of person is one who is afraid of his own shadow*
>
> (DICK 1977, 102).

> *... the paranoid sees hostile forces in the world and weaves them into a satisfying conspiracy*
>
> (KIRMAYER 1983, 170).

> *Drugs are dangerous, yes, and certainly some more than others, but what is the danger specific to drugs?*
>
> (LAMBERT n.d.).

> *Why do humans so often desire things that engineer their own repression and slavery?*
>
> (LAMBERT n.d.).

> *... just something of an adventure, what we call space opera*
>
> (Philip K. DICK Interview, Festival du Livre de Science Fiction, September 1977).

INTRODUCTION

Bob Arctor knows the farm, he likes it there; it is familiar, it is comfortable. It seems that he has been at the farm for a long time now but this may simply be a product of his inability to live beyond the moment. That is okay. Spending days toiling between rows of corn is comfortable. His overalls are comfortable. He likes sleeping in the small clean shack, and his days working the rows of corn permit a calming vista towards the far off mountains. "Where is this?" He cannot remember a more tranquil time. He cannot remember any other time at all.

The scene switches to someone from Arctor's past whom he knew as Donna. Her real name may be Audrey. Donna / Audrey sits with a colleague in a fast-food restaurant:

> "So tell me, are they getting paranoid about him?" She asks.
> "Not at all, the guy's so burnt out."
> "And we're still convinced they're growing the stuff."
> "They have to be. Who else?"
> "I just wonder if it even matters."
> "It matters Audrey. It matters if we can prove that New-Path is the one that is growing, manufacturing and distributing ..."
> "How does he look? I mean do you think he is going to be able to pull through for us?"
> "I guess we can hope that when he finally gets in there a few charred brain cells will flicker on and some distant instinct will kick in."
> "It's just such a cost to pay."
> "Yeah. But there is no other way to get in there. I couldn't and think how long I tried. They got that place locked up tight. They're only gonna let a burnt out husk like Bruce in. Harmless, you have to be or they won't take the risk."
> "Yeah, but to sacrifice someone ... a living person without them ever knowing it. I mean if he'd understood, if he had volunteered. But he doesn't know and he never did. He didn't volunteer for this."
> "Sure he did. It was his job."
> "It wasn't his job to get addicted. We took care of that ... shit we are colder than they are."
> "I don't think so. I mean, I believe God's m.o. is to transmute evil into good ... and if he's active here he is doing that now ... although our eyes can't perceive it. The whole process is hidden beneath the process of our reality ... it will only be revealed later ... "

In the following scene the camera cuts back to Arctor working in the cornfields. He is drawn to the small blue flower at his feet. The small blue flower becomes a carpet of blue flowers beneath the corn. He thinks that it is somehow important; but the large man in a suit looking down at him interrupts his reverie, limited as it is. The man is Donald, the Executive Director of New-Path:

> "You are seeing the flower of the future."
> Where did he come from? Arctor is unperturbed.
> "But not for you Bruce."
> Bruce, is that his name?
> "Not for me." Nothing really perturbs him these days. There is a vague memory that something should perturb him but that memory is fading along with the blue flowers.
> "No, you've had too much of a good thing already," laughs Donald. "Get up, get up. Stop worshiping. This isn't your god anymore, although it once was."
> "Gone." Arctor looks down at where the flowers once were. "The flowers are gone."

"No, you just can't see them. Back to work."
"I saw."
"Back to work, Bruce." Donald walks out of the corn and back to his car. "I saw death rising from the earth ... from the ground itself ... in one blue field."

Figure 1. *A Scanner Darkly*, the animated movie

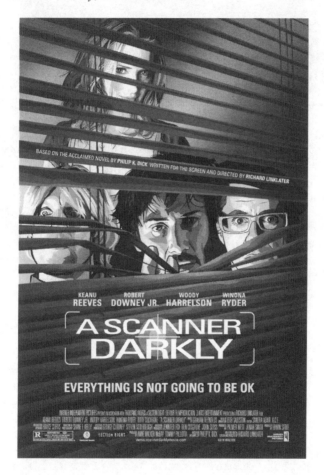

Richard Linklater's filmic adaptation of Philip K. DICK's novel about duplicity within duplicity, *A Scanner Darkly*, follows the plotline of the novel closely and ends almost identically. We are drawn to the duplicity outlined in the story between personal choices, corporate controls and state surveillance; and, we are particularly intrigued by the ways Linklater visualizes DICK's so-called space opera. Our interests in this movie are in the way that Linklater deals with the larger socio-spatial contexts of drug use and addiction and the chimera of capitalist and government control over the culture of addiction.

Figure 2. Fred / Bob Arctor lecture on drug addiciton

In the following sub-sections of the paper we look through the lens of Deleuzian theory at the ways Linklater visualizes the spatiality of DICK's portrayal of individual and societal paranoia and schizophrenic delusion. Our hope is that doing so provides clarity and insight into the varied social and spatial relations between cultures of addiction, corporate greed, and state surveillance that we address. DELEUZE's philosophical work is, in itself, a theoretical and philosophical technology we play and work with to illuminate the ways socio-spatial relations are connected to drug addiction. The end point of this experiment may very well be – to paraphrase Bob Arctor – to show that what we know about this film and these subjects "is very little, and often we get that fragment wrong." That said, we end the paper with some speculation (and hope) by returning to the emancipatory socio-spatial contexts that the notion of recovery offers and suggesting that *A Scanner Darkly* depicts both an illness as well as a remedy to some of neoliberal capitalism's excesses.

The paper is divided into four main sections. In the first, we connect the broader narrative of drug use and addiction flowing through the film to some of the duplicitous social, political, and pathological geographies deeply embedded in the workings of America's 'War on Drugs'. We are particularly concerned with elaborating on the notion of 'duplicity within duplicity' as it intersects the societal, enforcement and corporate workings of drug addiction being elaborated in the film. In the second, we draw from theoretical works of DELEUZE and GUATTARI to develop a relational understanding of schizophrenia and drug use – with a focus on affect and the production of desire / difference. In the third, we continue working from conceptual ideas on affect, difference, and drug using bodies presented in the previous section, but, more specifically, addresses the way in which the spatialities of paranoia, surveillance, non-moralist spatial politics / ethics of drug use and neoliberalism connect to the visual geographies in the film. And, in the fourth, we explore how the visual geographies of the film enable the film's affective capacity to engage with social spaces engaged with drug addiction off-screen.

SCANNING DARKLY

A Scanner Darkly is, perhaps, DICK's most autobiographical work. Prior to writing the book, DICK had his literary finger on the societal pulse of cold war paranoia, a condition where "betrayal and patriotism are mutually reciprocal and virtually indistinguishable" (UMLAND 1995, 3). DICK points out that *A Scanner Darkly* is an amoral, anti-drug rendering of what he perceived to be the relational and societal consequences of his and others' chronic drug use during the 1960s and 1970s (see DICK 1977, Author's Note). From DICK's life as an amphetamine addict, some of his most inner thoughts and feelings about the people he loved and used drugs with, as well as their growing paranoia over Nixon's drug policies of the 1970s emerge in this book (see WARRICK 1987). While harrowing, humorous and dark, *A Scanner Darkly* is not so much an anti-drug story or a book written simply to circumvent the endemic subculture of drug use in America. Rather, it is a drug narrative that gives rise to much more complex socio-political and psychological geographies of drug use that take into account the emotional experiences of drug users as they meet psychosis and the various tangential, but equally important, layers of governance, technologies and scales of control and surveillance connected to America's war on drugs; but also – it may be argued – its contemporary war on terror as well as any form of warmongering that attempts to winnow profit from others' distress.

Arctor's suburban house in Anaheim and his roommates, Barris and Luckman, bear some resemblance to DICK's milieu and acquaintances after his first divorce. The book, and the movie, have a post-script listing friends who died because of substance abuse: "This has been a novel," DICK (1977, 276–7) states in the end author notes, "about some people who were punished entirely too much for what they did." The book is also about the times: "I myself, I am not a character in this novel; I am the novel. So, though, was our entire nation at this time … And nature cracked down on us. We were forced to stop by things dreadful" (DICK 1977, 276–7).

A Scanner Darkly is not a narrative about a 1960s counter-culture. Linklater and the actors that play Arctor, Barris and Luckman – Keanu Reaves, Robert Downey Jr. and Woody Harrelson respectively – note, during special DVD features that accompany the movie that they believe *A Scanner Darkly* is very much about our times. Set in California sometime in the near future, it deals with a society increasingly addicted to technology – especially visual surveillance – and the narcotic Substance D. The effects of Substance D are never precisely articulated in either the book or movie. Nonetheless, it is highly addictive as are other drugs mentioned such as heroin, methamphetamine, opium and hash. As Barris states early in the movie, "there are no weekend warriors on D, you are either on it or you haven't tried it".

An optional special feature accompanies the DVD that switches on commentary during the movie. This feature enables the viewer to engage with the dialogue between Screenwriter / Director Richard Linklater, Actor Keanu Reeves, Producer Tommy Pallotta, Isa Dick Hackett (one of DICK's daughters), and, Philip K. DICK Historian, Jonathan Lethem. There is some suggestion during the dialogue that Substance D creates a Winnicotian *transitional space*, somewhere between a seeming outer reality and a seeming inner-self through which play is enabled (WINNICOTT 1971). For DICK (1977, 276), child-like play is the temporary outcome: "For a while I myself was one of these children playing in the street; I was, like the rest of them, trying to play rather than grow up, and I was punished." For DICK, Linklater and Lethem, the outcome of the escape to a drug induced transitional space is not growth and a redefinition of self as suggested by WINNICOTT, but rather, schizophrenic delusions and paranoia. Lethem goes on to argue that Substance D relates metaphorically to certain aspects of capitalism and consumer pleasure, while also having the characteristic of a pharmaceutical product, with the properties of a street-drug, created and distributed by one company.

The main 'duplicity within duplicity' of *A Scanner Darkly,* then, is that the company that provides rehabilitation from the drug – New-Path – is also its producer and distributor. And, rehabilitation through New-Path – as Arctor's story epitomizes – ultimately provides slave labor for fields producing the blue flower that is the base of Substance D. The irony of the narrative is that the end point of Substance D addiction – paranoia and schizophrenic delusions – is also the context of the society portrayed in *A Scanner Darkly.* In order to look more closely and critically at the spatial and social form(s) of paranoia and delusion expressed in the film, in the following section we sketch out a theoretical platform using the work of DELEUZE and GUATTARI upon which our analysis of *A Scanner Darkly* finds support.

SCHIZOID GEOGRAPHIES

The work of DELEUZE, as spatialized by DELEUZE and GUATTARI, offers an interesting way of contextualizing spaces of addiction. We find this work particularly appealing for our purposes because it draws, in convoluted and yet inimical ways, upon DELEUZE's early work on cinema and points to later discussions (most often amongst students of DELEUZE and GUATTARI) on ways larger neoliberal processes embedded in global capitalism – and particularly the corporate / state apparatus – opportunistically create addictive societies (DELEUZE and GUATTARI 1983, 1987; MASSUMI 2002; MALINS 2004; BONTA and PROTEVI 2005). What follows is a sketch of a theoretical framework derived from DELEUZE and GUATTARI that is also (in the manner of DELEUZE and WINNICOTT) an experimental play on understanding larger societal spaces and modes of encounter with drug addiction. The notion of experimental play does not detract from the serious connection we seek to make between the relations of individual choice, cultures of addiction and the corporate / state apparatus; rather, it enables us to embrace the contradictions inherent within ways of countering the chimera of contemporary neoliberalism. In many ways we see *A Scanner Darkly* as a call to arms but also a capitulation, a surrender; and, borrowing from DICK (1977), a *"[m]ors ontological,* Death of the spirit. The identity. The essential nature." This paper is not about using *A Scanner Darkly* as a way to address the ineptitude of the 'war on drugs' and its insubstantial effects, but rather it foments around an appreciation of the moral duplicity embedded within neoliberal social and spatial structures connected to drug addiction.

In *Thousand Plateaus* (1989), DELEUZE and GUATTARI outline five body types: hypochondriac, paranoid, masochistic, schizoid, and drugged. In developing a geography of the drugged body, we begin by elaborating the schizoid body – one of the defining characteristics of what DELEUZE and GUATTARI dub a nomad philosophy. Nomadism, they argue, is a means through which schizoids wage war against their internal organs (i.e. brain) to prevent their body from turning inward on itself toward a catatonic state. Schizoids must constantly keep their bodies outwardly active, continually producing desire and sets of new spatial, social, and corporeal relations to, as Doreen MASSEY (2005) suggests, become the new.

DELEUZE and GUATTARI's (1983) notion of the schizoid body can be better understood when distinguished from the psychoanalytic treatment model of schizophrenia. For example, the conceptualization of the unconscious is central to the psychoanalytic treatment of schizophrenia. Psychoanalytical readings of the unconscious encode it as a place or space to observe and control oppositionally from outside. Moreover, psychoanalytical treatment models for schizophrenia rely on the externalization of controlling devices such as drugs and electric shock therapy to sedate and represses what they deem to be the schizoid's abnormal libidinal desires being expressed in and through the mind, body, family, and society.

In contrast, DELEUZE and GUATTARI (1987) celebrate the nomadic tendencies of schizoid bodies for their continuous mind-body movements, creativity, production, and activeness in the formation of body, society, and space. They develop, in a partial and experimental way, an ethical discussion on drugs in relation to schizoids by arguing that drugs impose themselves on the interior spaces of the body-location: where inner desires are produced and extend outward. Because it surrounds the ethical conceptualization of the schizoid body engaged with drug therapy, what we are concerned with here is how drug therapy works to suppress the body's own production of desire (vitality). DELEUZE and GUATTARI argue that psychoanalytically motivated drug treatment for schizophrenia often leaves in its wake a completely de-territorialized body or social space. The total collapse of subjectivity, or complete de-territorialization, leads bodies to passive, non-active or non-affecting states with other bodies and spaces – 'social catatonia.' Catatonic spaces / bodies imagined in this way are unable to produce anything real or lasting without the external aid of drugs. What becomes exceedingly important, is not so much the qualitative differences between drugs or drug using bodies, but the effect drugs are having on body-to-body and body-to-space relations.

Figure 3. Substance D: the flower of the future.

Drugs also affect the perceptive relations between drug users and social space(s). BONTA and PROTEVI (2005, 146) argue that, "slowing down can be just as effective a means of de-territorialization or de-stratification as speeding up, for it is the shift of the intensive differential rates of change that wrenches a body out of its old habits, that free it from the basin of attraction of a singularity." Different drugs, when conceived as effecting and differentiating forces, alter the speed at which the consuming bodies move through and connect with other bodies and social spatial assemblages. In this way, drugs not only enhance the body's aesthetic (perceptive) and emotional (connective) relations with society, space, and other bodies (assemblages); but also perform political ethical actions in terms of smoothing over the existing power structures (striations in space) operating on their lives and bodies as well as affecting their capacity for future action and differentiation. This is why DELEUZE and GUATTARI, in *Thousand Plateaus*, argue that smooth spaces 'cannot save us' and that there is a need to map out the 'productive' tendencies (ethics) of each 'smooth' space (i.e. drug using). And, importantly, smooth spaces of liberation and movement can, in time, become striated spaces of constraint and control. With addiction and social catatonia, drugged bodies join with chemical assemblages to enervate any movement towards differentiation and the becoming of the new.

The schizoid-geographies we elaborate through the visual acuity of *A Scanner Darkly* echo the affective contexts of becoming other (into addiction and then, through recovery, from addiction) in the sense that we accept (and yet we do not claim to understand) the importance of winning though defeat, gaining power by letting go, realizing self through sharing and community, accepting past failures and future fears through the lens of the here and now, and elaborating equality through difference. These schizoid relations are part of the visual geographies of the film. Like other works of DICK that are visualized through cinema – *Bladerunner (1982), Minority Report (2002)* – *A Scanner Darkly* is about the identity politics and larger, darker forces that manipulate, or try to manipulate, those politics.

Technology is a large part of these schizoid relations. Early in the movie we see Arctor in his role as narcotics agent, Fred. He is wearing a *scramble suite*, which presents to the viewer millions of fractural representations of body (especially facial) and clothing features. The viewer encounters a constantly changing visage: factures of different faces, demeanors and clothes show up every second or two; constant re-identification, transformative embodiment, instant de-recognition and depersonalization. The scramble suit is a technology designed by the narcotic enforcement agency so that their undercover agents can continuously change all facial and bodily comportment. The suit has no means of personal identification and thus no selfhood or image that can be tied down or voice that can be recognized (Almost – In a wonderful nod to Hitchcock and his ego, pieces of Philip K. DICK show up through the scramble suite from time to time). The suit offers no objective viewpoints, but rather a body performance where identities blur and realities shift. The suit creates a body in a constant state of becoming 'other.'

Figure 4. Arctor's boss Frank / Donna in his / her scramble suite

Figure 5. Arctor's scramble suite morphs for a second into Phillip K. DICK

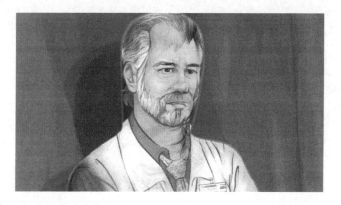

Schizophrenia is not only embodied in the scramble suite, it is prescribed by Arctor's job as a narcotics agent known as Fred. Later, when in recovery from Substance D, Arctor is known as Bruce. His boss, known in his scramble suit as Frank is also Donna, the women with whom he wants a relationship. She is also Audrey who meets with a colleague in the fast-food restaurant to discuss the plight of Bruce at the New-Path facility. If DELEUZE's work points to becoming 'other' as a liberatory experience, *A Scanner Darkly* portrays a graphic dystopian othering of schizophrenia perpetrated by work and technology.

Throughout *A Scanner Darkly*, DICK and Linklater comment on paranoia and differentiation from the dialectical image of the 'double'. The lead character, Arctor / Fred / Bruce, is a doper, drug narcotic officer, and slave laborer. In the beginning of the film, Arctor is an undercover narcotics agent named Fred sent to spy on drug dealers, specifically those who deal Substance D. At the same time, Arctor is a chronic user of Substance D and many other drugs. Arctor's drug use, at least in the way we read DICK and Linklater, was about changing his perceptive field

– Winnicottian transitional space – in order to de-territorialize the dual consciousness of Fred and Bob. Arctor's drug use made what was commonly imperceptible to Fred (life as a drug addict and dealer) perceptible and what was imperceptible to Bob Arctor (narcotic surveillance and control) perceptible.

This notion of the 'double' that DICK uses in *A Scanner Darkly* is common to many characters in his other literary works. UMLAND (1995, 3) notes that "DICK's fiction is populated by assassins (Keith Pellig in *Solar Lottery*, Spence Olham in *Imposter*, Joe Candella in the *Man in the High Castle*), informers (Kathy Nelson in *Flow my Tears, The Policeman Said*), double agents (Donna Hawthorne in a *Scanner Darkly*, Vivian Kaplan in *Radion Free Albemuth*), agents with blown covers (Douglas Quail in *We Can Remember it for you Wholesale*), and triple agents (Roni Fugate in the *Three Stigmata of Paler Eldritch*)." With Arctor, DICK creates a particularly convergent transitional space that annihilates (WINNICOTT's term is "kills") the social and psychological boundaries between what is typically perceived to be two entirely distinct spaces – interiority and exteriority. Arctor, as drug user, and Fred, as narcotics agent, are not enclosed or closed off from one another but flow, intermix, and absolve each other. Over time, as the narrative unfolds, this schizophrenia breeds self doubt, paranoia, and confusion. DICK (1977) wonders,

> How many Bob Arctors are there? A weird and fucked up thought. Two that I can think of ... The one called Fred, who will be watching the other one, called Bob. The same person. Or is it? Is Fred actually the same as Bob? Does anybody know? I would know if anyone did, because I'm the only person in the world that knows that Fred is Bob Arctor. But, he thought, who am I? Which one of them is me?

The notion of Arctor spying on himself is confounded in a particularly poignant scene where he has a romantic moment with Donna that ends when she is unable to have intimate body contact because she has ingested too much cocaine. Arctor storms out of her apartment and ends up in his house with another woman who is more interested in his drugs than sex. After they make love, Arctor turns to the girl and watches her morph into Donna. The explanation is that this morphing is a drug-induced illusion. Later, however, Fred / Arctor watches the sex act he had with the woman through a *holoscope* (a holographic image maker) that was installed to survey Arctor and his roommates.[1] What does the scanner see? It depicts the girl morphing into Donna in precisely the way Arctor remembers. He isolates the image of the girl from the holoscope and creates a three-dimensional hologram. What does the scanner see? Darkly? The three-dimensional image of the girl morphs into Donna. Arctor rewinds and fast-forwards watching the naked schizoid body change back and forth. In the end, Arctor ponders – as part of the illness and remedy, as part of the striations and smoothings, does the scanner see clearly or darkly?

> What does the scanner see? Into the head? Down into the heart? Does it see into me, into us? Clearly or darkly? I hope it sees clearly because I cannot any longer see into myself. I see only murk. I hope for everyone's sake the scanner does better. Because if the scanner sees only darkly the way I do then I am cursed and cursed again.

1. WARRICK (1987, 159) notes that "the scanner...assumes the role in the novel almost as important as any of the characters."

CONSUMED BODIES, STRIATED SPACES, AND DRUG USE

When Fred / Arctor is given a psychological test by a couple of doctors as part of his assessment, the first shadowed object he is asked to identify is a Coca-Cola bottle. In this scene we are not only reminded of how contemporary consumerism, tied to the production of an addictive society, is mobilized in part by insidious corporate advertising strategies entirely orchestrated to produce desire for an object, thing, activity, or relationship. DELEUZE (1962) suggests that the desire for, and consumption of, drugs and other material assemblages such as Coca-Cola and plastic surgery rests on the idea that the body (including the social body) we are given (inherit / possess / produce) is somehow insufficient to deal with the participatory pressures that beset us in today's modern, urban, capitalist landscapes. In stark contrast, DELEUZE and GUATTARI (1987) argue that the body alone, without drugs, is itself capable of meeting these challenges of producing desire and affective relations: "The body's active forces make it a self and define the self as superior and astonishing" (DELEUZE 1962, 39). That said, the notion of inadequacy problematically situates the context of desire that bombards us from media advertising as we strive to consume various things in order to create a 'superior body' within an emergent 'super society' (see DELEUZE 1962).

If *A Scanner Darkly* is about schizophrenic bodies, it is also about societal paranoia. Paranoia, in *A Scanner Darkly*, is often expressed alongside the constant surveillance (real and imagined) endured by the film's characters. Near the beginning, a scene shows Arctor walking down the street, talking on his mobile phone. As he talks, the shot cuts to a large room full of people, computers, and visual images. A surveillance technician ties into the mobile net and satellite imagery in order to triangulate Arctor's position. After some trial and error, the technician sees him walking down the street on the screen. Then, the technician uses facial-feature recognition technology to pull-up Arctor's FBI file. She ultimately dismisses the telephone call as innocuous. Beyond her seat, we see rows of technicians and banks of surveillance imaging equipment. Public spaces are surveyed through satellites and cell networks; private spaces are monitored through holoscopes.

Figure 6. Globally Positioned Drug Surveillance.

In *Thousand Plateaus,* DELEUZE and GUATTARI (1987) differentiate two kinds of spaces: smooth space and striated space. Smooth space is, they argue, "directional not determinable, filled by events far more than by formed or perceived things. It is a space of affects, more than one of properties" (DELEUZE and GUATTARI 1987, 479). Striated Space, however, is canopied by the measurable, visible, perceptive, or surveyed qualities deriving from it. While both spaces exist in mixture, smooth space is best characterized as nomadic and striated space as sedentary and, therefore, enervating.

The liberatory potential of drugs has the potential to move people and alter spatial relations in two ways. First, people use drugs and alcohol to alter the way that their minds and bodies perceptively, emotionally, and affectively engage with striated (surveyed) environments. Second, mind-altering substances alleviate the pressures of neo-liberal cities that demand constant social and economic participation, rigid body and space autonomy, self-control, and personal responsibility (see HARVEY 2005). These movements are part of what DELEUZE and GUATTARI (1987) call lines of flight, and are liberatory to the extent that they stay on this side of addiction. Spacing-out is good if it moves a body and space away from striations:

> The drug user creates active lines of flight. But these roll up, start to turn into black holes, with each drug user in a hole, as a group or individually, like a periwinkle. Dug in instead of spaced out. Micro-perceptions are covered in advance...by hallucinations, false perceptions, fantasies, waves of paranoia (DELEUZE 2006, 153).

And so, drug and alcohol use is both an illness and remedy to the extent that it enables lines of flight but does not create a hole – a total collapse of subjectivity. MALINS (2004, 90) points out that it is important " … to retain at least some links with the social world, with organization and subjectivity … [w]ithout such links a body becomes incapable of forming new assemblages, of differing from itself and creating new lines of flight. And without such links a body loses all political and strategic power."

The question DELEUZE raises with a drug using and / or schizoid body centers on the type of affective relations it has with other bodies and socio-spatial assemblages. Addiction and substance abuse have the potential to become problematic in that what begins as a nomadic trajectory has the capacity to fall, "... into a breathless void, into death" (DELEUZE 1995, 113). They note further that a completely (de)-territorialized body (and space) is incapable of affective relations with other striating, (re)-territorializing, and hierarchical forces that help make up the world and give rise to the production of desire and body / space differentiated relations. In the same way that space is expressed as both smooth and striated, a body is both a territory and a force – both striation and smoothing are required for change (DELEUZE and GUATTARI 1987).

In a particularly humorous scene, Barris shows up at the house with a recently purchased eighteen-speed bike. As he shows it off to Arctor and Luckman, the scene unfolds to exhibit the paranoia of the group against everything including their collective community. Luckman counts the gears and, using the cogs as his guide, finds only nine – three on the front derailleur and six on the back. They then discuss the larger corporate plot that may well be in evidence from this finding. With a characteristic fervor, Luckman blurts out "Well let's just go rescue those orphaned gears dude" as he heads to the door. In essence, the group's paranoid delusions may apply to anything.

As Lethem points out on the DVD commentary, the roommates are in a state of radical disjunction, which also is a protest expressing their feeling about reality in general. If there were a missing ingredient for a recipe in the kitchen, it would be construed as a conspiracy; and this is, literally, a line of flight. By being readily able to find a conspiracy in seeming missing gears they are galvanized into group action. Luckman heads for the door to rescue the orphaned gears, pulling the rest of the group with him. They are always wrong yet they are always right. In the commentary track, DICK's daughter points out that he continually vetted the FBI for the file they had on him. When he eventually received the file there was nothing in it besides letters he had sent accusing his roommates of drug dealing. Duplicity within duplicity. Yet, from his earliest writing in the 1950's, DICK presaged a number of problematic changes in society such as the privatization of the public sphere, and the corporatization of surveillance technology.

Figure 7. Gears and conspiracy theories.

DELEUZE and GUATTARI (1987) argue that, with drugs, body movements become reified and stuck in habitual relations with the world and themselves; moreover, as paranoia emerges, bodies' movements in society and space become predictable and their destinations knowable. The roommates actions over the bike gears, and later when their car breaks down on the way to San Diego, are knowable and predictable, and, while endearing also verge on the pathetic. In the context of the film, we are drawn to the ways that drugs become the external source of producing desiring relations and, as such, limit thought and action, snip extensions, and smother the creative potentiality for affective relations and corporeal differentiations. The following section addresses the relationship between the production of moving 'drugged' imagery or visualization of addiction, as aesthetic, and the affective relations being constituted with social and moral spaces engaged with drug addiction off screen.

VISUALIZING ADDICTION AND MORAL DYSLEXIA

Linklater uses a film technique known as interpolated rotoscoping – an animation method that digitally repaints or traces conventionally filmed live-action – to create the visual narrative for *A Scanner Darkly*. Inspired by Frank Miller's graphic novels (cf. *Sin City* 2004; cf. AITKEN 2007), rotoscoping requires hundreds of hours of animated interpolation to produce one minute of film. It differs from Miller's starkly shadowed film-noire technique by using line animation, nuanced shading and color. At first glance, the power of this technique seems to lie in its ability to artistically present visual fluidity between wakefulness and dreams, between desire and inhibition, between reality and delusion. But the animation technique Linklater employs is not merely about tracing or representation of such visual fluidities, or that which the viewer can see and feel, as an animated alternative to the original spaces of the cinematic 'reel' (or the 'real' of DICK's original literary text as modified into a film). Filmic animation such as this takes, by its very doing or making, a new line of flight in filmmaking. With every tracing, a new image-space is created. With every animated image-event in *A Scanner Darkly*, emerge new formations, new movements, and changed expressions of the inner and outer worlds / spaces of paranoia, of drug addiction, as well as of the connecting and contextualizing suburban landscapes of Southern California. Whether or not the animation technique successfully developed new ideas about possible composite relations between filmmaking and animation artistry (in order to evoke a believable and knowable drugged landscape) is secondary to the affective relations Linklater's animated worlds give rise to within and outside the film itself. In suggesting this, we argue against HOPKINS' (1994, 53–55) famous indictment of animation as providing a diminished impression of reality that is less likely to enable a willing suspension of disbelief. Since HOPKINS wrote his classic semiotic appraisal of iconic illusions embedded within cinematic places, two things have happened. First, computer aided graphic imaging has changed the ways we suspend our disbelief; second, our post-structural theorizing (drawing largely from the work of DELEUZE) has enabled a fuller elaboration of affective aspects of image events.

We argue that, with interpolative rotoscoping, there is a particular cinematic / animation performativity that is critical for conceptualizing drug addiction spaces. Filmic animation comes together and oozes, estranges, distorts, warps, confuses and / or obscures the relational qualities within and between every frame, body, space, place, and landscape expressed in the film. Likewise, viewers engage the animated image space in a variety of ways. Their imaginations must be ready to toil as they also take an active role not only in experiencing and trying to make sense of the alternative realties being expressed in the film but also in creating them. Therefore, like the waves of paranoia vibrating throughout the film, within Linklater's animation is a particular performative (affective) uncertainty that flows and moves, always enabling a capacity of / for differentiation. Affectively, Linklater's animation "pulls" the viewer into an imaginative or laborious relation with the obfuscating and changeling image spaces and moving bodies of drugs, addiction, paranoia, and surveillance. By doing so, the animated worlds created by

Linklater move beyond HOPKINS' iconic illusions as mere indexical relationships (a mimetic canvas) to the extent that liberatory landscapes emerge. CURTI (2008) notes that animated landscapes have corporeal vitality; they are living and endeavoring things. The animation derived from *A Scanner Darkly* is an entirely new world – a differentiated body – that nonetheless relates in important ways to DICK's original literary work and to the original live action sequences from which it is created. Filmic animation of this kind (and that found in other films enhanced by computer graphics), when viewed through the lens of Deleuzian critical theory, has the capacity to challenge traditional ways of both understanding film and how geographers read concepts such as space, place, landscape, and body in film.

We argue that *A Scanner Darkly* articulates a visual aesthetic that is meant to shock the social body that encounters it. In a Deleuzian sense, assemblages of images and viewers are mutually co-constituted so that there is a combined movement forward in both social and filmic space. The notion of a shock, or a collision of ideas and image-events, was first established by Russian filmmaker theorist Sergie EISENSTEIN who used montage and other cinematic techniques to heighten social, economic, and political acuity in his filmmaking (EISENSTEIN 1991, also see DELEUZE 1988). The difference, however, is that EISENSTEIN's cinematic work was based on pre WWII dialectical notions of a passive or thoughtless social body where a particular sequencing of imagery (montage) could be used to move society to some form of political action and thus create social change. Within DELEUZE's language of cinema and montage (see DELEUZE 1988 and 1989) is a heightened acuity of an active social body encountering an active image space – a collision of affective bodies whose movements into one another mutually affect the formation of one another. In this way, viewers, like filmmakers or image spaces themselves, become active in producing thought, ideas, action, and nomadic life both in and outside of the filmic space. Each line of flight taken, each trajectory of image into society and vice versa, allows their becoming other (filmic and social).

The issue of moral dyslexia is highlighted in the suburban visual aesthetic of Arctor's home. *A Scanner Darkly* resonates with DICK's other novels, in particular, *Do Androids Dream of Electric Sheep*. Unlike the film, *Bladerunner,* that is based upon it, this book is set in suburban, not urban, Los Angeles. In the novel, the protagonist "bladerunner" cop lives the post-apocalyptic suburban dream where keeping up with the neighbors is to buy the latest android animal; he dreams of having a sheep (After the Coca-Cola bottle, the image Arctor is faced with during his psychological test is a sheep).

Figure 8. Arctor's suburban idyll morphs into a drug-addicted space

In *A Scanner Darkly,* DICK envisions the near future in suburban Anaheim. In a particularly poignant scene, Arctor dreams a part image of living the suburban idyll with wife and children, that fades out into the decrepit lawn and house his home has become. Later in the movie, in a moment of seeming lucidity, Arctor walks from his office back to the house and, in voice-over, comes to the conclusion: "Something big is definitely going down in this house ..." The irony is that he believes the duplicity is focused on Barris, not on himself. He continues to wonder as he walks up the driveway: " ... this run-down, rubble-filled house with its weed-filled yard and cat-box that never gets emptied. What a waste of a truly good house. So much could be done with it. A family and children could live here. It was designed for that. Such a waste. They aught to confiscate it and put it to better use."

Figure 9. A waste of a truly good house

These moments in *A Scanner Darkly* open up an innate desire for truth. The narrative of the film, as expressed in scenes like this, can be seen as the creative endurance of Bob Arctor. And, while the desire to endure does not overtly seem to trump Arctor's desire for truth about his social world of drugs, enforcement and government conspiracy in growing Substance D, *A Scanner Darkly* can be read as a unmitigated critique of "the work of truth" (FORD 2005, 66). Indeed, despite the fact that all the characters in this film do not necessarily function well in society (as individual, friends, co-workers, lovers, etc), they do find a way to endure. Even as a lifeless body, DICK's rendering of a drugged body can still endure. Such a rendering has important ethical considerations for a society steeped in capitalist and neoliberal values. In *A Scanner Darkly,* to endure, however, does not necessarily mean to be alive from the Deleuzian sense of an affective or acting body. As DICK shows us, even dead things and dead people can endure. The social reproduction of junkie (or those who move only for the junk) produces nothing new relationally other than competing forms of (in)sanity – difference predicated by degree (or lack) and not kind.

Fred and Bob Arctor's (un)-consciousness, while initially projected as dwelling within one body, is being defined and expressed by a form of movement, duration, or a process of differentiation concerned merely with the before(s) and after(s) of drug use. Although Fred was Arctor, he initially watched the scanned imagery taken from his home, from one moment to the next, as if he had never lived what he was watching. With the constant dividing of space and time or mind and body going on in this film, with each division, there is a passing of judgment. Passing judgment on a thing, person, activity, and state of affairs; however, like drug use can only be located in the perceptive realm. Yet, this is what DICK seems to want us to question. Arctor annihilates judgment of himself(s) with each hit of Substance D and each time he slips on the scramble suit.

The shadowy, vicious, and tragic culture of chronic drug use, recovery, capitalism, and governance expressed in DICK's drug narrative visualizes the contaminating, degenerative, and paradoxical affects of cold war paranoia connected to drugs.

At times, the debilitating feelings of distrust, wariness, and suspicion connected to spaces of drugs dominate the film's narrative. The social landscape of drug addiction, first painted in words by DICK in 1977 and later re-animated into moving images by Linklater, is like a predatory animal whose sole action is to devour the life producing qualities of those bodies who traverse the space too long. That said, the portrayed social world of drug addiction is not meant to be simplistic, dualistic or bounded by some archaic Cartesian thought progression regarding the emotional and political aspects of the film's conspiratory and alterating 'drugged' movements. Linklater and DICK create a world of drugs that sheds morality for ethics and playful or recreational drug use for conspiracy and power.

Expressions of paranoia exhibited by (Arctor / Fred / Bruce, Luckman, and Barris) are not merely emotional spaces limited to these three drug users, but also a feeling permeating the walls of rehabilitation (New-Path) and local and federal narcotic enforcement institutions. And, it is through a particular emotional and affective reading of this film that the spaces of drug use (in the home, streets, bathrooms, cars, work, etc), rehabilitation (New Path) and narcotic enforcement breed a new form of politics and ethics. None of the three spaces (drug use, rehab, enforcement) expressed in this film are distinct or independent from one another. DICK and Linklater remake these social fields as continuously and translucently folding back and forth into one another. Indeed, one of the more interesting critiques DICK and Linklater raise in *A Scanner Darkly* relates to the emotional and relational moving spaces (imagery) of 'drugged' psychosis.

Characters in *A Scanner Darkly* move and function as partial addicts and psychotics, narcs and roommates, friends and lovers, co-workers and co-conspirators. Their identities, like the spaces they traverse as well as the drugs they ingest and desire, are never fixed but, rather, are mobile; it is their combined complex mobilities and their inability to connect to, or feel themselves move in and out of, these spaces relationally that contribute to their affective-less state in which they can not truly love and trust one another. Their social relations lack empathy. This lack led KIRMAYER (1983, 170) to note in regards to DICK's work in *A Scanner Darkly*, "the complexity and confusion of the social world forces on us a kind of extraversion in which the cause and control of our lives seem to lie wholly outside ourselves, with the powerful Other. This is a setting ripe for paranoia." Said differently, not only do the characters of this film struggle to not 'see' or 'feel' what is right in front of them, their paranoia does not allow them to affectively engage or communicate with each other. Nonetheless, there is a sense of conspiratorial community – as suggested by some of the comic antics of the roommates.

KNOWING VERY LITTLE AND GETTING THAT FRAGMENT WRONG TOO

> *It is our belief that the issue of drugs can be understood only at the level where the desire directly invests perception, and perception becomes molecular at the same time as the imperceptible is perceived*
>
> (DELEUZE and GUATTARI 1987, 283).

> *Real or unreal, originating within the percept system or received validly by the percept system because, say, of some chemical agent not normally present and active in the brain's metabolism, the unshared work that we call 'hallucinatory' is destructive: alienation, isolation, a sense of everything being strange, of things altering and bending – all this is the logical result, until the individual, formerly a part of human culture, becomes an organic 'windowless monad.' It does not matter that his reasoning faculties are impaired, it does not matter whether or not he feels adequate emotion. He may display moods and feeling that to us can't be accounted for. But we are not perceiving what he is; the emotions are almost certainly appropriate in relation to what he perceives, i.e. experiences*
>
> (DICK 1996, 173).

Extending from the works of SPINOZA and his definition of *substance* (SPINOZA 1996, also see CURLEY 1994 and DELEUZE 1970), drugs function as an external, affective, or nomadic body. Each time a character in *A Scanner Darkly* snorts coke, drops a tab of acid, smokes hash, or takes a pill of Substance D they encounter another affective body (i.e. drug). Like with any meeting of two affective bodies (drug and user), there is a particular relational convergence, or an encounter, that creates a transitional or differentiating space. In the encounter, the drug and drug user, as two affective bodies, undergo corporeal transformations. Deleuzian scholar Greg LAMBERT (forthcoming) states that taking drugs is, "not without its own dangers. Sometimes the relations combine in such a way to cause my body to decompose, destroying 'its own relation' and the parts to be combined with this new, more powerful body, that severs former relations that belong to the former body, the so called 'body proper', and its parts."

In *A Scanner Darkly*, we are conditioned to a particular ethic in the form of the drug Substance D. Substance D is an organic, governmentally grown and distributed drug that slowly destroys the corpus of the brain, the affective and affecting relational bridge between the two cerebral hemispheres. For DELEUZE and GUATTARI (1987) the brain (unconscious) is a factory for producing thought and thus moving the body towards action and new sets of relations. At first glance, DICK would have us believe that Substance D will merely result in creating two independently functioning minds within one brain (body), each hemisphere in competition with the other – able to think and act independently. Such a bifurcating competition, however, is what DICK describes as the death of the spirit – a spatial enclosure of parts to its whole.

The tragedy of chronic drug use visualized by DICK and Linklater is clear, although the story of *A Scanner Darkly* ends with possibility and hope as Bruce / Arctor / Fred stoops to pick up a blue flower and put it in his boot. He is at the New-Path facility, the one place in the world that is not scanned and surveyed, the one place he can move nomadically, where he can actively create smooth spaces, produce desire, a new body, a new identity, and new sets of social relations. With each step in Arctor's recovery he forms a new (social and spatial) path, "A present for my friends," he thinks as he looks forward inside his mind, where no one could see, to a Thanksgiving break where he may meet Audrey / Donna and may give her the flower. This is the hope behind the narrative, that corrupt corporations / governments can be toppled by a committed group of individuals. Yet, with Arctor's future unclear, we are reminded that there is a difference between knowing the path to recovery and walking, feeling, and creating that path.

REFERENCES

AITKEN, S. (2007): Dreams and nightmares as part of the order / disorder of the city. HUBBARD, P., T. HALL and J. R. SHORT (Eds.): *The Sage Companion to the City*. London, 373–388.

BONTA, M. and J. PROTEVI (2004): *Deleuze and geo-philosophy: A guide and glossary*. Edinburgh.

CURTI G. H. (2008): The ghost in the city and a landscape of life: a reading of difference in Shirow and Oshii's *Ghost in the Shell*. *Environment and Planning D: Society and Space* 26 (1), 87–106.

CURLEY, E. (Ed.) (1994): *A Spinoza reader: The ethics and other works of Benedict de Spinoza*. New Jersey.

DELEUZE, G. (1962): *Nietzsche and philosophy*. New York.

DELEUZE, G. (1970): *Spinoza: Practical philosophy*. San Francisco.

DELEUZE, G. (1988): *Cinema one*. St. Paul.

DELEUZE, G. (1989): *Cinema two*. St. Paul.

DELEUZE, G. (1995): *Negotiations: 1972–1990*. New York.

DELEUZE, G. (2006): *Two regimes of madness: Text and interviews 1975–1995*. Los Angeles.

DELEUZE, G. and F. GUATTARI (1983): *Anti-Oedipus*. Minneapolis.

DELEUZE, G. (1987): *A thousand plateaus*. Minneapolis.

DICK, P. K. (1977): *A scanner darkly*. Great Britain: Gallancz and Orin Books.

DICK, P. K. (1996): Drugs, hallucinations, and the quest for reality. DICK, P. K. and L. SUTIN (Eds.): *The shifting realities of Philip K. Dick: Selected library and philosophical writings*. New York, 167–174.

EISENSTEIN, S. (1991): *Selected works: Towards a theory of montage*, eds. GLENNY, M. and R. Taylor. London.
FORD, R. (2005): Deleuze's dick. *Philosophy and Rhetoric* 38 (1), 41–71.
HARVEY, D. (2005): *A brief history of neoliberalism*. Oxford.
HOPKINS, J. (1994): Mapping cinematic places: Icons, ideology, and the power of (mis)-representations. AITKEN, S. and L. ZONN (Eds.): *Power, place, situation and spectacle*. Lanham, 47–68.
KIRMAYER, L.J. (1983): Paranoia and pronoia: The visionary and the banal. *Social Problems* 31 (2), 170–179.
LAMBERT, G. (n.d.): *This is my body on drugs*. Forthcoming. (Permission from author – 9/2007)
MALINS, P. (2004): Machinic assemblages: Deleuze, Guattari and an ethico-aesthetics of drug use. *Janus Head* 7 (1), 84–104.
MASSUMI, B. (2002): *Parables for the virtual: Movement, affect, and sensation*. Durham.
MASSEY, D. (2005): *For space*. Thousand Oaks.
SPINOZA, B. (1996): *Ethics*. Translated by E. Curley. New York.
UMLAND, S.J. (1995): Introduction. UMLAND, S.J. (Ed.): *Philip K. Dick: Contemporary critical interpretations*. London, 1–7.
WARRICK, P.S. (1987): *Mind in motion: The fiction of Philip K. Dick*. Carbondale and Edwardsville.
WINNICOTT, D. (1971): *Playing with reality*. London.

Susan P. Mains

'ENGLISH FEVER':
DOCUMENTING THE CARIBBEAN DIASPORA IN *THE COLONY*

INTRODUCTION

The negotiation of media representations can be a complex and challenging process. Mainstream mass media is frequently critiqued for an inability, or reluctance, to make connections with the communities that it seeks to explore and / or exploit. As such, despite media's potential for opening up spaces of public debate and testimony for diverse experiences and identities, minority groups have pointed to a need for it to engage and depict a more nuanced understanding of the dynamic nature of social and spatial relations. A need for more diverse systems of representation is particularly evident in relation to images of migration. In the context of Caribbean migration, for example, media representations have played a pivotal role in translating (and erasing) personal diaspora narratives and, more generally, challenges faced by migrant communities. In this chapter I explore the role of media, particularly documentary film, as part of a process of translation and democratization. I focus specific attention on the possibilities for articulating and remembering more diverse Caribbean stories of mobility, transnationalism, citizenship, and community.

My discussion focuses on Philip DONNELLAN's documentary for the BBC, *The Colony*[1] (1964) – a complex case study that crystallizes contemporary anxieties and geographies of migrant lives. As a social documentary, *The Colony* unearthed and interrogated ways in which anti-immigrant sentiments fuelled public debates and broadcasting. The BBC first broadcast the film on terrestrial television, 16 June 1964. The film set the groundwork for DONELLAN's next film, *The Irishmen: An Impression of Exile* (1965), which examines Irish workers in London, as well as a further body of work examining a range of communities who had largely been ignored by mainstream British media (DUGUID 2003). DONELLAN's exploration of how images of colonialism resonated with different communities was striking for its focus on the everyday experiences of migrant workers and the locales they produced and traversed. Filmed in black and white, with dramatic and haunting

---

1. The Colony is held in the archives of the British Film Institute (BFI) in London, UK. The film, along with other documentary materials held in this national archive, can now be viewed online if you are based at a UK school, college, university library or public library at http://www.screenonline.org.uk/. This paper is part of a larger project examining the film and newsreel archives in BFI Collections, particularly those depicting West Indian-UK relations. Viewings of all footage listed under related subject categories were undertaken while working as a BFI Research Officer during 2000–01, and as part of a UWI New Initiative Grant in the Summer of 2003.

cinematography of solitary industrial landscapes and migrant workers, the film documents the stories of several individuals from different Anglophonic Caribbean islands as they re-tell their first impressions of England – and Birmingham – where they then resided.

The process and practice of migration is intricately intertwined with ties to place and community. These connections are significant not only in relation to present-day interactions, but also to ways in which concepts of place and identity are constructed through memory and have been interwoven with images of empire and post-imperialist nation-building. In the context of Caribbean-British relations, migration has been a key component of individual, national, and transnational identities. By focusing on *The Colony* and exploring documentary coverage of Caribbean migration to the UK, I illustrate how memory and narratives of migration inform, reflect, and shape connections to place and imperial identities. In my analysis of selected documentary film footage broadcast in post-WWII Britain, attention is paid to ways that specific images are informed by, and resistant to, prescriptive notions of the gendered and racialised 'colonial subject.'

Documentary films can provide a complex and useful context for understanding dialogues with place, identity, and representation. In addition, use of migrant oral histories in documentaries offers a process of recognizing and reconstructing memories of journeys and challenges faced by émigrés. I suggest that the process of narrating, recording, and broadcasting also produces new journeys and migrant geographies; and, as such, illustrates the dynamic nature of memory and ongoing negotiations with place and transnational connections. The process of re-telling and re-presenting migrant experiences unearths emotional and emotive landscapes that complicate and enrich our understandings of mobility and the visceral – and visual – presence of imperialism and geographies of exclusion (SIBLEY 1997).

For this exploration, I provide a theoretical context for examining links between mobility, place and representations of imperialism by drawing on poststructuralist understandings of identity and space as well as links between narratives of nation and citizenship. This is followed by an in-depth analysis of *The Colony*. I selected this film because of its provocative, and often resistant, content that challenges dominant mainstream media images of immigrants as being vague and inarticulate. These images provide important pedagogical tools for understanding empire – and post-imperial imaginings – as a lived, complex experience that produces provocative cultural geographies.

THEORETICAL FRAMEWORK:
VISUALIZING (POST) IMPERIAL GEOGRAPHIES

Phillip DONNELLAN produced *The Colony* as Jamaica was extricating itself from British control of the island. Concurrently, other European nations were gradually relinquishing their territorial claims while still using imperialist ontologies for conceptualising power and space. As critical cultural geographers have noted, during much of the last century – and one could argue, still to this day – there has been a tendency to view the world as consisting of distinct zones of space, largely controlled by the state. Such depictions of space fail to explore how certain identities or regions have been produced and challenged through forums, such as post-colonial community organizations, or through popular media, such as mainstream cinema or local and regional newspapers (JACKSON and PENROSE 1993). For many former colonies, the period leading up to and following independence has often resulted in an almost schizophrenic existence punctuated by media stories, both critical and supportive, of the former imperial power. News media and particularly visual media such as film play an important role in conveying both the contested identities that emerge during such periods of transition and political transformation – eras at "the end of empire." In addition, imperialist visions of spatial relationships depicted in film, such as those frequently aired in UK newsreels and bolstered by anti-immigrant politicians such as British MP Enoch Powell's nativist policy drives during the 1950s and 1960s, frequently fail to engage with the ways notions of citizenship and representations of space, countries, and borders metamorphose at different moments – through transnational political, media, and artistic movements for example (MCKERNAN 2003). Indeed, until relatively recently (with increasing globalization of media content due to changing technology and economic systems), even in times of political instability policy makers and media organizations have tended to assume that national identity and territory are relatively stable concepts with borders defined by the respective governing power (SHAW 1996). The production and consumption of media images of place, however, transcend political jurisdictions and exist beyond the contexts in which they were produced. I argue that movements of people and cultures challenge dominant notions of borders by examining ways that representations, both of Caribbean migrants and the spaces with which they have been associated, can not only be stereotyped but also destabilized in the context of documentary film.

Moving image media has not only been important in constructing imperial narratives about colonies, landscapes, and migrant communities to a broader public, but also has been a significant medium for communicating these stories through discursive strategies that (implicitly and explicitly) rely on specific nationalist notions of gender and race (ROSE 2001). In an examination of stereotyped Irish identities in British and U.S. media, for example, WALTER (1997, 354) notes, "Irish men have received the full force of these derogatory racialized characterizations. In part, this reflects the masculinity of Britishness and the exclusion of all women from English national identity." Accepted codes of representing Irishness became particularly important in signifying and placing specific marginalized immigrant identities. By "fixing" Irish identities in this manner, British and U.S. media simultaneously reinforce and locate dominant cultural identities that are coded as nationalistic, patriotic, and safe. This fixing often appears at moments in which hegemonic political identities seem most under threat such as during periods of economic or political instability.

Representation, therefore, is as much about depicting and communicating identity as it is about a process of reinforcing, challenging, and producing new identities (JONES and NATTER 1999, 1993). In turn, each representation is open to a variety of interpretations and readings feeding from and fuelling additional representations in an infinite number of overlapping connections. To establish meaningful representations, codes of communication have to be identified – and these are dependent on relational identities. For example, a central component of imperialist and anti-imperialist struggles has been an implicit understanding of the power of depicting the state as a natural entity by relying upon commonly agreed upon symbolism and imagery in which different social groups have invested (HALL 1997; DALBY 1996).

HALL (1997, 28) defines such practices of representation as "the production of meaning through language...meaning is produced by the practice, the 'work,' of representation." In other words, by producing a national body of programming or promoting a cinematic tradition in a particular region, a certain kind of identity or type of community character may be made visible and legitimated above others. At the same time, representation is important for the process of producing and mediating identity and space. As JONES et al. (1997) note, examining representational practices has been particularly important for feminist theorists when questioning and challenging gendered or sexed codes and identities embedded in a variety of media. In undertaking an exploration of feminist approaches towards representation, they point out three key questions that emerge from these analyses:

> 1) who has the (social) power to represent?; 2) what is the form and content of the representation?; and 3) what are the reception contexts – or "readings" – of the representation, including the intended and unintended social outcomes? It is in all three questions that we find that feminist scholars do not simply analyze texts for their intrinsic value as "art," but understand them as sites through which gendered and sexed social relations are produced and reproduced within society at large (JONES et al. 1997, xxxii).

This statement suggests that, in order to understand how empire and the decline of specific imperial visions have been constructed, there is a need to critically read the production of specific imperial depictions of cultural and national identities and to unearth images of resistance that challenge these dominant ideas. An aspect of this critical reading involves interrogating ways in which former colonies and migrants to the UK were depicted in film through the use of specific exclusionary discourses. *The Colony*, by heavily relying on largely ignored and often poignant stories of individual migrants, provides an innovative example of resistance and narration challenging dominant depictions of migration, colonialism and Caribbean identities in the UK.

By understanding identity as relational and constantly under negotiation, we can investigate the shifting and fluid nature of migration to and from the Caribbean and its associated visual representations thus avoiding the limitations of a singular view of this cultural landscape. Often, visual media are used in attempts to fix and locate identities and subject positions as in depictions of indigenous Caribbean populations as "exotic" or naïve in 19th century British art. These efforts, however, are always open to challenges and can never be permanently stabilized – nor are their meanings completely defined (ROSE 2001; HANNA 2000). This inability to completely fix identities and positions is because although "nodal points" become moments in which some degree of demarcating identity is established, identity is temporary, never complete, and still part of an ongoing state of flux (MOUFFE

1993). In her analysis of racialised and sexualized colonial imagery, for example, MCCLINTOCK (1995, 41) points out the power of visual media in contributing to images of "non-Western" cultures as being "out of place":

> Africa came to be seen as the colonial paradigm of anachronistic space, a land perpetually out of time in modernity, marooned and historically abandoned... In the industrial metropolis, likewise, the evocation of anachronistic space (the invention of the archaic) became central to the discourse of racial science and the urban surveillance of women and the working class.

Even while repressive, however, women's "different" sexual characteristics and work activities often challenged patriarchal and colonialist norms (through social and personal independence) thus creating new spaces. Examining a similar process of *displacement* in later years – in news media in the UK during the 1950s and 1960s wherein immigrants were depicted as being both out of time *and* space (CARTER *et al* 1993; JAMES 1992) – expands these ideas. Silencing and feminizing hierarchies were given even greater force with the ongoing development of visual media technologies such as television and film.

Ironically, while supported by – and in spite of – its kinetic characteristics, in certain instances documentary film provided a form of moving museum; encapsulating in a tightly contained format carefully selected material that could be transported to various venues but still collectively consumed in a manner that was highly stylized, catalogued and controlled, and which *placed* migrants in very specific ways. Simultaneously, however, living exhibits (where "native" groups were dressed in traditional costumes and included as a "live" part of the exhibition) and documentaries that tried to show the everyday life of colonial subjects, unintentionally produced the result of humanizing marginalized populations – thus calling into question previous systems of representation (KIRSHENBLATT-GIMBLETT 1998).

Despite its limitations as a process of communicating narratives and establishing a rallying cry for nation building projects (particularly during WWII), film provided a significant and engaging medium. In cataloguing a shift from print to mechanical media prior to the war, BENJAMIN (1968) noted that cinema, in particular, had power to nurture both a collectively passive audience and a broader mass resistance through subversive representations. Given its factual appearance, documentary film seems to offer an immediate and dynamic chronicle of social and political changes that is validated through the power of visual imagery (HALL 1997). Commenting on BENJAMIN's work, STEINER (1999, 88) notes that for the theorist, the illusion of accuracy and authenticity in art and moving image media are central concerns:

> [Benjamin's] essay, in other words, is an extended discussion of standards – exemplars we employ in determining the kinds of things and sorts of relations that we have a legitimate claim to call "genuine" or "real." According to Benjamin, the authentic is equivalent to the auratic, and it is for him the "aura" of art that declines in the age of mechanical reproduction.

It follows, therefore, that film makers and television programmers fuel certain consumption patterns that are partially based on "imagined" realities – often idealized and over simplistic – which are frequently far removed from their lived uniqueness and complexity. However, since visual media is not under the purvue of one single producer and can be read by an audience in many different ways (or by the same audience in contrasting ways given a change in context) I suggest that counter hegemonic images can also be made more easily reproducible (although with more struggle and less financial support) and can, like *The Colony*, pose avenues for critical engagement with exclusionary state-dominated representations.

CHANGING PLACES, RESISTING EMPIRE: MEMORY, BORDERS AND *THE COLONY*

The Colony emerged in the early 1960s – a period in which there was a growing hostility toward Black residents and Caribbean migrants and a call by several conservative politicians to alter the nature of existing West Indian-UK political ties. There also was a push by several right-wing organizations to limit the British government's responsibilities for Commonwealth countries, particularly by restricting the number of migrants allowed to relocate to the UK as reflected in the Immigration Act of 1962 (CHAMBERLAIN 1998; JAMES 1992). Links between the West Indies and Britain extend through many centuries of shipping, slavery, trade, colonialism, and, more recently, tourism. During World War I and II, many Caribbean nationals lent their support to allied troops, fighting on behalf of Britain and France (and the Caribbean). Then, as a migrant labour force, they formed a key component of the post-war economic and social reconstruction (CHAMBERLAIN 2001)[2]. Indeed, WAMBU (1999, 22) notes that Caribbean migrants, who began arriving in 1948 on the ship *Empire Windrush*, pushed the UK into a more reflective mode: "If British identity has changed and become more forward-looking and gently inclusive over the last fifty years, a large part of the reason has to be attributable to the presence of the 'Windrush generation' and the discourse of freedom and equality they brought with them to the heart of Empire." Yet, despite this in-depth interweaving of transatlantic cultures and a growing Caribbean presence in key metropolitan areas in the UK (e.g. London, Birmingham, and Manchester), the experiences and voices of Caribbean migrants have seemed conspicuous in their absence from postwar twentieth century mainstream media (HARRIS 1993). The development of a post-imperial (or postcolonial) spatial imaginary exploring what it means to be Caribbean or a migrant has been slow as this development is hindered by longstanding and ongoing global economic and political inequalities that are often embedded in lingering imperial discourses that continue to inform visual images of nationhood in the UK.

In 1958, riots in Nottingham and London were fuelled by a group of Whites attacking a White Swedish woman married to a Black Jamaican man in Notting Hill, West London aggressive policing practices, inflammatory statements by far right-wing politicians, economic recession, groups of nativist White male gangs intimidating West Indian residents in Notting Hill, and an increasingly frustrated and excluded Black population. These race riots pointed to a serious need for dialogue,

---

2. For a more detailed socio-demographic discussion of Caribbean migration see CHAMBERLAIN (2001), THOMAS-HOPE (1999), and MAINS (2002).

political change, and a re-evaluation of what being British meant (FRYER 1984). For, although many migrants already felt a strong connection to the UK prior to migration, and particularly to England[3] – having effectively grown up through a transplanted English educational system – following WWII many West Indian settlers were informed that their Blackness was seen as disqualifying them from belonging to a British community. The imperial nation had been willing to claim West Indians as colonial subjects when they were "over there," but now that they had actively, and physically, laid claim to this connection, the hostilities that migrants met on arriving at the other side of the Atlantic – both in terms of personal interactions and increasingly restrictive policy changes – meant that this notion of citizenship was not only relational but arbitrary, being embedded in racialised notions of citizenship and territoriality.

The Colony is unusual for documentaries of its time that usually contained an authoritative and often paternalistic narrative voiceover as a frame of reference. This technique can be noted in educational films of the British Colonial Film Unit that sought to teach (presumably White) viewers about the unfamiliar places and subjects, such as colonial territories and Black migrants, with whom they were becoming acquainted. In contrast, DONELLAN allows the film's narrative to be guided by its central subjects as they discuss their travels. Migrants' stories are intercut with footage of them working or with their family at home and are punctuated with images of the urban landscapes in which they have struggled. In the tradition of social realist cinema, the film works as a form of visual anthropology and cultural geography drawing attention to the ways in which media images are constructed while engaging with the complex and nuanced experiences and places through which the practices of migration and citizenship are enacted.

As *The Colony* explores the physical and cultural geographies of working class migrants, reflecting on how they have not only re-situated themselves since migrating, but also how they view their identities in relation to the UK, DONELLAN illustrates the concepts of memory and citizenship as part of ongoing negotiations that are linked to changing connections with place. The film's subjects offer not only a diversity of viewpoints but also vocations – Stan Crooke is a railway signalman from St. Kitts, Victor Williams a Jamaican bus conductor, Polly Perkins a Baijan nurse, Bernice Smith a Jamaican teacher, Pastor Dunn a Jamaican preacher, and the Stewarts a family of singers from Trinidad. Each raises questions

---

3. The reference to England rather than Britain is a significant one in that it also reflects a discourse of internal colonialism wherein a London-centric government framed discussions of "British" politics and media – thus, England, became the referent for the UK, despite internal tensions about such a claim to authority. Interestingly, at the same time as growing migrant populations in the UK highlighted the need for a reexamination of migration policies and cultural diversity, nationalist movements in Scotland, Wales and Northern Ireland, were also attempting to challenge the hegemony of what was viewed by activists as an Anglo-centric and geographically exclusionary elite. As I have argued previously (see MAINS 2003), many parallels exist in the ways in which race and region have been framed as "special interests" by British broadcasters and policymakers – increasingly illustrating the centralized control and power dynamics of culture industries.

about how the Caribbean has been generalized as a single place and culture. As DUGUID (2003) notes in relation to the range of stories and perspectives shown in the film:

> Most importantly, the film features a very diverse range of views and experiences, demonstrating the absurdity – as one participant points out – of Caribbean immigrants from different countries and very different backgrounds being seen, and coming to see themselves, as a single group.

In order to provide a more detailed analysis of *The Colony* and how memory and migration are used in its critique of imperial / post-imperial landscapes, the following discussion is divided into key themes that frame the film's narration: family and community, and work and leisure.

REMEMBERING AND REPRESENTING FAMILY AND COMMUNITY

For several participants in *The Colony*, the act of remembering ties to material landscapes and past experiences with family overseas and in the UK is an important part of testifying to their challenges and successes as individuals as well as charting new cultural geographies. Discussing a project that explores migration, memory and transnational links to family among Asian women in London, Divia TOLIA-KELLY (2001, 117) states:

> ...I think that's part of the experience of migration, that you can't take much when you leave. All you can keep is your memories of places and various small objects that trigger those memories. If you're a member of a diasporic group, there's a way in which you make connections with other people with the same experience.

Remembering events, connections to specific kinds of music, and favourite places and images can all play an important role in maintaining and recreating ties to transnational communities. Memory is inherently spatial. It is embedded in specific places and contexts and enables us to affect cultural geographies that provide nodal points, or touchstones, to identity and space. Furthermore, I suggest that memory is a dialectical construction of the present: it resituates the past thus enabling us to make present identities fit into particular narratives and vice versa. Memory is also inherently contradictory: it includes specific stories while excluding others, embraces both pleasure and pain, and is a means of claiming cultural and political citizenship – but at the same time citizenship incorporates a system of borders and limitations. When thinking back to being a child and the lessons he was taught growing up in the Caribbean, one participant in *The Colony* states: "England was a paradise...you could live without misery...[now] I'm finding out for how I thought it was." Another reflects on the UK being depicted as the "Mother Country" and singing "Land of Hope and Glory," yet learning on arrival that many politicians were attempting to restrict migrant access to the UK.

As testimonies to memories of travel, media images of migration such as *The Colony*, are a form of visual and audio citizenship that help foster a sense of collective identity through the recognition of specific experiences; their legibility and resonance affirms and / or contests social and political values. Media images also can alienate audiences through a limited range of corporate, gendered and racialised images. Despite nativist and imperialist trends noted earlier, however, *The Colony* provides a useful means of the former – of giving voice to migrants memories – during a process of travel (migration) that often denied social and legal rights. This process of giving voice through the film involves exploring and understanding images of Caribbean families and the production of new family relations and relationships in the migrants' native and destination country.

In relation to film representations of place and community, MORLEY (1999, 153) states that the concept of home (or family) "simply cannot be understood except in relation to its outside(s)." Although this theme is addressed more indirectly than in other contemporary media, which tended to focus on the Black family as a dysfunctional and often pathologised entity (FRYER 1984), DONNELLAN subtly illustrates the significant role of external tensions, supportive extended families, and the ways in which new families and communities are created. As CHAMBERLAIN (2001, 45) notes, "[m]oving the emphasis on family structure as a fixed entity with immutable spatial and temporal boundaries to one which looks at the family as a fluid and permeable state, transversing geography and generations enables a more effective exploration of how the family functions". On the one hand, for example, a responsibility towards families in the Caribbean is seen as a crucial motivating force for migrants and part of a transnational family dynamic. This responsibility can be seen when one interviewee states that, before leaving Jamaica, he was told, "When you go to England, try your level best to remember your father." On the other, racist assumptions about what a Black family is, or what a migrant worker looks and sounds like, means that being "at home" often involves complicated negotiations of power and space.

The family can be seen as reflecting and encompassing a certain form of citizenship: a shared identity that recognizes individuals as part of a larger whole. At the same time, this requires acceptance (or the rejection) of certain attitudes and practices. Gender is an important part of this familial form of citizenship and specific depictions of gendered identities can be noted in the film. For example, as an interviewee in one scene speaks, his partner sits silently on a bed holding a child on her knee; in the group debates about West Indian identity the discussion is among male adults; and, in other scenes, women tend to be interviewed individually outside places of paid employment. One female interviewee from Trinidad states that in her home island parents were very strict with their daughters. They worked in nursing or teaching or got sent to sewing school; later, women were usually housewives. While these images and gendered spaces may have been depicted to illustrate an upstanding morality for young Black Caribbean women and their similarities with White British women, they also serve to illustrate the ways in which male voices have been privileged in public spaces and associated with degrees of flexibility and mobility different than that of women's.

As the film begins, the opening inter-title states, "Birmingham Colony – 1964," and shows an image of the city centre and an array of Victorian buildings – whitewashed and impressive in their architectural solidity. As the camera pans across the buildings, a female upper-middle class English-accented voice talks about the difficulties of children who are waiting to be adopted and states, "[a] section of children are not considered eligible for adoption... they are coloured and half-caste... I feel very deeply about this because I'm coloured myself." As the narrator says the latter words, the image shifts from one of grand architecture to one of a well-dressed middle-aged Black woman sitting in a room as she talks about her experiences of being Black in the UK. The contrast in voice and image is striking: a relatively unshakeable architectural landscape with an established imperial history, a narration about the fragile existence of a marginalized (and voiceless) group, and the image of a woman who visually could be viewed as vulnerable, but through her calm and steady words depicts a clarity and concern that depicts strength and conviction – and in doing so, subtly and symbolically challenges the assumptions that are embedded in many exclusionary Victorian moralities (signified by the initially solid image of the buildings). The placement of mixed race and Black children was a lengthy, complicated, and often-ignored process. This constraint worked against the re-creation of stable family environments. Thus, while a discourse of happy nuclear families and moral education was promoted throughout the Commonwealth, public notions of desirable children and family structures were being used to circumscribe the private lives and spaces of British Black and Afro-Caribbean youth (CHAMBERLAIN 2001).

DONNELLAN uses what appears to be unrelated, or contradictory, visual and oral representations throughout the film in ways that encourages the viewer to re-read the cultural landscapes revealed and to make more insightful connections as the stories unfold. Given when the film was made and the very limited positive representation of middle or upper class Black British residents in film and television, the delayed viewing of the narrator as the film begins is used to illustrate viewer assumptions about both who is speaking and what the accent connotes – a White upper class philanthropist. In so doing, DONNELLAN begins the documentary with a pedagogical lesson about class and prejudice in the UK as well as the audience's own knowledge, images of race, and willingness to unreflectively consume these ideas.

In his study of exilic filmmaking, Hamid NAFICY (2001) refers to critical and counter-Hollywood productions as accented cinema. Although not an exile himself, DONNELLAN's opening scene, above, can be read as a form of exilic production. DONNELLAN not only illustrates that his film can be read as accented in terms of the aural and visible presence of its central subjects, but also points out that all speech and images are accented. Even though some forms of speaking may be categorized as neutral or unaccented – they are accents so ubiquitous and dominant that they go unnoticed – these forms of speaking also have an inflection and are spatially and culturally produced. This recognition is important and runs parallel to discussions about the need to recognize White identities as being racial constructs; not only racial identities that are depicted in dominant discourses as different or, for example, Black. In recognizing this aspect of identity lies the possibility for a more comprehensive understanding of all forms of speech and language, and of how they are interpreted and valued; not as natural characteristics, but as part of ongoing social productions embedded in discourses of power.

I suggest that, in film, memory also functions as an accent: it leads to an emphasis on certain details, a specific version of a story, a particular kind of intonation when story-telling; and, it is necessarily selective. Furthermore, as DONNELLAN illustrates, memory helps construct, lay claim to, and articulate certain experiences that are both unique and collective, and that are spatially grounded – the accent *locates*. *The Colony* incorporates a range of pleasant, sad, and poignant memories from a range of participants with a diversity of Caribbean and British accents. These participants articulate the changing and varied relations and families of which they are a part. One couple, for example, sits on a tidy but small bed with their young child and explain that, before they came to England, they were told it would be, "Paradise... but every-one has to struggle in life." The diverse representations draw attention to ways in which Caribbean communities have been generalized as a singular identity. In addition, conversations, such as the one below, illustrate that, through a process of unifying against racism and exclusion, migrants become part of an extended family; even if these families grapple with the internalization of colonial markers:

> *Stan Crooke [*in close up – *a signalman from St. Kitts discussing West Indian identities in the UK with other male documentary participants]*: On first coming here, we were all sort of a, we had our insularities. What I notice nowadays, the West Indian is no longer considering himself a Jamaican, a Trinidadian, Barbadian, Kittician, Antiguan. We are all, we are subtly, but inexorably being, considering ourselves as, we're all coloured people.

Images from the opening segment of *The Colony* and the above discussions, depicting how West Indians were struggling to feel at home in the UK, point to the psychical and structural impacts of colonialism and the decolonization process. Stuart HALL (1999, 37–38) refers to these impacts when reflecting on his conflicts with his family and his reasons for leaving Jamaica:

> When I was seventeen, my sister had a nervous breakdown. She began a relationship with a young student doctor from Barbados. He was middle-class, but black, and my parents wouldn't allow it. There was a tremendous family row and she, in effect, retreated from the situation into a breakdown. I was suddenly aware of the contradiction of a colonial culture, of how one lives out the colour-class-colonial dependency experience and how it could destroy you, subjectively... It broke down forever, for me, the distinction between the public and private self. I learned about culture first, as something which is deeply subjective and personal, and at the same moment, as a structure you live...But it crystallized my feelings about the space I was called into by my family. I was not going to stay there.

National adoption policies, imperial educational curricula, institutionalized racism, and conflicting family aspirations, all combined with individual prejudices, are only a few examples of ways that colonial and post-imperial relations are represented. DONNELLAN's film shows that the emotional and structural limitations of British culture necessitated ongoing self-reflection that was rarely shown on mainstream media coverage of immigration. For example, during one discussion with a group of men from different Caribbean islands, the issue of future race relations emerges combined with a debate about integration. Despite disagreement, there is a consensus that youths could experience better race relations in the future because it is not they who are innately prejudiced. Rather, prejudice is something learned from adults who can inject this "poison into children... it's not the children, it's the parents."

Mixed race and Black West Indian migrants often also found themselves having to negotiate between imperial values and post-colonial aspirations, and, to see their identities as symbolic of inbetween spaces and transgressions that challenged the binary thinking of black / white, us / them, local / foreign – particularly when they had families of diverse backgrounds. DONNELLAN illustrates ways in which spatial imaginaries and identities are key components for resolving these tensions when he highlights several participants stating that it is the identification of migrants as "strangers" – or, as out of place – that is problematic. In footage of Black and White residents walking, shopping, or talking in the commercial streets of Birmingham, the film includes several female and male interviewees stating that getting to know neighbours who live on the same street is crucial to combating hostility and ignorance. This recognition points out linkages between large-scale policies, attitudes, and local landscapes.

DIALOGUES WITH WORK AND LEISURE

Many images of Caribbean migrants in *The Colony* focus on the arena of work. Throughout the film, there are depictions of key participants engaged in different areas of work (or dressed formally outside of workplaces discussing their experiences). Participants are shown changing signals at a railway line, talking with nurses and pushing a patient in a wheelchair in a hospital, teaching young Black and White children in a classroom, and collecting fares on a public bus. Throughout the film, DONNELLAN returns to a group of Black West Indian men discussing a variety of reasons to work in the UK or travel to the country. Reasons include: national service, hope for self improvement, new opportunities, and, simple curiosity – or what was known as English Fever – a desire to experience the Mother Country (in its imperial centre) firsthand. These diverse images of migrants working, and reflecting on work, challenge dominant images of foreign labourers as dependent on social services (a common nativist claim) and show instead skilled, articulate and productive members of a society who are actively involved in a range of urban spaces. In a sense, these are images of British Commonwealth subjects who are continuing to work for the Empire – an empire now seeking to reduce this allegiance. The contradictions within these post-imperial relationships also can be seen when a West Indian curator walks through a museum of mechanical inventions. Reflecting on the nature of creativity and industry, he states that, in order to invent, peoples' minds had to be open, then asks, "but, are they open now?"

One particularly poignant image that is repeated in the film – and which most explicitly challenges the stereotype of the illiterate migrant manual worker – is that of a smelter who is surrounded by heavy machinery in a dimly lit setting, while, in his voiceover, he contemplates the betrayals and disappointments of the colonial education system:

> Sometimes we think we shouldn't blame the table. Because it's we that have come to their country and trouble them. On the other hand, we think well, if they in the first place, had not come to our country, and spread their false propaganda we would never have come to theirs. But them say, if we had not come we would none be the wiser, we would still have the good image of England, thinking that they are what they are not. And, the English would be as ignorant as us.

It appears that DONNELLAN is informing his audience that many of this host nation's population still are unaware of Caribbean culture and migrant experiences. In this sense, the film is a direct attempt to challenge this ignorance.

In the film, images of people working look almost painterly – creating a somewhat stoic and melancholy image – and usually are accompanied by voiceovers of the migrants being interviewed. Simultaneously, these images highlight, with a few exceptions (such as people talking while walking down the main street), the limited interactions between White and Black populations. These limited interactions surface more directly as Stan, the signalman, describes the ways that Blacks and Whites may work together but rarely converse or socialize outside of the work environment. Stan notes that, while he may sit next to co-workers on the train, as soon as they reach the station the contact is over: "This matter of integration is very difficult...we don't get together outside of work... If there was a club I would attend, but I wonder – would they attend? We don't seem to have many things in common."

The use of voiceover and close-ups not only is effective in depicting the film's subjects and migrant stories as being reflective and deeply personal, but also in emphasizing a sense of distance and dislocation between people and the surrounding environment – of being out of place (CRESSWELL 1996). Depicting faces in detail during everyday interactions in the street gives the audience a sense of viewing private and intimate moments – even when in public contexts. The idea of migrant labourers and families suddenly becomes humanized and more visible. The images are diverse: a White woman, frowning, stands alone looking around her while she waits with prams outside a shop; a Black and White man walk together laughing and talking; as the former waves to another passing on a bike, a group of Black and White people, silently bearing the cold weather, stand on the sidewalk waiting for a bus. This diversity gives the viewer a sense of many different and often unspoken lives existing in close physical proximity, but, at times in socially parallel or conflicting worlds.

Series of still shots with ongoing background street noise are also used to highlight the disjuncture – of both time and space – and hostility that many migrants experience. In one series there are: images of foggy urban streets combined with a voiceover; images (from the perspective of the passenger) in rapid succession of arriving in a train station while whistles blow in the background; a man shouting "taxi, taxi;" a view of walking up stairs and then one of emerging from the station; and, a brick wall along a sidewalk on which "Blacks go Home" is painted. DONNELLAN uses stills to highlight key points or moments of conflict, and to emphasize the flexibility needed to adapt to the rapidity of street life in Birmingham. In contrast, work locations are almost idealized as spaces of solitary contemplation away from the tensions and disorder of public space.

While work environments are consistently visible throughout *The Colony*, connections between work and leisure, and the creation of social spaces that foster greater interaction between native and migrant populations, is less clear. This lack may be DONNELLAN's response to stereotypes of migrants as simply "hanging out" or "having fun" at the taxpayers' expense. Even more significantly, however, it suggests limited opportunities for entertainment and relaxation, given participants' work and family commitments, as well as White wariness of what were perceived as Black social events (GILROY 1994). A fear of socializing and working with migrants is framed as pointing to a lack of symbiosis and the need for a more organic, holistic culture. A male Jamaican migrant refers to this lack of integration in a monologue. Dressed in a suit and carrying a sheaf of notes under his arm, he comes into a room, sits on the bed, looks into the camera, and says:

> You see, the Englishman is a very funny creature. He likes his change of scenery, he likes the variety in his life. He like – as a matter of fact, in England, you have a country of variety. The changes of the season and it is part of the – it has entered into the peoples themselves. Yet the Englishman, or the White man for that matter, doesn't want the variety of the human specie. He likes to see white only. He can't admit that the same variety that makes the world possible and beautiful in all other aspects [image switches to a view of a Black person with White people waiting for a bus] is the same thing that applies to the human race. There must be variety. It can't just be all White or all Black.

The terms used in this monologue are direct and pose a challenge to viewers to think about the inconsistencies of how White British residents interact with Blacks and to reflect on what diversity means – and when it is considered beneficial. This challenge also points to ways that Blackness has not been seen as part of Britishness – despite colonial claims to imperial territories, and, regardless of whether a person has migrated to, or been born in, the UK. The speaker sits in a private room. His location suggests that he is willing to expose these private thoughts and aspects of his life, but, in doing so, is in a position of vulnerability. Several scenes include participants speaking directly to the camera, an act significant for claiming a space and stating, 'I socially and legally belong here' – or, 'I am a citizen.' At the same time, images of the street illustrate the reality of an urban setting that is becoming increasingly diverse and that need not always involve confrontation.

Other links between work and leisure are made indirectly, for example, between historical events and present landscapes in Birmingham. The film is bookended with images of empire that continue to mark the built environment and that reflect hidden landscapes of industrial work: Victorian statues are used at the outset of the documentary, and, the grounds and interiors of Aston House – a mansion estate now open to the public – are used in the conclusion. As the camera pans across the extensive gardens of Aston House, we see a racially diverse group of school children learning about the imperial history of the building – but specifically about the house's English pedigree, fixtures, décor details, and dates of paintings. A Black Caribbean couple joins the group as it winds its way through the house; and, the man's voice becomes the narrative voiceover as the tour guide fades into the background. Although the guide fails to mention the labour and suffering upon which many imperialists built their wealth, the narrator does not:

> *[Image:* close up: *A young Black child looking at a painting in the staircase of Aston House]*
>
> *Voiceover:* One doesn't put slavery on their mind, but if they read history it's something that they've got to look back on to. What I am proud about my forefather is: [image changes to a still drawing of a slave ship] although they have passed through such difficult time, they haven't lost the value, the value of human living. When they could not express it in words, they put it in song.
>
> *[Narration changes to the Stewart Family group singing "Going along the Road," then concluding titles.]*

DONNELLAN uses his key participants to illustrate the sub-text of slavery and forced work implicit in the landscape of the museum. He highlights the uneasiness of the space by depicting it as a place now used for recreational visits and educational purposes; but, which exists precisely because it excluded and marginalized Black colonized populations as well as working-class, White social groups – descendants of whom now walk through its halls. Despite the immense symbolic materiality of this exclusion, the voiceover and accompanying singing suggests that the powers of creativity, music (and love – as suggested earlier by an interviewee), can be far more pervasive and empowering. As GILROY (1993) notes in his study of transatlantic movements, people produce and disseminate non-material artifacts that transform places and identities. Music – which punctuates the film with traditional Trinidadian songs – forms a bridge across cultures, and suggests that emotional generosity and celebration can be more powerful, and useful, than force and cement.

CONCLUSION

> *Loneliness is an inevitable outcome of transnationality, and it finds its way into the desolate structures of feeling and lonely diegetic characters*
>
> (NAFICY 2001, 55).

This chapter has been part of an ongoing journey towards interrogating varied ways that migrant stories are documented, framed, and embedded in changing social / political contexts that transcend national boundaries. In an era when individual mobility frequently is hailed as a positive endeavour resulting in access to a range of social and economic opportunities, it is important to examine contrasting and conflicting ways that mobility has been experienced. Efforts to represent transnationality may illustrate the arbitrariness of national borders and imperial territories, and, the possibility for their transgression; they also, however, point to the places and identities that become compromised or left behind through pressures to belong, or, to create new life stories and cultural geographies.

The ability to visually represent places and cultures is an important component of communicating and legitimating claims to space and identity. Through the documentary film, *The Colony*, Phillip DONNELLAN illustrates that claims to citizenship, place and identity inherently are contested and more complicated than they first appear. His documentary acts as a testament to a diversity of experiences for Anglophone Caribbean migrants – while depicting these émigrés as multidimensional characters and pointing to the failure of contemporary British popular culture to engage with these social groups in a constructive, meaningful way. DONNELLAN illustrates the transformation of family and community support systems that creates new spaces of hope and reassurance. At the same time, his images of migrants working and discussing the segregated nature of leisure activities, point to ways that racism and social exclusion have shaped the formal and informal spaces of migrant, urban life. In *The Colony*, stories are told on multiple levels through a combination of striking visual and oral representations highlighting ways that migrant experiences cut across a range of class, employment, residential, and material landscapes. Although just one example of film being used to read and speak "against the grain," the documentary is a significant contribution and provides a model for critical and politically progressive filmmaking – contexts in which migrants are frequently marginalized, or, rarely part of an ongoing dialogue.

REFERENCES

BENJAMIN, W. (1968): The Work of Art in the Age of Mechanical Reproduction. ARENDT, H. (Ed.): *Illuminations*, 223. New York.
CARTER, B., C. HARRIS and S. JOSHI (1993): The 1951–55 Conservative Government and The Racialisation of Black Immigration. JAMES, W. and C. HARRIS (Eds.): I*nside Babylon: The Caribbean Diaspora in Britain*. London, 55–71.
CHAMBERLAIN, M. (2001): Migration , the Caribbean and the Family. GOULBOURNE, H. and M. CHAMBERLAIN (Eds.): *Caribbean Families in Britain and the Trans-Atlantic World*. London, 32–47.
CHAMBERLAIN, M. (Ed.) (1998): *Caribbean Migration: Globalised Identities*. New York.
CRESSWELL, T. (1996): *In Place / Out of Place: Geography, Ideology, and Transgression*. Minneapolis.
DALBY, S. (1996): Crossing Disciplinary Boundaries: Political Geography and International Relations after the Cold War. KAUFFMAN, R. and G. YOUNG (Eds.): *Globalization: Theory and Practice*. New York, 29–42.
DUGUID, M. (2003): The Colony (1964). *Screenonline*. London. http:// www.screenonline.org.uk
FRYER, P. (1984): *Staying Power: The History of Black People in Britain*. London.
GILROY, P. (1993): The Black Atlantic: Modernity and Double Consciousness. London.
GILROY, P. (1994): Urban Social Movements, "Race" and Community. WILLIAMS, P. and L. CHRISMAN (Eds.): *Colonial Discourse and Post-Colonial Theory: A Reader*. New York, 404–420.
HALL, S. (1997): The Work of Representation. HALL, S. (Ed.): *Representation: Cultural Representations and Signifying Practices*. Milton Keynes, 1–74.

HALL, S. (1999): The Formation of a Diasporic Intellectual I. WAMBU, O. (Ed.): *Empire Windrush: Fifty Years of Writing about Black Britain*. London, 86–90.
HANNA, S. P. (2000): Representation and the Reproduction of Appalachian Space: A History of Contested Signs and Meanings. *Historical Geography* 28, 171–199.
HARRIS, C. (1993): Post-War Migration and the Industrial Reserve Army. JAMES, W. and C. HARRIS (Eds.): *Inside Babylon: The Caribbean Diaspora in Britain*. London, 9–54.
JACKSON, P. and J. PENROSE (1993): Placing "Race" and Nation. JACKSON, P. and J. PENROSE (Eds.): *Constructions of Race, Place and Nation*. Minneapolis, 1–26.
JAMES, W. (1992): Migration, Racism and Identity Formation: The Caribbean Experience in Britain. *New Left Review* 193, 15–55.
JONES, J. P. and W. NATTER (1999): Space "And" Representation. BUTTIMER, A., S. BRUNN and U. WARDENGA (Eds.): *Text and Image: Social Construction of Regional Knowledges*. Leipzig, 239–247.
JONES, J. P. and W. NATTER (1993): Pets or Meat? Class, Ideology, and Space in Roger & Me. *Antipode* 25 (2), 140–158.
JONES, J. P., H. NAST and S. M. ROBERTS (1997): Thresholds in Feminist Geography: Diffference, Methodology, Representation. JONES, J. P., H. NAST and S. M. ROBERTS (Eds.): *Thresholds in Feminist Geography*. New York, xxi–xxxix.
KIRSHENBLATT-GIMBLETT, B. (1998): *Destination Culture: Tourism, Museums, and Heritage*. Berkeley.
MAINS, S. (2003): 'The Future of Multi-Ethnic Britain': Media, Diversity, and Regional Identity. RALPH, S., H. MANCHESTER and C. LEES (Eds.): *Diversity or Anarchy*. Luton, 225–232.
MAINS, S. (2002): Mobility and Exclusion: Towards an Understanding of Migration in the Context of Jamaica. *UN WIDER conference report on Poverty, International Migration and Asylum*. Helsinki.
MCCLINTOCK, A. (1995): *Imperial Leather: Race, Gender and Sexuality in the Colonial Contest*. New York.
MCKERNAN, L. (2003): Topical Budget: British Identity and Empire. *Screenonline*. London. http://www.screenonline.org.uk
MORLEY, D. (1999): The Mediated Home. NAFICY, H. (Ed.): *Home, Exile, Homeland*. New York, 151–168.
MOUFFE, C. (1993): *The Return of the Political*. London.
NAFICY, H. (2001): *An Accented Cinema: Exilic and Diasporic Filmmaking*. Princeton.
PINES, J. (Ed.) (1992): *Black and White in Colour: Black People in British Television Since 1936*. London.
ROSE, G. (2001): *Visual Methodologies*. London.
SHAW, M. (1996): *Civil Society and Media in Global Crises*. London.
SIBLEY, D. (1997): *Geographies of Exclusion*. New York.
STEINER, C. B. (1999): Authenticity, Repetition, and the Aesthetics of Seriality: The Work of Tourist Art in the Age of Mechanical Reproduction. PHILLIPS, R. B. and C. B. STEINER (Eds.): *Unpacking Culture: Art and Commodity in Colonial and Postcolonial Worlds*. Berkeley, 87–103.
THOMAS-HOPE, E. (1999): Return Migration to Jamaica and its Development Potential. *International Migration* 37 (1), 181–207.
TOLIA-KELLY, D. (2001): Intimate Distance: Fantasy Islands and English Lakes. *Ecumene* 8 (1), 112–119.
WAMBU, O. (1999): Introduction. WAMBU, O. (Ed.): *Empire Windrush: Fifty Years of Writing about Black Britain*. London, 19–29.
WALTER, B. (1997): Gender, "Race," and Diaspora: Racialized Identities of Emigrant Irish Women. JONES, J. P., H. NAST and S. M. ROBERTS (Eds.): *Thresholds in Feminist Geography*. New York, 339–360.

FILMOGRAPHY

DONNELLAN, P. (1964): The Colony. BBC Films: London.
DONNELLAN, P. (1964): The Irishmen: And Empression of Exile. BBC Films: London.

Mita Banerjee / Peter W. Marx

ALLY LIVES JUST NEXT DOOR...
GERMAN-U.S. RELATIONS IN POPULAR CULTURE

INTRODUCTION

Where does Ally McBeal live? The answer to this question is really quite simple. As we all know (or are supposed to know) Ally, the famous U.S. lawyer, lives in Boston. Leaving the sure ground of fiction; however, the question becomes more difficult. What (and where) is the place of fictitious characters? Obviously, fictional characters are living in our collective imagination – at least those who are successful enough. How do these characters affect our imaginative geography though? Furthermore, what does the spatial order of popular culture tell us about the cultural order of our societies?

This paper traces the presence of "ethnic" characters in German popular culture by investigating the spaces in which these characters can be found. Most importantly, we suggest that this spatial investigation of difference turns the established paradigm of ethnic or minority studies on its head. Rather than focusing primarily on the context of the production of these images, the question of whether or not these films were conceived by an ethnic or a "mainstream" director, we explore the circulation of 'Otherness' that manifests itself in the visual instances of the 'Other's' presence in the mainstream. For that purpose we analyze the successful German TV series *Edel & Starck* as well as the TV movie *Alles getürkt* (2002), a 'mainstream' film made by a German-Turkish director, Yasemin SAMDERELI.

Our reading of ethnicity as being spatially performed levels the difference between mainstream representations of ethnicity, such as *Edel & Starck,* and films by ethnic directors themselves. Reading popular culture as a terrain of cultural negotiation implies that there is, in fact, a continuum between these various texts, regardless of their authors / directors. Importantly, a sense of the *presence* of ethnic communities thus emerges in-between mainstream and alternative representations of ethnicity. Ethnicity, in the German cultural imaginary, is constituted solely by neither discourse, but, rather, by both. To see ethnicity as a fusion of the two discourses, is to refuse to see them in opposition to each other, even though they are. A trans-national cultural studies approach, however, may look for ways in which mainstream discourses and alternative representations can be fractured to enable a clearer expression of ethnicity.

In order to more closely consider the question of 'cultural presence' in the mainstream, we first must look at the means of spatial representation in mainstream movies and television. In the TV show, *Ally McBeal*, the primary means of spatial orientation used is inserting small sequences showing well known and picturesque views of the buildings and cityscapes the story's heroes live in. These sequences, that combine pictures with musical themes, provide the essential deictic information for the viewer, indicating, space, time, and season. While these inserts might be considered irrelevant or simply marginal, during the story they become metaphors for the world our heroes are living in. After a while, we recognize the court where Ally McBeal and her allies fight their professional battles, the office building with those characteristic windows we know from the inside shots, or the route to Ally's home – although we seldom see our protagonists on these routes or entering these buildings.

At a dramaturgical level, these sequences serve a number of functions. Due to the cost of TV productions, most series are filmed in studios, thus guaranteeing availability of the best lighting and weather conditions. The short sequences, once filmed, are repeated again and again, con-necting these fictional people and their setting to our daily-lived environment. We recognize Boston and its skyline and realize that these filmic characters live there. At the same time, the money for expensive location shots is saved. On a more differentiated level, these sequences serve as a transition from one level of the story to another, or, as an explanation for a time change. Their main purpose, however, seems to be to increase the illusion of place and location for the audience.

When considering the semiotic level and looking more closely at these sequences, we realize that the sequences obey certain patterns of representation: one of the main tools for spatial orientation – although this may sound contradictory – is the fragmentation of buildings, places and cities. The sequences are in a precarious balance between their recognisability and more general symbolic character of spaces as such. Thus, we might read Ally's Boston as the prefiguration of the U.S. East Coast (non New York City) metropolis. At this point, we might make a twofold observation. On one hand, we could trace, up to a certain extent, a complex imaginative geography of the U.S.: Boston, the lawyer city; Chicago, capital of TV medicine; and New York – a cosmos of its own, inhabited by freaks such as *Seinfeld*, *Friends*, and *The Buchmans*. On the other hand, these series, through their characters and location sequences, perpetuate the myth of metropolitan life.

We therefore can consider these sequences as being on the borderline between fiction and reality, fulfilling a paradoxical task. While functioning as indices of reality for the fictional construction, at the same time they increasingly become elements of a specific cultural code that marks the genre, and, to a certain degree, the specific television series. By showing Boston, we not only recognize Ally's Boston, but also Ally. The manifold tourist enterprises offering tours through "Seinfeld's New York," prove that this border is permeable from both sides.

A discussion of popular culture in the twentieth century implies talking about the U.S. dominance of popular culture – cultural imperialism. Here, we do not want to consider the economic or political impacts of this imperialism, but rather to concentrate on its impact on dramaturgical and fictional constructions. In this light, German TV culture can be understood as an echo of U.S. originals. In particular, since the emergence of commercial television twenty years ago, German television has been deeply influenced by U.S. models. This influence includes not only importing TV series and films, but also adapting successful models.

These interrelations were discussed quite critically in the 1990s. The situation, however, has changed slightly. The series *Ally McBeal*, in particular, caused a change in perspective. After the first season's broadcasts, an increasing number of people confessed to watching the series. The audience included German parliament members from all political parties. *Ally McBeal* gained attention and importance due to two main reasons: its unusual dramaturgy and visual code that constantly broke the conventions of TV realism, and by making questions of female identity topical.

This successful model found its echo in German television, in the series *Edel & Starck*, which, since 2002, has been shown on channel SAT.1, German cable TV. Apart from several minor changes, the series' main features clearly remind one of *Ally McBeal*. Situated in the milieu of metropolitan lawyers, the predominant model of realism is questioned if not destroyed. What is of particular interest, however, is that even the visual code of the small deictic sequences is markedly similar those in *Alley McBeal*. Berlin is represented in similar fashion to Ally's Boston – passing metro trains on bridges, fragmented buildings (emphasizing some decorative details), and even the pan shots across water features. This latter shot is especially remarkable since, unlike Boston, Berlin is not a major port city.

Here the deictic devices no longer refer to a realistic environment but open a new level of reception for the audience: it is obvious that they do not simply try to evoke Berlin, or the atmosphere of German metropolitan life, but rather openly allude to Ally's Boston. This allusion requires some kind of popular cultural literacy; and, it Americanizes Berlin or visually constructs a global metropolitan sphere. Reminding us of *Ally McBeal* is surely not only meant to play with our expectations as media consumers, but also to contain a message about the interrelation of the U.S. and Germany on the level of popular culture.

In discussing mass media, we should return to the question of cultural predominance and ask for its outlines. Arjun APPADURAI (1996) suggests that the global distribution of mass media products does not simply entail a univocal response. He argues that the model of stimulus and response is highly inappropriate. He also suggests that consuming Western mass media might create a diasporic realm for smaller communities. In this light, media consumption can be considered as a form of cultural communication:

> There is growing evidence that the consumption of the mass media throughout the world often provokes resistance, irony, selectivity, and, in general, agency. ... It is the imagination, in its collective forms, that creates ideas of neighbourhood and nationhood, of moral economies and unjust rule, of higher wages and foreign labor prospects (APPADURAI 1996, 7).

While APPADURAI's argument focuses on diasporic spheres and migrant cultures, we seek to broaden this perspective. To what extent do these imaginative realms affect the outlines, and even concept, of mainstream and cultural centre? What happens if these borders are trespassed from one side to another and former marginal groups or characters enter the centre stage of mainstream cultural imagination? In this case, importing U.S. popular culture is not a mere economic phenomenon but should rather be considered with respect to its cultural echoes and effects. Such is the goal of this paper.

Our point of departure is the question of representing ethnic characters in these series. While in the U.S. multiculturalism in series is common and – as an experience of daily life – also taken for granted, ethnic characters are still highly remarkable on German television. Germany's cultural identity is still based on the nineteenth century concept of an ethnically homogeneous nationhood; thus ethnic communities are still regarded as dubious and marginal.

Our concern is twofold. First, by focusing on the spatial coding of ethnic figures in German popular culture and the circulation of 'Otherness' in mainstream media, we are interested in the concept of mainstreaming minorities. Second, taking our cue from APPADURAI, we are, therefore, also concerned with the intersection between media and mass migration. As APPADURAI (1996, 6) proposes –

> electronic mediation and mass migration mark the world of the present not as technically new forces but as ones that seem to impel (and sometimes compel) the work of the imagination. Together, they create specific irregularities because both viewers and images are in simultaneous circulation. Neither images nor viewers fit into circuits or audiences that are easily bound within local, national, or regional spaces.

What is at stake in such a reading is, in fact, a form of inclusion through circulation. By focusing not on the absoluteness of space (the Oriental bazaar vs. the authentic space of the Turkish home) but on the ways in which these spaces are fractured from within, we trace a gradual inclusion of Turkishness into the German mainstream. This paper focuses solely on Turkishness because, in the filmic narratives to be discussed, ethnicity is equated with Turkishness. The Turkish-German community is the largest ethnic community in Germany; this demographic presence may account for the fact that Turkishness has become synonymous with ethnic Germany in the realm of popular culture. Where other ethnicities (such as Asian characters) surface in filmic narratives, they still are confined to the culturally inassimilable. In this paper, we argue that this inassimilability is beginning to give way in the case of a Turkish presence in German popular culture, a slippage that is marked by visual (and, we will argue, *spatial*) irony and a certain self-reflexivity of the filmic narratives themselves.

Moreover, we argue that this mainstreaming of minorities in German popular culture is inseparable from a transnational dimension. The allusion, especially in *Edel & Starck*, to U.S. popular culture seems to enable a spatial estrangement from Germanness. As Germanness is estranged from itself through U.S. popular culture, a mainstreaming of Turkishness, ironically, becomes possible. We use an approach that Jigna DESAI (2003) calls a "transnational cultural studies": an analysis of the ways in which the role of ethnicity is articulated through a cultural imaginary that is specifically German, but at the same time takes into consideration the intersection of this imaginary with global discourses of racialization and democratic inclusion. As DESAI (2003, ix) points out, "[t]he 'beyond' in this context signals an investment in mobilizing an analysis of cinema to ask questions regarding significant cultural, political, social, and economic processes of globalization." The increasing appearance of ethnic characters in German TV series requires attention. These characters can be seen as exploring the outlines of an imaginative transnational sphere whose concrete conditions have to be adjusted to the single criteria of consumption. They embody social change in Germany and explore the possibilities and chances of multiculturalism by performing the limits of acculturation, assimilation, and rejection.

WHERE DO THE TURKS LIVE?

We should modify our initial question to "Where do the Turks live (in German TV)"? To explore the traces of this special sphere, we start with an incidence from *Alles getürkt*, which can be translated as "Everything is fake," a film made in 2002 by Turkish German director Yasemin SAMDERELI. The story is an ironic mixture of detective story and romantic comedy. The protagonist, Olaf Stern, is an undercover German policeman masked as a Turk. He falls in love with a young Turkish woman who, disappointed by German men, is waiting for her Turkish Mr. Right. Apart from its main plot, the film negotiates cultural borders and makes use of collective stereotypes and imagination.

At the beginning, the film introduces the interactions of Olaf and his Turkish friend by showing Olaf helping the latter with an advertising campaign for his new café:

Olaf: What a stupid day. First work, and now this. And actually, why do you get to be the @-man? I'd look much better in that costume. At least there's some dignity in it. But, no, I had to be the stinking Döner sandwich.
Friend: Can you tell me what walking around like this has to do with dignity?
Olaf: The @ symbolizes communication in the 21st century. Internet, World Wide Web. The new media. It's the symbol of a new era. And what does a Döner sandwich symbolize? Garlic breath, mad cow disease, junk food and grease stains.

This short sequence offers a kind of cultural confrontation where the two main characters symbolically don costumes, the @-sign and the Döner sandwich, the latter becoming the epitome of Turkish everyday life and culture. Yet, the mask is inverted: the German complains about having been made to dress up as the Döner, that he thinks stands for unhealthy fast food while the @-sign stands for connectedness and open-mindedness. In doing so, he reveals himself as narrow-minded by not realizing his masquerade itself is a symptom of cultural border crossing.

The setting of the sequence is critical – the inner city. We discover the protagonists amidst strolling pedestrians. Visually, they can be read as carnevalistic flâneurs. Obviously they are city dwellers whose costumes are extraordinary at the first glance. Yet, on a deeper level, they might be considered the expression of an underlying conflict that is not only situated in the inner city but is also characteristic of its cultural sphere: multicultural encounters are shown as problematic, although funny in a certain way.

The crucial point of *Alles getürkt* is the masking of Olaf as Cem Yilmaz: Olaf considers the undercover mission not only as a professional challenge and career opportunity but also rather enjoys the adventure of crossing ethnic and cultural borders. The key film sequence is Olaf's infiltration of the Turkish greengrocers' environment. Here, the film superimposes the confrontation of police and criminals as an intercultural encounter.

This sequence confronts us with the 'real' Turkish world within German society. In contrast to the argument about Döner and @-man, situated in the middle of urban life, this 'real' sphere is hidden, suspicious, and dangerous. Its Oriental character is stressed by the use of music and noisy sound effects that clearly evoke the impression of a bazaar. The entrance of 'our' hero is marked by a dark tunnel that functions as a liminal space of this *rite de passage*. The protagonist is changing his cultural identity, although he has to remind himself of this new identity by repeating again and again: "My name is Cem and I am a Turk."

This Oriental world is the underworld of the city life – representing the dark side and subconsciousness of multiculturalism. This dark side not only implies criminal activity (one of the greengrocers is a smuggler) but also its moral and psychological status. It is clearly marked as a libidinous space: the elderly trader praising his apples – in a heavily accented mixture of German-Turkish slang – appreciates his apples as well as the bosom of a young, blond woman ("You also have nice apples...!"). Her bewilderment and even anger can be seen as representing the irritated mainstream accidentally trapped in this Oriental chaos. The trader's punishing his obviously innocent employee for his own act not only stresses the arbitrary moral standards of the inhabitants of this sphere, but also reminds us of the stock figure of the Oriental Sultan (and proverbial "ordre de mufti") who is tied not to any standards or rules but only his own needs and wishes.

The use of cultural stereotypes goes even further. If we keep the European canon in mind, the fruit trader gains an additional symbolic level: praising his apples, he reminds us of the Biblical serpent in paradise, seducing the blond (German / mainstream) Eve. It is evident that to a great extent the construction of the Turkish / Oriental 'other' space requires the repertoire of the cultural canon, stereotypes and collective imagination.

The topos of the bazaar is absolutely synonymous with patterns of Western Orientalism: it is represented as a pre-civilized sphere, mirroring suppressed (Western) desire. This sphere of demand and seduction is shown as categorically separated from the mainstream world: the tunnel clearly emphasizes not only the danger of transition but also stresses the character of this cultural border.

Alles getürkt imagines multiculturalism as an encounter of clearly divided and separate spheres: the German sphere (police department), the fruit market / bazaar, and the pedestrian area. The latter realm is staged as the contact zone or battlefield: it is not only the symbolic argument of Döner sandwich and @-man, but also the narrative construction of the film that fuels this clear division: the genre of the police story (including the initial sequence of Olaf Stern, alias Cem Yilmaz, being on patrol). The street is thus shown not only as a sphere of contact and exchange but also one of threat and danger. In the hierarchal spatial order of the genre, this threat is situated in the 'Oriental' underworld.

The extent to which the programmatic idea of the film – subverting clichés by presenting the good and honourable Turkish father and the beautiful and desirable young Turkish woman – is in turn subverted by its own dramaturgy (with its implicit geography) and its visual language is remarkable.

THE 'AUTHENTIC' SPACE OF THE 'OTHER'?

While the visual imagery and spatial topography of the Turkish German film *Alles getürkt* can be seen to undermine its progressive message, we now turn to the opposite scenario. In the mainstream production *Edel & Starck*, the spatial coding of the filmic narrative can be said to support the tricksterism of its plot, or at times, to be more progressive than the plot itself.

At first glance, the following scene seems to be in keeping with the space of ethnicity as a parallel universe. The scene is set in a Turkish bath – the epitome of Oriental voluptuousness. There seems to be a congruence of setting and character. The ethnic character is at home in the Turkish bath; it matters little whether this bath is actually in Berlin or elsewhere. Ethnicity forms a spatial enclave in the Western metropolis; it is timeless, ahistorical, and spatially autonomous. The Turkish character in the Turkish bath doubly reinscribes the dissociation of ethnicity from the German mainstream. In a sense, the ethnic character goes with the décor of the Turkish bath; he authenticates this space of 'Otherness.' Read on this level, the trope is that of the Orient's seductiveness. The ethnic 'Other' lures the mainstream – in the guise of the well-to-do lawyer, Felix Edel – into the space of the subconscious, a sphere of lust, nakedness and Dionysian pleasure. Ironically, this rite of passage into Oriental space is physically challenging for the mainstream character: Felix's labored breathing is evidence of the fact that, for the mainstream, this spatial initiation is by no means a facile one.

Edel's case – a porn star's claim that her colleague sexually harassed her outside the set – makes it necessary for him to engage in an on-set investigation. It is at this point that Edel's case, for Otto, becomes the mainstream actualization of the Harem fantasy:

Felix: This is an entirely normal case.
Otto: You will interview witnesses. Porn babes. Felix, you are going to heaven!
Felix: Otto, that's a tough business.
Otto: It's heaven. A harem, a harem full of professional babes. You have to tell me everything. No, better, you have to take pictures.
Felix: Otto, you're out of your mind.
Otto: Take me along. Of course! You're going to take me along!
Felix: I don't think Allah is going to approve.
Otto: Allah wants his children to be happy, especially his male ones. You're going to take me along.
Felix: I'm not a harem guide!
Otto: You're my friend, right?
Felix: Yes, I am your friend.
Otto: Then take me with you. I'll be your assistant.
Felix: That's out of the question.
  ...
Otto: You're going to heaven and you want to leave me here? Here? You're

>   taking me along. Take me to heaven! That's your duty as a friend and
>   as a Christian.
> *Felix*:   Otto! [*Dives*]

On the surface this dialogue seems in keeping with the trope of the voluptuous Oriental. Otto's helpless begging to be taken along, however, subverts this cliché. It is Otto, the Oriental, who wants to be initiated by the mainstream character into the spaces of secular pleasure in Berlin. Moreover, Otto's helplessness can also be read as a sign of his cultural illiteracy in matters of a secular Western world. The incongruence of a porn set and the religious transfiguration of an Oriental Harem that will eventually lead to Otto's disillusionment ("Felix, this was not paradise") implies that Otto is at a loss to understand the German mainstream surrounding him.

However, the very language in which Otto attempts to persuade Edel undermines the cliché of the Oriental displaced in – and at odds to comprehend – the West. Where the mainstream invokes the Koran ("Allah would not want Otto to enter the set of a porn film"), the ethnic character answers by quoting the father of German Protestantism, Martin Luther himself: it is Edel's duty as a Christian ("Freund und Christenmensch") to take him along. The ethnic character thus in fact betrays a dual cultural literacy – a literacy that fundamentally undermines the cliché of his being outside Western space as symbolized by the Turkish bath. Where a mainstream audience, prompted by the Oriental bath, expects the religious cliché – Otto's invocation of Allah – this audience is faced with an ethnic character speaking in the dominant culture's own voice: the voice of Martin Luther. Otto's reaction to Edel's words confirms the clichéd assumption of the Oriental's voluptuousness, but the language in which this confirmation is phrased subverts the cliché. The filmic narrative of *Edel & Starck* uses visual clichés – spaces of visual difference triggering Orientalist codes – only to subvert these codes. It is Otto's dual cultural literacy, then, that makes him a trickster figure who is simultaneously at home both in the Turkish bath and outside it. It is through this trickster literacy, then, that the narrative of *Edel & Starck* subverts the authentic space of the Turkish bath even as it inscribes it.

At this point popular culture emerges as a sphere of spatial negotiation. To read Otto's character only on the level of the cliché would erase the ways in which the narrative subverts its own coding of ethnicity as stereotypical. This coding, in turn, is unreadable without the spaces which ethnicity is ascribed in the cultural imaginary of German popular culture. This simultaneous presence of stereotype and unpredictable, performative ethnicity is inseparable from the idea of mainstreaming. What reading the narrative of *Edel & Starck* against the grain implies is that mainstream narratives about ethnicity simultaneously point to ways in which their own coding of ethnicity falls short. The question of whether such a reading against the grain is prompted by the narrative itself or can only be read into it, then, is at once an indication of the extent to which a particular ethnic group or character has become part of the German cultural imaginary. This participation as being mainstreamed, in turn, is constituted through space: the question of whether or not a space remains marginal to the German nation or, as a liminal space, opens up potential for spatial and cultural negotiation.

This reading of the mainstreaming of ethnicity in popular culture thus follows the practice of what Jigna DESAI, following Homi BHABHA, has called a search for the beyond; a search in which popular culture becomes a space both of inclusion and exclusion. The idea of mainstreaming, then, views this practices of exclusion and inclusion as mutually constitutive. As Homi BHABHA puts it,

> We find ourselves in the moment of transit where space and time cross to produce complex figures of difference and identity, past and present, inside and outside, inclusion and exclusion. For there is a sense of disorientation, a disturbance of direction, in the 'beyond'... (Quoted in DESAI 2003, ix).

Crucially, in contrast to the Oriental marketplace, the Turkish bath is thus no longer a truly heterotopic space. Rather, the Turkish bath is an Oriental (and colonized) space that has been deprived of its 'Otherness' and has hence been transformed in what could be termed a non-threatening heterotopia. The concept of heterotopia, of key concern for our discussion of ethnicity in German popular culture, is defined by Michel FOUCAULT (1986, 24) as follows:

> There are also, probably in every culture, in every civilization, real places – places that do exist and that are formed in the very founding of society – which are something like counter-sites, a kind of effectively enacted utopia in which the real sites, all the other real sites that can be found within the culture, are simultaneously represented, contested, and inverted. Places of this kind are outside of all places, even though it may be possible to indicate their location in reality. Because these places are absolutely different from all the sites that they reflect and speak about, I shall call them, by way of contrast to utopias, heterotopias.

In *Edel & Starck*'s Turkish bath, then, Orientalism has become a matter of lifestyle and Oriental décor which the mainstream and its ethnic Others can *share*. It is still a heterotopia, a space completely apart from other spaces (the court, the law firm), but it is no longer threatening. What is striking is that Oriental props are thus seen as markers of a cosmopolitan lifestyle. Yet, ironically, the narrative self-reflexively establishes a contrast between the false cosmopolitan (Edel) and the true cosmopolitan, the Turkish German trickster figure Otto. Even as Edel pretends to be a cosmopolitan well versed in the Koran, Otto tells him what Allah *really* thinks.

The question that the filmic narrative seems to ask, then, is what happens if there is an ethnic person in an ethnic space that, having been mainstreamed, is no longer seen as ethnic? Ironically, Otto's presence serves to re-ethnicize the Turkish bath: he thus introduces an element of authenticity. Yet, this authenticity is simultaneously subverted. Otto, as a trickster figure, effortlessly crosses the spaces between the heterotopia that he himself has just created by re-ethnicizing the Oriental décor and the mainstream. Where Edel is a would-be cosmopolitan, Otto is the real border crosser. This, in fact, could be termed the chaos of heterotopia, a heterotopia that has begun to slip. Authenticity is at the same time both inscribed and subverted. Otto not only tells Edel what Allah really thinks, but adds the advice of Martin Luther to further his own ends; he wants to be taken along. Far from being a token of cultural inassimilability, the ethnic 'Other' quotes its core values back at the mainstream. The Muslim 'Other' instructs the lapsed Christian. Otto, as a trickster figure, is simultaneously outside and of the mainstream. He is a trickster who brings about spatial instability; he can re-ethnicize and de-ethnicize spaces at will. A trickster character that at first seems to authenticate rather than subvert heterotopic spaces hence brings about spatial instability and a subversive heterotopia. Spaces can thus be seen to trigger expectations; ethnic characters found in German popular culture can then undermine or manipulate these expectations. It seems in instances of mainstreaming Turkishness in *Edel & Starck* that, through self-irony, the narrative rehearses the disruption of our expectations of the Oriental.

In contrast to *Alles getürkt* and its univocal spatial order, *Edel & Starck* also shows to what extent the 'Other' affects the mainstream. Edel is no longer master of the situation, but rather is losing control (of the 'Other' as well as of his own cultural legacy). His conspicuous corporeal affectedness can be read as a symptom of cultural change. In contrast to Olaf Stern, who consciously masks himself as a Turk, Felix's cultural foundation seems unsettled.

TRANSITION: THE DIFFERENCE OF URBAN WEIRDNESS

The next scene takes this breaking up of the stereotypical coding of ethnicity – its correlation with ethnic spaces – one step further. The ethnic character's difference is levelled the moment he enters the space of an urban culture that is itself considered neurotic, freakish. Once again, the ethnic character's voluptuousness is inscribed on the surface level. Yet, this time, he is the object, not the subject of the desiring gaze. Edel has to defend a male client who works in a striptease bar. Where Otto initially is appalled by the idea of Edel's female colleagues embarking on an onsite investigation, he is left to wonder about the appeal of striptease for women. Once again, it is the ethnic character who leads his mainstream friend to explore bodily pleasures, or rather, their physical expression. This exploration, however, is also a self-commodification. Taking the cue from the professional German Chippendales watched by Edel's female colleagues, Otto makes Edel join him in exploring the role of male sex appeal as commodity. It is at this point that he loses his ethnicity. Otto, who had initially confirmed the stereotype of the Turkish macho man by scorning male striptease as gay, is now asking Edel to judge the suppleness of his own movements.

>   *Otto*: Tell me, Felix, how do you think I move?
>   *Felix*: Before or after you've had six glasses of beer?
>   *Otto*: Usually.
>   *Felix*: Like everyone else.
>   *Otto*: Do I not somehow lack – suppleness?
>   *Felix*: Well, some men are a bit awkward in their hip movements.
>   *Otto*: I'm a Turk; we are not awkward in our hip movements.
>   [*They start dancing.*]
>   *Woman*: I saw light from outside. And the door was open.

Otto is once again a trickster figure who leads Edel to do a dance that is readable simultaneously on two levels. On one level, their striptease is a tribal dance – the 'Other' teaches his mainstream friend how to shed inhibitions occasioned by Western civilization ("Ich bin Türke, wir sind nicht steif in den Hüften"). On another level, however, Otto leads Edel into the space of popular culture – a space of commodification. By implication, Otto is at home in both ethnic and mainstream spaces at once. Otto and Edel become objects of a metropolitan gaze on the lookout for visual pleasure; for popular culture is a profoundly urban space and male striptease a lifestyle in a liberal urban community. Through the urban space of a striptease bar, then, the difference between the mainstream and ethnicity is levelled. Both Edel and Otto become urban in their shared eccentricity. Ethnicity loses its meaning because the urban community itself is exotic. But who is the recipient of this visual pleasure? As a woman client looking for Edel's colleague, Sandra Starck, enters the office, she becomes an unwitting and unwilling audience of this urban performance of self. It is through her bewildered gaze that the half-naked Edel and Otto are exoticized in their shared urban freakishness. The woman's gaze is thus in fact mainstream, a gaze under which Edel and Otto appear exotic, freakish. The difference between Edel and Otto, between mainstream and ethnic character, is thus no longer applicable.

The context of this impromptu striptease; however, needs to be considered. For even before Edel and Otto discover a common rhythm through their tribal / urban dance, their differences have been annihilated by the male bonding of home improvement. By tearing out the office wiring, even though neither of them have a clue about electrical engineering, they stripped the office space of its professional specificity, and respectability. In one respect, the tribal dance about to be performed is thus preceded by a breaking up of order. In another, however, home improvement also levels the difference between Otto and Edel, between the affluent lawyer and his professionally challenged friend. With a power drill in hand, all men have been created equal. This stereotypical space of masculinity as home improvement, however, is simultaneously undermined by the performance that follows, male striptease. *Edel & Starck* thus inscribes spaces of authenticity – the Turkish bath, the gender solace of a construction site – only to subvert them. In or through this subversion, urban space emerges as a space of cultural negotiation. This urban space, importantly, is a transnational space; it is devoid of a specifically German connotation. It is connoted, however, as fundamentally Western.

We thus find ourselves in a different kind of heterotopia: the heterotopia of urban craziness. Otto has shed his ethnicity by moving into the space of urban weirdness: this heterotopia is not an ethnic one. By creating a visual and spatial simultaneity between the tribal dance and the spectacle of commodification, the filmic narrative rehearses the slippage of scripts of difference. The ethnic and the mainstream character, moreover, converge in a spectacle of commodification that is enabled by U.S. popular culture. Otto can become a sex bomb only through the background presence of Tom Jones. Ironically, in the German context, Tom Jones loses his ethnicity; he is coded only as American – an Americanness enabling a Turkish character to shed his Turkishness. What this requires of a German public, of course, is a pop cultural literacy in American terms; a literacy which is also at the core of *Edel & Starck* as a German spin-off of *Ally McBeal*.

MULTICULTURAL UTOPIA: SPATIAL ABSENCE OR VIRTUAL ETHNICITY?

What then is the ethnicity, which emerges from this renegotiation of ethnicity in urban space? In the following scene from *Alles getürkt*, popular culture, and American popular culture, emerges as a thirdspace in between ethnic authenticity / difference and a German mainstream – a thirdspace in which intercultural romance is possible only through a cliché from iconic U.S. pop cultural. If the mainstream character can play Turkish, he might as well pass as an American cowboy.

> *Olaf* [*to his horse*]: We've got the music. It'll be like in the Wild West. But I mustn't forget the music.
> *Father*: What's that noise? ...
> *Nihan*: Cem! Olaf...
> *Olaf*: I know I hurt you. [*In Turkish*] But believe me, I wanted to tell you.
> *Nihan*: It doesn't work. We don't belong together.
> *Olaf*: Yes, we do, and how we belong together. I like Turks, your way of life, your humor, your language. But the best thing about Turkey, Nihan, that's you. You're moody, you always want to have the last word, ... but the time I've spent with you was the best time of my life. Marry me. Please. I love you. And now I'm going to take you away, whether you want it or not. Come on, before I fall from this horse. Please. Lütfen. [*Reads to her father, in Turkish*] With Allah's help and the blessing of the prophet, I've come to ask you for your daughter's hand in marriage.
> *Father*: [*in German*] What? You mean con man. Never!
> *Olaf*: Come into my arms, princess.

Ultimately, both Turkish authenticity and American cliché are said to be out of place in contemporary German urban culture. In this scene, both ethnicity and the mainstream are readable only as cliché, and are emptied out through this caricature. The mainstream suitor who formerly donned Turk face to propose to his Turkish lover has now assumed an American disguise. Yet, surprisingly, this American disguise turns out to be authentically Turkish. His lover has told him of her own parents' romance which Olaf, alias Cem, seeks to re-enact. Turkish traditional romance is thus a Hollywood style fairy tale to begin with – Olaf / Cem enters Turkishness by authenticating the cliché. Similarly, while he addresses his fiancé's father in Turkish, invoking Allah, the father angrily rejects his suit in German. Significantly, the thirdspace in *Alles getürkt*, thus, is that of parody. While in *Edel & Starck*, metropolitan culture takes the place of authentic spaces, *Alles getürkt* can deconstruct these spaces through parody, yet, there is nothing to put in their place. A German / American / Turkish cowboy and his Turkish bride on a white horse that hates Turkish music remains the deliberately incongruous tableau of the transcultural romance of the future.

Parody is also at the heart of another space in *Alles getürkt*: a space that sheds its liminality and goes mainstream. For this is the culmination of ethnic role play, of a travesty which began with a mainstream character in a Döner disguise and a Turkish character walking the streets as the living epitome of global cyberspace. The Dönernet café is the ultimate fusion of Turkish cliché and its subversion. It is a space in which Turkishness exists only virtually, in which it simultaneously enacts and subverts its difference. As the Turkish equivalent of McDonald's, the Dönernet café is global Turkishness, an ex-ethnic space turning the world into its playground. In this instance, too, transnational spaces are created through a reference to American popular culture; this transnational space, in turn, can serve to create the basis for mainstreaming ethnicity. Having shed its niche as ethnic petty economy, ethnicity has become part not only of the German, but the global mainstream. The Dönernet café fuses the predictable – the correlation of Turkishness with Döner – with the unpredictable: global Anatolia. A mainstream audience enters the café expecting to find rural Anatolia and finds itself in an urban cyberspace made in Berlin.

Yet, to return to Olaf's travesty of Turkishness as an American cowboy, we are left with a suspension of difference through absurdity. This is no longer the heterotopia of ethnicity; instead, there is a categorical rupture. Ethnicity seems feasible only as staged; the happy end of multiculturalism can be conceived only as a utopia, a virtual space. As FOUCAULT (1986, 24) has claimed,

> Utopias are sites with no real place. They are sites that have a general relation of direct or inverted analogy with the real space of Society. They present society itself in a perfected [here: multiculturalist] form, or else society turned upside down, but in any case these utopias are fundamentally unreal spaces.

Multiculturalism, in *Alles getürkt*, is feasible only as hysterical syncretism. This syncretism, in turn, is once again enabled by American popular culture. This space of an American / global popular culture, then, serves not a transnational utopian device, but as alienation effect. In SAMDERELI's film, the fusion between ethnicity and the mainstream can be imagined only as parody – a suspension in which the filmic narrative bears out the literal meaning of utopia, a space that does not exist. We have thus come from the heterotopia of the Oriental bazaar to the subversive heterotopia of the Turkish bath and the transitional space of urban weirdness to an absence of spatial location. In *Alles getürkt*, multiculturalism exists outside the real world precisely because it is conceivable only in virtual space. We suggest that what is striking is that a non-mainstream cultural production can not conceive of the realization of a multicultural fusion of the mainstream and its 'Others.' This realization, however, does seem feasible in a mainstream cultural production.

THE LOCUS AEMONUS – 'PARADISE NEXT-DOOR'

As we have seen, these film and television series use different spatial metaphor strategies to locate minorities in their relation to the mainstream: *Alles getürkt* makes extended use of clichés, trying to overcome them through exaggeration. *Edel & Starck*, in contrast, consciously deconstructs the well-known sphere of Western urban life, by creating liminal spheres that subvert the cultural order of mainstream and minority. Both strategies have difficulties: while *Edel & Starck* relies on the trickster character of Otto – rather than presenting him as an equal partner in private as well as professional matters – the multicultural vision projected by *Alles getürkt* seems to be all too unreal with its exaggerated, even hysterical, clichéd scenes.

In contrast to *Alles getürkt*, *Edel & Starck* not only confines itself to deconstructing well-known places, but also engages in creating a visionary space. Our final example is taken from the last episode of the 2003 season of the series. This episode features Edel's attempt to escape his professional daily life after a putative defeat in court. Felix Edel buys a yacht, docked at a small lake near Berlin, so that he can sail to the Caribbean. Remarkably enough, it is Otto who suggests the purchase. Consequently, both of them start living on the yacht. Step by step, the yacht and pier become the center of an increasing process of social erosion. One character after another leaves his or her post and joins the happy community – the secretary, judge, other colleagues. This transformation can be seen in their changed outward appearance as well; gown and business suits become Hawaiian shirts and shorts. Only Sandra Starck remains steadfast, but increasingly upset by this loss of work ethic. Finally, she tries to convince Felix to come back:

> *Sandra*: You can't do this. You can't do this!
> *Felix*: Do what?
> *Sandra*: This! You can't just hang out like this. Who will do all the work? You are the pillars of society. You've got responsibilities. You can't just put on these – ridiculous shirts and sit on this boat. You can't do that.
> *Felix*: Why not?
> *Sandra*: Because – if everyone did that...
> *Felix*: Well, there are some people who don't. You, for example.
> *Sandra*: Yes.
> *Felix*: Yes, you, with your Prussian Protestant work ethos.
> *Sandra*: Oh, Felix, that's not nice of you. Don't you think I'd like to do this too? Do you believe I get up every day thinking, I like getting up, I love going to work? I'd also like to stop worrying about tomorrow, but you can't live like that. And Felix, I'm so tired of it. I'm so fed up with the fact that you can always afford these pranks and I have to wipe up after you. And then I end up looking your anal aunt. You're coming with me now. You can come back to the boat on the weekend, but now you're going with me. We have a case to argue. And by the way, the presiding judge is you, Judge Moosleitner, so I'd be happy to see you in court. Come on Felix, let's go.

The sequence initially shows a close-up view of her boots as she is getting out of her car. This is hardly accidental. It emphasizes the underlying pattern of discovery and exploration. Beginning with the contrast of boot / car and nature in the initial close-up view; we experience Sandra Starck as the interloper in this community. She embodies not only duty, professionalism, and business, but also urban civilization. This is why she is shocked when she realizes that nearly all her (male) colleagues are involved. The visual code used in this sequence mirrors Sandra's impression of astonishment and even anxiety. The audience's perspective is that of discoverer. We experience the grotesque characters, like that of the judge whom we see only from the waist up, and the out-of-fashion clothes they all wear. The fragmentation of bodies and their unusual costuming is a sign for the grotesque body – thus the small community by the lake might be regarded as the carnivalesque counter-world of daily life. Similarly unusual is Felix Edel's appearance. He comes up from the lake – reminding us of the instance when he descended in the Turkish bath that he visited with Otto. Here the situation has changed significantly, however. The space is no longer a cultural one, but nature itself.

What is Otto's position in this Dionysian idyll? He is again shown as a trickster. He is not tied to the law of nature; he is a real interloper, who can appear and vanish whenever he wants. Thus, to a certain extent, this yacht adventure seems to obey his master plan – while he was often shown as being in conflict with the major institution of mainstream society, the judiciary, his idea of buying the ship has torn down the foundational pillars of this society. His revolution is seduction, but not under the signum of Orientalism but rather in the light of Western popular culture. He stages the Caribbean next-door to Berlin and offers an alternative way of life. He is not himself the embodiment of subconscious longings, but rather uses the Western imaginary of the Caribbean paradise. He enters this sphere without himself being subject to its conditions. Through Otto's mediation, the Wannsee becomes both an ethnic and a transnational space.

Facing the happy, neglectful, and relaxed community, Sandra loses her countenance and cries (like a child) about the useless men, blaming them for destroying everything while she tries to maintain the unquestionable necessity of Western civilization. Felix Edel is perfectly right when he reveals this behavior as being "Prussian and Protestant". The back sliding savages, former representatives of Western civilization, are not interested in being discovered at all. They are not even interested in the interloper herself.

When Sandra exits, frustrated and angry, it is Otto who admonishes Felix Edel to follow her. "Do not let her go in this mood. Be the man whom I respect so much." Here, the trickster takes back his own creation. He disenchants the dream of ultimate freedom and leisure time by reminding Felix not of his duty, but of the foundation of his (cultural) identity.

CONCLUDING REMARKS

In our analyses we tried to show the extent to which spatial setting of films and their characters define the characters' cultural and social position. While German popular culture is modelled after successful antecedents in U.S. popular culture, the mere transposition of patterns and techniques does not necessarily imply that the underlying cultural concepts are also transferred. Instead of assuming an effect of homogenization, we experience an adaptation that mirrors the specific cultural and social conditions of each society. Thus, while the filmic narratives pretend to envision a transnational and intercultural sphere of agency, they, in fact, fuel a process of adjusting these models to the German context.

Our focus has been on the representation of ethnic characters and the question of to what extent they gain access to the mainstream via these models of popular culture. Comparing *Alles getürkt* and *Edel & Starck*, it became obvious to us that ethnic characters (and the idea of cultural borders) in Germany are still determined by the dominant idea of an ethnically homogeneous nationhood. Ethnic characters dwell in marginal spaces, like the fruit market or Turkish bath, and the encounter of mainstream and ethnic communities is still marked as exceptional. The dramaturgy and plot lines also reveal difficulties in envisioning a multicultural society. While *Alles getürkt* attempts to offer a happy ending by exaggerating stereotypes and clichés that stage the happy consummation of a Turkish-German love story in the setting, costume, and patterns of U.S. Western films, *Edel & Starck* exhibits the subversive vibration caused by an ethnic trickster. Both models, however, contain ethnic characters whose cultural mobility and social agency is limited compared to that of the mainstream characters. To ask about mainstreaming these ethnic characters, also is to envision a time when they will no longer be confined to heterotopic or utopian spaces but be an intrinsic part of German society itself.

Considering the slowness of political discussions and the anxiety shown towards embracing the multicultural reality by German society, these examples from popular culture indicate a sustainable, although subterranean change. While Otto is still a trickster character, he may eventually come to be seen as the ironic and comic forbearer of a successful and popular Turkish lawyer defending his grotesque but likeable German clients.

REFERENCES

APPADURAI, A. (1996): *Modernity at Large: Cultural Dimensions of Globalization*. Minneapolis.
DESAI, J. (2003): *Beyond Bollywood: The Cultural Politics of South Asian Diasporic Film*. New York.
FOUCAULT, M. (1986): Of Other Spaces. *Diacritics* 16 (1), 22–27.

Stefan Zimmermann

LANDSCAPES OF *HEIMAT* IN POST-WAR GERMAN CINEMA

INTRODUCTION

This chapter illustrates the link between national cinema, cinematic landscape and national identity. It also offers insight into film history by exploring one of the few truly German film genres, *Heimatfilm*. Although concentrating on the historical geography of a cinematic genre and the alteration of its represented landscapes, cinematic geography is not simply a disassociated reading of entertaining texts. Rather, it studies cultural documents, thus allowing insights into the historical construction of regions and their inhabitants as well as the visual heritage of a represented nation. By looking at the historical geography of an entire genre and the variations that occurred during its existence, cinematic geography can be seen as a tool used to gain understanding of these historical dimensions. Following BRUNO (1997, 2002), LUKINBEAL (2004, 247) posits that movies may be seen as today's "social cartography of meaning creation and identity formation" at multiple scales. Visual art forms are often consumed without any critical scrutiny or verification. The normative statements, deriving from visual media, often are transferred into the taken-for-granted consciousness of the recipients and, therefore, need further analysis.

The subsequent reading of a cluster of films is only one approach towards genre cinema from a geographical perspective. Films are visual legacies of the existential orientation of a cultural era. As such, this reading, which explores *Heimatfilm*, also offers an excursus into film history. Hence, this chapter tries to demonstrate how a specific geographic reading of one, or a group of films, might help dismantle dominant ideologies and alternate forms of social contestation. As geographers look at cinematic landscapes, they must take into account several factors that limit the creation of represented settings. These factors include the directors' ideas, the technical development of the cameras and the possibilities of post-production and market needs. All cinematic products, including the movie itself and the connected merchandise, are products of their time. *Heimatfilm* and its represented landscapes are no exception. Geographic research on film can contribute to a better understanding of cinema's influence on society and provide access to a nation's history via its visual heritage. This chapter provides a geographic, interpretative film analysis that seeks to understand the German *Heimatfilm* by interpreting the different landscapes within that genre (cf. ZIMMERMANN 2007). The seminal work of HÖFIG (1973), a film historian, provides the basis of this paper and demonstrates that research on cinematic geographies is not carried out only by geographers.

POST-WAR GERMAN CINEMA

German cinema lost its high position in world cinema after the Nazis came to power (KRACAUER 1984). This decline continued after Germany's defeat in WWII until the 1950s. When the Nazi party came to power in 1933, many talented German filmmakers had already left the country (ELSAESSER 1989). As a result, there was a lack of gifted filmmakers with the needed skills to produce films that could bring back the glory of German cinema's early years. Available filmmakers, producers and writers had either started their careers during the Nazi reign or were inexperienced beginners who were highly involved in the propaganda machinery of the National Socialists (KASCHUBA 1989).

In the early years of the Federal Republic of Germany, as in most other countries involved in WWII, cinema audiences longed to see images of an undamaged world. Between the war and the formation of the new state, the so-called *Trümmerfilm* or *Rubble film* made an impact on Germany's cinematic agenda. This genre used the destroyed cityscapes as background and setting for its often ruthlessness and rather realistic films. The films were interesting on an artistic level but not too successful in terms of box-office takings. In addition to these films, early post-war cinema in Germany consisted of reruns – specifically, movies chosen from the allied victors and low-budget German productions.

1950's German cinema in general and the *Heimatfilm* in particular, offered an apparently perfect alternative to everyday life. The decade was marked by hopelessness, despair and shame. The dreamscapes of cinema helped audiences escape memories of the 'Third Reich', the occupation, and the hardship of living in destroyed cities – the remnants of WWII (BLIERSBACH 1989). Going to the movies was much more than an escapist act; the movies offered home, shelter and entrance into a new life. Because of this, cinema going peaked in Germany during this era (Figure 1). In the context of the times, cinema needed to be sheer entertainment while offering a life different from that being experienced daily. German cinema used – as did most national cinemas – social purposes as a means of enlisting local audiences (O'REGAN 2002, 156). Movie theatres showed a wide variety of films from different genres and countries thus helping transport to, and instil in, audiences the *new ideology* of the allied countries – democracy (HÖFIG 1973).

Heimat and the Genre

Heimat is a difficult word to translate. Homeland is a rough, but unsatisfactory translation. The German word *Heimat* means country, part of a country, or place where one was born, grew up, or feels at home as a result of continually residing there (cf. MORLEY and ROBINS 1990). Many of the German films made in the 1950s are called *Heimatfilms*. In this context, the expression, *Heimat*, is rooted in loving human relations, not in a mythological connection to the soil as it was in the former Nazi ideology. This difference allowed a second *Heimat* for those who had been driven from their home (BOA and PALFREYMAN 2000). Post-war German and Austrian *Heimatfilm* used its scenery, its landscapes and simple narratives to convey a profound message – the 'secret' mission of nation building.

Figure 1. Cinema visitors and screened films in Germany.

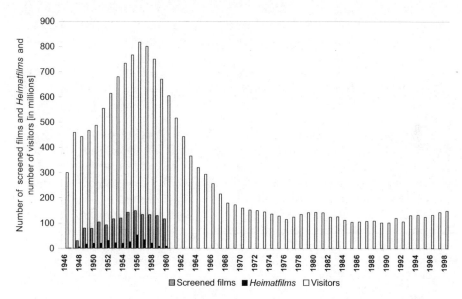

Source: HÖFIG (1973, 166) and Deutsches Filminstitut (2004)

A cinematic landscape is a filmic representation of an actual or an imagined environment viewed by a spectator – nothing more and nothing less – at first sight. HOPKINS (1994, 49) suggests a cinematic landscape is a very sophisticated and powerful form of representation because of the medium. Movies have helped establish specific landscapes and brought them into national consciousness. Landscape is central to the formation of cinematic space (ESCHER and ZIMMERMANN 2001). BALÁSZ (1924) argued that in a good film the spectator should be able to foresee the character of a scene just from reading the landscape and that the poetic possibilities of landscape were not fully exercised. In 1924, it was definitely true that landscapes' potential were not used to their full extent. It took several more years to develop these possibilities. Today, some genres are organised around their distinctive geography including Hollywood and Italian *Westerns*, Eastern German *Mountain Film*, and German *Heimatfilm*. The various uses of landscape through the period of *Heimatfilm*'s existence highlight the importance of landscape for this genre (BLIERSBACH 1989).

The basic ideas and motifs of this genre derive from numerous influences. One influence is the idealization of *Heimat,* or homeland. This idealization is demonstrated by characters finding hope, acceptance and balance only within very pure Arcadian environments, usually 'virgin' landscapes, where the main characters (often hermits) could find themselves and be left alone by an ignorant society. KOEBNER (2002) showed that *Heimatfilm* had its roots in other cinematic genres and was not only a phenomenon of the 1950s; its origins can be traced back to the late 1920s and early 1930s. The 1920s' *Bergfilm or Mountain Film*, and the early 1930s'

Operetta Film (in which the homeland is represented through folk-music, folkloristic narratives and popular tunes) are seen as predecessors of *Heimatfilm*. *Mountain Film* included elements of adventure films and melodramas, and usually took place in the high mountain region of the Alps. A quest for authenticity pushed the barriers of technical development; and new cameras and ground-breaking filming techniques were developed. Arnold FANCK's and later Luis TRENKER's and Leni RIEFENSTAHL's *Mountain Films* are often regarded as the earliest examples of *Heimatfilm*.

Nature plays a key role in *Heimatfilm*. GREIS (1992) argued that the genre applied the condensed aesthetic means of 1930s' and 1940s' documentary film. Nature was reduced to only a setting and lost the former sumptuousness of the genre's predecessors. Nature was replaced by landscape and thus could be interpreted only in a sentimental way (GREIS 1992). Landscapes were used to reinforce the characters' emotions (HÖFIG 1973). Positive characters had very close ties to nature that could not be explained by rational means (GREIS 1992). The preservation of nature was one of the important commandments of early *Heimatfilms*. Considering that the films appeared while German cities were being reconstructed and the Federal Republic of Germany was being founded, this message appears strange. Conservation simply did not seem to be an important priority for society at that time.

Heimatfilm was most popular in the 1950s and seemed to answer major *Zeitgeist* issues. The period of the *Wirtschaftswunder*[1] in West German politics was characterised by the conservative governments of Konrad Adenauer and Ludwig Erhard. In terms of social issues, after WWII, there were approximately ten million refugees in West Germany from Germany's former Eastern territories (cf. HARRIS and WULKER 1953). West Germany was a country caught between its past and future that could not, and did not want to, face up to its past. Instead, it concentrated on achievement and, thus, on the future.

Heimatfilm is one of the only original genres created in Germany and often is compared with the American Western because landscape and national identity play a central role in both genres (GÖTTLER 1993). From the early fifties to the early sixties, *Heimatfilm* was characterized by peaceful and mostly idyllic rural life with splendid landscapes such as the Alps and the moorlands of northern Germany (HÖFIG 1973). In terms of narrative, most films were simple love stories or heroic tales in which the good guys always won. After the Nazi reign and the terror of war, German audiences longed for uplifting films about beautiful people doing self-determined things in even more beautiful environments.

A shift in the films' locales from cities to rural areas was essential in order for filmmakers to provide a positive image of the country within, and outside of, Germany. The small, enclosed world of the village, with its firmly fixed values handed down from the past, was a contrast to everyday life in the Federal Republic

1. *Wirtschaftswunder* is the German word for the "economic miracle" or, the fast economic development after WWII partly due to aide provided by the United States and the Marshall-Plan.

of Germany. The landscape, with its beautiful scenery, would in today's terminology be called a fantasy – something removed from the reality but pleasant to see. There also was a patriotic fervour in these films. Movies in this genre were made for people who had grown up between 1920 and 1940 and had been influenced strongly by Nazi ideology. To them, these films were a kind of nostalgic throwback to the idyllic past rather than a reminder of Germany's defeat and eventual destruction in the Second World War. These films were trying to present the traditional values of the pre-Nazi era by depicting beautiful mountain landscapes, traditional festivals and country fairs, colourful costumes and dances, folk music, and romantic sentimental affairs between Cinderella and Prince Charming-like characters. The younger generation, however, was not particularly drawn to *Heimatfilm* and its narratives involving sentimental or melodramatic themes and relationships.

Heimatfilm confirmed an idealised world, idyllic landscapes and forests as well as healthy, happy people. Although the genre re-presented a Germany that did not exist outside the imagination, it was able to instil a new sense of home in Germans and refugees alike. The films helped create an imaginative community (MORLEY and ROBINS 1995). At the same time, these films were symptomatic of the German people's unresolved feelings regarding their recent traumatic past. This context made the success of *Heimatfilm* possible.

KRACAUER (1963, 1984) argues that films mirror the society in which they are made and more directly reflect the mentality of that society than any other form of mass media. Using national cinema as a research object, its films tell much about the represented and depicted nation and society as well as how these specific insights were made accessible (SILBERMANN 1970).

Of approximately three hundred *Heimatfilms,* few can be considered high art (HÖFIG 1973), nor are they either distinctive in their narrative structure or very reliable in their depiction of landscape. One can use the ideas behind the cinematic landscapes, however, to gain insights into the state of German society in the 1950s (TRIMBORN 1998). Looking at Germany's destroyed cities; it is not surprising that these locales never played a vital role in a genre that was supposed to entertain. Movies that picked these settings as a central topic were too close to reality and were financial unsuccessful; quite the reverse of German / Austrian blockbusters like *Grün ist die Heide (Green is the Heath), Der Förster vom Silberwald (The Forest Warden of the Silberwald)* that were seen by millions of people. The latter film originally was shot as a documentary on alpine flora and fauna. Due to the high quality of its images, however, it was turned into a feature film by constructing a simple narrative that was embedded in brilliant nature cinematography. Even so, across Germany twenty-two million spectators went to the cinemas to see the movie in the 1950s (HÖFIG 1973, 176).

LANDSCAPE DEPICTION AS A TOOL

Researchers have used a variety of approaches in order to investigate and understand cinematic landscapes and their uses (cf. HIGSON 1984; KENNEDY 1994; ESCHER and ZIMMERMANN 2001; LUKINBEAL 2005). Looking at a genre or genre-specific feature, one can see how landscape might be used as a tool for analysing feature films. Landscapes give meaning to cinematic action and place the narrative within a particular scale and historical context. Looking at cinematic landscapes from an historical point of view KRACAUER's (1984) idea of film as a mirror of society is made more easily accessible. Both landscape and film are social constructions. Thus, movies are products of their time and understanding the depiction of landscape within films offers insight into society. Cinematic landscapes of national cinema reflect a nation's state of development and can help analyze a genre and make it comparable to other films.

LANDSCAPES OF *HEIMAT*

Cinematic landscapes can be studied from various perspectives; it is difficult to tell which is the most appropriate. The way that landscapes are depicted, cinematically constructed and represented in *Heimatfilm* throughout the 1950s, raises questions about the fusion of landscape and film as well as the hybrid nature of the genre. The genre's cinematic landscapes need to be seen as a mirror of a society as well as the mental and emotional needs of West Germany's post-war generation. The use of landscapes within the genre varied throughout its existence. BRAUDY's (1977, 22) argued that films can be seen as a mirror or window in time foreshadows KRACAUER's (1984) proposal. It might be argued that film is accepted too readily as a window on reality without noticing that the window has been framed in a particular way that excludes as well as includes. Reading cinematic landscapes offers an insight into society but also can open a chapter on historical geography – a chapter that has long been thought only accessible by means of written sources. In the following, cinematic landscapes of *Heimatfilm* are investigated, focusing on the narrative function of the landscape as metaphor and spectacle (ESCHER and ZIMMERMANN 2001; LUKINBEAL 2005). Geographic reading of visual media as a research method is also used because, "looking seeing and knowing have become perilously intertwined" (JENKS 1995, 1). The boundaries between different categories of cinema's adoption of landscape are a bit blurred. However, although different films might contain elements of more than one ascription, they usually can be brought into a broader context.

Heimatfilm not only mirrored society; it seemed to affect society as well. The narrative usually contained a desire to return to traditional values predating WWII. In so doing, it sought to allow Germans to feel a sense of pride in traditional values. The genre allowed an acceptable form of naturalism built on a moral landscape, a Heimat.

Characters within the Landscapes

Landscapes are phenomenon not only seen and perceived by individuals but also largely constructed through personal cognitive processes. Similarly, cinematic landscapes are not only seen – as a mixture of material and nonmaterial landscapes – by a large audience (a collection of individuals); but also are portrayed and already consumed by several involved agents (cf. ESCHER and ZIMMERMANN 2001). Within *Heimatfilm*, audiences were confronted with specific characters who used landscape as a playground and who also functioned as support for the films' representation of landscape. Not only were cinematic landscapes used as foils for characters' emotions, but also, archetypal characters supported the cinematic landscapes' strong sense of place.

These characters reflected many realities of post WWII Germany. One main character was the almost omnipresent forest warden – usually the only one who could wear a uniform without arousing negative emotions in the audience. Single mothers were also part of the narrative – in keeping with the fact that more than three million German soldiers were killed in action as well as a comparable number of civilians (BOA and PALFREYMAN 2000). Another consequence of the war was numerous orphans. Therefore, from the beginning through the heyday of the genre, orphans played a vital role. Another group of characters, travelling musicians, emblemized displaced populations and usually were depicted as clownish vagabonds. BOA and PALFREYMAN (2000, 93) called them "timeless wanderers in the Romantic tradition" adding that these nomadic figures can be seen as the archaic embodiment of a landscape. The eccentric and wise hermit, who played an important role by functioning as mediator between society and intruders to the rural locale, was another character brought into play. These loners were the only older people acceptable to the audience (HÖFIG 1973) as they usually lived on the margin of society and had no connection to the Nazi regime and its hegemonic organization.

A common denominator throughout *Heimatfilm*, was the nebulous concept of a common culture – excluding the twenty odd years leading to, and during, the war. The idea of homelessness as a collective experience helped establish some sort of mutual approach towards the new country people were living in. In 1950, the young Republic had to cope with more than eight million displaced people and nearly two million fugitives (KOEBNER 2002, 250). Every single cinema-goer knew someone who had lost his home. Hence, homelessness and loss of roots, in geopolitical terms, became part of people's identity. Re-integration was a task for the young Republic and the film industry. Audiences, especially the older generation aged forty and over, cherished these films. They used the cinema as a place of both escape and entertainment without giving much thought to the subliminal messages the films contained. Foreign movies were shown, but were most favorably received by younger audiences (HÖFIG 1973).

Landscape builds *Heimat*

Landscape as place provides narrative realism and helps hold the action in place (HIGSON 1984; LUKINBEAL 2005). MORETTI (1999) argued that every action of a narrative is bound to a specific place. These places could be found in *Heimatfilm's* constitutive landscapes, in the *hinterland* of the destroyed metropolitan areas, e.g. the moorlands of Northern Germany and the Bavarian and Austrian alpine region. In the heyday of the genre, from 1953 to 1956, landscape was used predominantly to emotionalize particular scenes and underline the importance of having a home and being rooted in a community. The new home used a set of metaphors, creating a genre specific sense of place. In retrospect, one can find evidence of the spiritual needs of the audience – the need to be part of a thoughtful community who live together with friends and family.

Society had gone through a loss of national identity and cinema offered a means of creating a new *Heimat*, or homeland, to the displaced population and refugees. The inhabitants of towns and cities had to adapt to the results of war and a *Heimat* had to be regained by finding a new identity. Cinema offered a means of creating a new *Heimat* by developing a new individual as well as group-specific identity. CHALMERS (1984, 93) observed another effect of identity deprivation was that

> ...even language no longer provided a 'home'. Even the image of Germany in the post-war period was part of this uprootedness. America [was] represented, for example, by the White House, England by Buckingham Palace..., France by the Arc de Triomphe.... Germany, however, [was always] represented by its division..., marking the absence of certainty about home: separation, expulsion, exile.

The movie *Am Brunnen vor dem Tore* (1952) grasped that specific uncertainty about home and depicted a world of brotherly love (somewhere in the Bavarian provincial backwater) in which Germans and English were beginning to work and plan together once more.

In the early period of *Heimatfilm* (1950–1952) landscape was a metaphor, a dreamscape, an imagined geography of another not yet accomplished world. Examples can found in *Schwarzwaldmädel* (1950), and *Grün ist die Heide* (1951). The major goal of these movies was to introduce audiences to a joyful, agreeable life by depicting people in a harmonious environment. Filming locations and narrative places had to be sought outside the bombed cities of Germany. These places could be found in the periphery of the coastal region, and in the northern German moorlands, Black Forest and alpine regions of Southern Germany and Austria. Small towns and villages were shown as offering home to the displaced (Figure 2). Interestingly, in reality, individuals tended to migrate towards metropolitan areas, not to the small towns of the hinterland as shown in the movies.

The landscapes offered only the framework for the narrative. Landscapes were mainly used as a metaphor for *Heimat* / home. Within the new positioning of the *Heimat*, the spectator can observe a change in its meaning.

Landscape is *Heimat*

The glory days of the genre did not last long. By the end of the 1950s, landscape depiction within the films had lost their power. These movies mastered the *Heimat* topic and with playful ease handled new forms of picture language and a more visualised sense of place. The cinematic landscapes offered merely the framework for the narrative and the metaphorical content could easily be decoded. In *Heimatfilm's* heyday, from 1953 to 1956, landscapes were used primarily as a metaphor for a newly developed home. Within the new positioning of the *Heimat*, a spectator could monitor a change in its signification. The cinematic landscape developed

Figure 2. Destruction in German Cities in WWII and major filming locations of the Heimatfilm, 1948–1960.

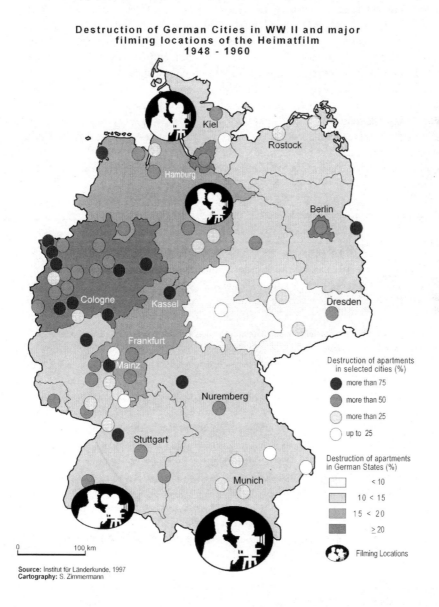

from its former role as setting and metaphor to a more pivotal and substantial role as actor. For example, in *Der Förster vom Silberwald*, the opening credits thank the astounding landscape for its beauty and help as an actor (HARRIS and WULKER 1953). Other excellent examples from this period are: *Wenn der weiße Flieder wieder blüht* (1953), and *Heideschulmeister Uwe Karsten* (1954).

Later, landscapes were cinematically and perceptually outlined by mentioning, rather than showing, them. Cinematic landscapes were produced within a discourse, a whole communication process that featured several artistic elements, including regional costumes, folk music and vernacular or regional dialects. Landscape, if depicted at all, became an aesthetic commodity. Through this process landscapes were woven into the concept of *Heimat* and became a cultural component of custom and tradition. In this cognitive process, cinematic landscapes became an ingredient of the new homeland that was finally found. From the early 1960s, the *Heimat* movement was forced into a defensive position and criticised for its backwardness as well as its tendency not to face everyday problems (KASCHUBA 1989). At the end of the genre's existence, a trend toward a more artistic and sophisticated conception of the entire setting and a perceptible partial adoption of political and social topics could be observed. Movies, belonging to this phase include *Geierwally* (1956) and *Heimat deine Lieder* (1959).

Landscape as Distance

By the end of the 1950s, movies of the genre were usually set in the touristic regions of Germany or Austria and featured the landscapes and locales of preferred travel destinations, as can be seen in *Im weißen Rößl* (1960) and *Der letzte Fußgänger* (1960). The depicted places were shown as simple backdrops and stages for pure entertainment. The result was a dramatic shift in narrative emphasis from community and nation building to promoting tourism. This shift changed the picture language within the *Heimatfilm* genre to a more artistic and vibrant approach. The cinema adapted to new, emerging needs of spectators, who, by then, had found their place within society and the new State. *Wanderlust* and pure entertainment replaced the desire to gain a new home; and the trope of making a journey simply for pleasure is found in the final *Heimatfilm* movies. Contributing to *Wirtschaftswunder*, travelling was affordable once again and consumerism had taken the place of earlier political agendas. Film inspired travelling and audiences soon experienced holiday destinations first hand. The new destinations – for filming and for vacation – could be found all over Europe; especially in Italy, Austria and Spain. In the movie *Auf Wiedersehen am blauen Meer* (1962) this new trope is portrayed in a rather absurd manner. The main character, again a simple huntsman, comes to know a swanky Italian girl who has just inherited a castle in her Italian home village. He follows her to Italy and has to cope with the new environment on all possible levels. *Wenn man baden geht auf Teneriffa* (1964) uses the cinematic language of *Heimatfilm* but depicts a group of high-school graduates on their holiday to the island of Tenerife and how they are confronted with, what is supposed to be, Spanish culture.

New places became a central feature of these latter films. Audiences could observe tourists and their newly encountered problems (e.g. new political and economical freedom as well as vague cultural understanding) while on holiday. The adaptation of *Heimat* and overcoming the search for the earlier, specifically cinema assisted *Heimat*, can also be seen as a reflection of the distance German society had travelled. At the end of the 1950s and beginning of the 1960s, society seems to have integrated into their new, altered homeland and communities. Landscape was no longer an influential narrative and metaphorical aspect within this process. *Heimatfilm* and its 'secret' mission of nation building was no longer needed.

CONCLUSION

Cinematic landscapes played a vital role in the German genre, *Heimatfilm*, not only as actor, but also, in various ways, as a means of expressing the status quo of post-war German society. *Heimatfilm* helped create West Germany's new collective social identity while literally giving a home (in theatres) to millions of refugees. The cinematic landscapes within this indigenous German genre can be seen as a mirror of, and role model for, post-war German society that offers profound insights into the desires of society. Landscape played an essential role by helping promote the idea of a new Germany. Cinematic landscapes functioned not only as spectacle but also as metaphor; and thus, can be used to measure the social condition of a nation. Furthermore, these landscapes functioned as a historic source, supply insights into the visual heritage of a nation and can help researchers understand existing national identity. During the era of post-war German development, society could be seen as being in urgent need of a healing sleep. Popular media aided this sleep, or psychic rest; thus, *Heimatfilm* helped create a civil society within the newly found state.

Today it is still possible to read cinematic landscapes of a specific genre as done above. The visualised landscapes of cinema and television should be observed for signs of hereditary images and narratives from *Heimatfilm*. To some extent, the genre still exists; although it appears in different forms and with other topics and cinematic styles. A common way of adapting the main features of the genre can be found in popular TV-productions (e.g. *Die Schwarzwaldklinik*, *Forsthaus Falkenau*). Many well-known German filmmakers such as Volker SCHLÖNDORFF have grabbed ideas from the genre and worked with them. Examples range from SCHLÖNDORFF's *Critical Heimatfilm* and Edgar REITZ's filmic novel trilogy *Heimat* to the *New Heimatfilm* of Joseph VILSMAIER. Today, elements of *Heimatfilm* are primarily important in terms of nostalgia and for understanding the history and geography of Germany. Perhaps, however, *Heimatfilm* could today achieve even greater prominence and notoriety than before. Many of us are looking for a peaceful world in which we feel rooted and know our home. It seems, though, that this *Heimat* has become the ultimate luxury for many individuals living in a globalized world.

ACKNOWLEDGEMENTS

I would like to thank Prof. Dr. Anton Escher and Catrin Burgemeister who helped with discussions on the topic and have always been willing to share their ideas. I would also thank the ZIS (Centre for Intercultural Studies) at the University of Mainz for their financial support of the Symposium "The Geography of Cinema –

a cinematic world," which was held at the Department of Geography in June, 2004. Further, I would like to gratefully acknowledge the editorial support of Christina Kennedy and Chris Lukinbeal.

REFERENCES

BALÁSZ, B. (1924): *Der sichtbare Mensch*. Wien.
BLIERSBACH, G. (1989): *So grün war die Heide... Die gar nicht so heile Welt im Nachkriegsfilm*. Weinheim and Basel.
BOA, E. and R. PALFREYMAN (2000): *Heimat – A German Dream. Regional Loyalties and National Identity in German Culture 1890–1990*. Oxford.
BRAUDY, L. (1977): *The world in a frame*. Garden City, New York.
CHALMERS, M. (1984): "Heimat: approaches to a word and a film". *Framework* 26 (7), 90–101.
Deutsches Filminstitut: www.deutsches-filminstitut.de/dt2ja0003b.htm. Last accessed 06/02/2004.
ELSAESSER, T. (1989): *New German Cinema: A History*. London.
ESCHER, A. and S. ZIMMERMANN (2001): Geography meets Hollywood – Die Rolle der Landschaft im Spielfilm. *Geographische Zeitschrift* 89 (4), 227–236.
GÖTTLER, F. (1993): Westdeutscher Nachkriegsfilm – Land der Väter. JACOBSEN, W., A. KAES and H. PRINZLER (Eds.): *Geschichte des deutschen Films*. Weimar and Stuttgart, 171–210.
GREIS, T.A. (1992): *Der Bundesrepublikanische Heimatfilm der Fünfziger Jahre*. (Phil. Diss.). Frankfurt / Main.
HARRIS, C. D. and G. WULKER (1953): The Refugee Problem of Germany. *Economic Geography*. Vol. 29 (1), 10–25.
HIGSON, A. (1984): Space, Place, Spectacle: Landscape and Townscape in the 'Kitchen Sink' Film. *Incorporating Screen Education* 25, 2–21.
HOPKINS, J. (1994): A Mapping of Cinematic Places: Icons, Ideology, and the Power of (Mis)representation. AITKEN, S.C. and L.E. ZONN (Eds.): *Place, Power, Situation, and Spectacle: A Geography of Film*. Boston, 47–65.
HÖFIG, W. (1973): *Der deutsche Heimatfilm 1947–1960*. Stuttgart.
JENKS, C. (1995): The Centrality of the eye in western culture. JENKS, C. (Ed.): *Visual Culture*. London, 1–12.
KASCHUBA, W. (Ed.) (1989): *Der deutsche Heimatfilm – Bildwelten und Weltbilder*. Tübingen.
KENNEDY, C. (1994): The Myth of Heroism: Man and Desert in Lawrence of Arabia. AITKEN, S.C. and L.E. ZONN (Eds.): *Place, Power, Situation, and Spectacle : A Geography of Film*. Boston, 161–179.
KOEBNER, T. (2002): Heimatfilm. KOEBNER, T. (Ed.): *Reclams Sachlexikon des Films*. Stuttgart, 250–253.
KRACAUER, S. (1963): *Das Ornament der Masse*. Frankfurt / Main.
KRACAUER, S. (1984): Von Caligari zu Hitler. Eine psychologische Geschichte des deutschen Films. Frankfurt / Main.
KRACAUER, S. (1996): *Theorie des Films*. Die Errettung der äußerlichen Wirklichkeit. Frankfurt / Main.
LUKINBEAL, C. (2004): The Map that Precedes the Territory: An Introduction to Essays in Cinematic Geography. *GeoJournal* 59 (4): 247–251.
LUKINBEAL, C. (2005): Cinematic Landscapes. *Journal of Cultural Geography* 23 (1), 3–22.
MORETTI, F. (1999): *Atlas des europäischen Romans*. Wo die Literatur spielte. Köln.
MORLEY, D. and K. ROBINS (1990): "No place like Heimat: Images of Home(land) in European Culture". *New Formations* 12, 1–23.
MORLEY, D. and K. ROBINS (1995): Spaces of Identity. *Global Media, Electronic Landscapes and Cultural Boundaries*. London and New York.
O'REGAN, T. (2002): A National Cinema. TURNER, G. (Ed.): *The Film Cultures Reader*. London and New York, 139–164.

SILBERMANN, A. (1970): Nationale Imagebildung durch den Film. SILBERMANN, A. (Ed.): *Die Massenmedien und ihre Folgen. Kommunikationssoziologische Studien.* München, 149–158.
TRIMBORN, J. (1998): *Der deutsche Heimatfilm der fünfziger Jahre: Motive, Symbole und Handlungsmuster.* Köln.
ZIMMERMANN, S. and A. ESCHER (2001): Géographie de la "cinematic city Marrakech". Cahier d' Etudes Maghrébines – *Zeitschrift für Studien zum Maghreb* 15, 113–124.
ZIMMERMANN, S. (2007): *Wüsten, Palmen und Basare – die cineastische Geographie des imaginierten Orients.* Dissertation. Mainz.

SELECTIVE FILMOGRAPHY

Schwarzwaldmädel (1950) H. Deppe
Grün ist die Heide (1951) H. Deppe
Am Brunnen vor dem Tore (1952) H. Wolff
Wenn der weiße Flieder wieder blüht (1953) H. Deppe
Der Förster vom Silberwald (1954) A. Stummer
Heideschulmeister Uwe Karsten (1954) H. Deppe
Die Fischerin vom Bodensee (1956) H. Reinl
Geierwally (1956) F. Cap
Der Schinderhannes (1958) H. Käutner
Heimat deine Lieder (1959) P. May
Wenn die Heide blüht (1960) H. Deppe
Im weißen Rößl (1960) W. Jacobs
Der letzte Fußgänger (1960) W. Thiele
Auf Wiedersehen am blauen Meer (1962) H. Weiss
Wenn man baden geht auf Teneriffa (1964) H.M. Backhaus
Heimat (1984) E. Reitz

THE READER

Christina Beal Kennedy

LIVING WITH FILM:
AN AUTOBIOGRAPHICAL APPROACH

> *To write is to choose.*
> *I've selected what matters to me.*
> *Others would choose differently*
>
> (THYBONY 1997, vii).

North Peak has been my sacred mountain since I found it when I was nineteen years old. North Peak and the surrounding area along the crest of California's Sierra Nevada affected me strongly. They piqued my curiosity about landscape and our relationship with it, leading me to study geography and environmental perception. Imagine my distress when, in the process of creating this paper, I discovered North Peak's marked resemblance to the Paramount Pictures icon I had seen hundreds of times in my childhood (Figure 1).

Figure 1. Similarities between North Peak in the Sierra Nevada and the Paramount Films icon. Drawing by Tina Kennedy.

INTRODUCTION

I don't know how much of what I say here is true. Our emotional states, personalities, and life experience can bias memories (LEVINE and SAFER 2002). Even the simple reflexive act of remembering can subtly alter memories themselves. Yet, as Momaday pointed out, "If I were to remember other things, I should be someone else" (JAY 1994, 203). I am not trying to prove causality nor claim that what I experienced is universal. Here, I tell a story of my experience of film during my formative years, from age three to twelve. What I offer is a case study based on my remembered life with cinema. And, by this process, provide gist for the mill of speculation on possible relationships between film, emotions, actions, place, and identity formation; on the conscious and subconscious impacts of film on our daily lives.

Situating Self

I'm a humanistic geographer. As such I'm concerned with values, meanings and emotions; our relationship to places; and the 'growth of the human soul' (SELL 2004) and human potential (TUAN 1976). From a humanistic perspective we can look at film as a meeting between audience and director / producer that is a dialogue about potential life situations, experiences, emotions, and concerns that fulfill certain needs and are meaningful to us as human beings (SINGER 1998). Because I'm telling a story about cinema and places, I use both a narrative-descriptive and autobiographical approach. Geographers are beginning to look seriously at the relationship of narrative and place (cf. JONES 2004; PRICE 2004; SPRENGER 2004; CURRY 1999). Stories, and dramatic narratives, can both create and maintain places (TUAN 1991). Narrative is an integral part of Hollywood films; our experiences with films are also stories. By using a descriptive, narrative approach wherein complex phenomena are the focus and theories are in the background, rather than a standard theoretical one, I can explore the "ambiguity and complexity" (TUAN 1991, 686) of my early experiences with movies and tell a story that may help us better understand our experience of film as audience. Although this approach is less analytical than theoretical, TUAN (1991, 686) sees it as being more faithful to human experience because it allows the reader to see diverse yet related information rather than "rigorous explanation of a necessarily narrow and highly abstracted segment of reality."

Emotions

Although not a determinant, the act of engaging with movies may nudge us along certain paths in our lives; help shape the framework within which we "make sense" of, or through which we filter, our life experiences; and affect our sense of places and our identities (cf. CRESSWELL and DIXON 2002; IZOD 2000; ROEBUCK 1999; SINGER 1998; AITKEN and ZONN 1994; LUKINBEAL and KENNEDY 1993; BURGESS and GOLD 1985). In these developments, affect and emotion are critical. Traditional narrative film can be seen as an 'emotion machine' (TAN 1996) and, in Hollywood, new, improved methods of intensifying the filmic experience and the emotions aroused in that experience are continually being sought – quicker pace, louder sound, graphic level of violence, sex, and special effects (WEATHERS 2004). Narrative films obviously contain rational components – religious, philosophical and ideological content – that also affect both our identities and sense of places (MAST 2004). Emotions are, however, the heart of our social behavior and reasoning (DAMASIO 1994) as well as a critical source of energy and direction (MAIO and ESSES 2001). Emotions can lead to action by not only providing a readiness to act but by also fueling our decision *to* act (ZHU and THAGARD 2002). When we experience emotions induced by the experience of film, those emotions trigger an affective process that changes the memory of the images seen even as we watch. We filter those images and the story so that they conform to our own predispositions (IZOD 2000) through an active, if unconscious process. This suggests that the emotions aroused in our experiences in viewing movies have a significant role in the creation of our life-worlds and inform life-decisions – not always at a conscious level.

Although emotion and personal experience may be seen by some as contaminants in social sciences, thinking and feeling are not separate. Nor are our personal backgrounds incidental facts to our research but rather shape the processes of searching and discovering in complex ways. Indeed, "the process of thinking through issues is as important as any specific conclusions about those issues" (FREEDMAN and FREY 2003, 2).

SMITH (2001, 7) notes the "extent to which the human world is constructed and lived through emotions" and how in certain places and times we live "so explicitly though pain, bereavement, elation, anger" and love that "the power of emotional relations cannot be ignored." She calls for the recognition of "emotions as ways of knowing, being and doing in the broadest sense; and using this to take geographical knowledges ... beyond their more usual visual, textual and linguistic domains" (SMITH 2001, 9). One way of achieving this end may be through autobiographical writing.

Autobiographical Writing

Writing is a creative, fluid process in that we learn and change as we write. In autobiographical, qualitative writing, we place ourselves in our own text and thus make it transparent that we are writing from a specific viewpoint and time. This "frees us from trying to write a single text in which everything is said to everyone... Writing is validated as knowing" (RICHARDSON 2004, 476). In autobiographical writing we "let go of the myth of the coherent subject endowed with unquestionable authority..." (REAVES 2001, 14).

A criticism of autobiographical writing is that it is 'narcissistic' or 'mere navel gazing'. However, exploration and analysis of one's experience is different from self-adoration. Nor is analysis of one's experiences necessarily 'navel gazing'. The personal narrative is expression "of neither authorial authority nor of egoism.

Rather, the I is the voice of the individual from the margins... The 'I' says 'but in my experience...'" and is voluntarily open to a criticism of not being representative (OKELY 1992, 12).

In examining the role of film in our own lives and in others' we may be saying as much about ourselves as we are about the films, a risk that is difficult to take. I discovered that autobiographical writing is similar to an archeological dig into memories and understanding – a process that heightens some memories, dredges up others, and consequently, alters both understanding and the memories themselves – creating, perhaps, a mythography. If writing is, as RICHARDSON (2004, 474) claims, however, one way "to find something out", to "learn something I didn't know before I wrote it", this method is valuable. I learned that the formative power of cinema is likely stronger than I would ever have imagined.

CONTEXT: MY PERSONAL EXPERIENCE

"Childhood is neither outgrown nor fully known" as we grow beyond the social boundaries and constraints of our early life (NICHOLSON 2001, 128). Margaret MEADE claimed that the most important component of who we are is our childhood geography (WEATHERS 2004). COOPER MARCUS (1986) wrote about the importance of childhood landscapes in affecting our landscape preferences as adults. By twelve years of age, my only physical travel outside a forty-mile radius of my hometown was a trip, when I was two and a half years old, to the Oregon Coast – where I thought I was going to be swallowed by the ocean. As a child, movies were my main gateway to the world. As such, they were an integral part of my childhood geography, the Del Oro Theatre and places in movies, were major players in my childhood landscapes. Both my family and where I grew up were critical factors in my experience with film (Figure 2).

When Dad was courting Mom in the 1930s, if he wanted to take her to see a movie he had to take her parents and seven siblings as well. Dad and my Mom's family were scraping a living by panning for gold in the rivers of northern California or getting occasional work in one of the hydraulic gold mines that were still washing soils from the Sierra Nevada into the Central Valley. On one occasion, Dad drove Mom and her family thirty two miles down a narrow, curving mountain road from Camptonville to Grass Valley and the nearest theatres. They saw *Gone with the Wind* (1939) at the Strand. The Theatre was full, so they stood through the entire movie. When *Gone with the Wind* (1939) returned to Grass Valley in 1952, Dad went with us to see it again. That was one of only three times he went to the "show" with us.

I come from Grass Valley, California, a then isolated small town of 5,000 in the heart of the Gold Country. Aside from the bars or church events, going to the picture show was the only entertainment in town. A few "well off" people had televisions, but the Cinema was the important visual source of both news and entertainment. Movies changed three times a week. A show was a double feature, newsreel, cartoon, and occasionally a serial. There were many reruns, so the date a film was released and when it was shown at the Del Oro were often not related. The time period I primarily focus on here, however, is post WWII through the 1950s.

Figure 2. The three of us, (left to right) Mikel, me and Jack, in Oregon by the overwhelming ocean, 1949. Photo by Mabel Christina Beal.

My Dad worked seasonally as a logger or in sawmills, whenever work was available. He completed the tenth grade, my Mom the eighth. Mom was an exceptional housewife, seamstress, and mother. I had two brothers: Mikel, a year and a half older than I, and Jack, four years older. We were poor, but clean and not "beholdin'" to anyone. The Strand was gone by the time I was born, so in the first seventeen years of my life, every movie I saw was in the Del Oro Theater, on Mill Street. To me, the theatre and Public Library were the two most important downtown locations (Figure 3).

I cannot remember a time when I wasn't taken to the movies. The theatre was my Mom's escape from cooking, cleaning, sewing, and caring for us kids. Mom took us to the picture show once or twice a week when possible. So important was it to her that when our neighbors, members of the Pentecostal Church, convinced my brother Jack that he would "Go straight to Hell" if he kept going to movies, his pleas to stop going were ignored. To me the Del Oro Theatre itself was a magical place. It was elegant. There I heard classical music, at home only country. The walls were painted blue with ballerinas dancing through clouds, their arms gracefully

Figure 3. Grass Valley's Del Oro theatre in the "Gold Country" of California's Sierra Nevada foothills. Photo by Tina Kennedy.

raised and positioned. When the lights dimmed, heavy, red velvet curtains parted and the gateway opened into worlds different than mine.

I cannot imagine a life without cinema. Movies were a part of my reality long before books. Now I have a choice of what I watch; as a child I had none. Going to the movies was sometimes a pleasure and exciting, sometimes completely terrifying. The stories, places, and the theatre itself are mixed together in my memories, and, like all life experiences, especially childhood ones, are an integral part of my being. Film tied me into the zeitgeist of America for over half a century – Hollywood style, contributed to my sense of different places, informed my sense of aesthetics, and trained me in a particular way of seeing. I don't think it too strong a statement to claim my experience of movies was critical in the formation of my self-identity as well as image of, and consequent experience of places (Figure 4).

The first film I remember, when I was four, is *The Indian Love Call* or *Rose Marie* (1936) with Jeannette MacDonald and Nelson Eddy. Afterwards, I wanted to change my name to Tina Marie. My dream was to grow up and paddle a canoe through the Canadian wilds. In researching this paper, I discovered the movie was filmed, not in Canada, but at Lake Tahoe, a mere ninety miles from my home; a lake I first saw on my thirteenth birthday and experienced a strong sense of *déjà-vu*. Was the cabin in the film the template for my later home in Yosemite Valley and my current one in Flagstaff? What is the relationship between the hero, a Royal Canadian Mounted Policeman and my marrying a National Park Service Protective Ranger who, unfortunately, later transformed himself into a highway patrol officer? (Figure 5)

Figure 4. My cabin in Yosemite Valley, winter 1970 (center). My current home in Flagstaff, Arizona (lower right corner). Photos by Tina Kennedy.

Figure 5. Ray on horse patrol in Yosemite National Park. Photo by Tina Kennedy.

THE EFFECTS OF CINEMA

Why or how can cinema affect our lives? I suggest that five processes, or aspects of cinema, contribute to the impact films can have on us: 1) affect, 2) repetition, 3) introjection, 4) connecting story with place, and 5) symbolic content. Although I separate them out in the following, they are, to some extent, inseparable in most film viewings; and, the most powerful binding force amongst them is affect or emotion. In fact, Jung sees emotion as the chief source of consciousness (IZOD 2000). Films allow us to experience rapid, intense emotions that we may not experience or feel free to experience in our day-to-day lives. This is undoubtedly one of cinema's attractions (SINGER 1998). Films can also introduce us to new situations and allow us to practice for possible experience of those places, situations, and emotions (JOHNSTON 2000). As adults, although we experience intense affect when viewing films, we also can maintain a certain psychic distance from the narrative; and, moreover, are able to step back and examine, or think about, affect and our emotions. As children, we have few such skills and little experience with which to deal with the raw, intense emotions elicited by film (WEATHERS 2004).

Affect

Science fiction films were the bane of my childhood existence. Now, I understand that they were reflective of national fears resulting from the Cold War, the paranoia associated with McCarthyism, and fear of nuclear war and its consequences. Then, films like *The Attack of the Crab Monsters* (1957) simply terrified me. One movie was too terrifying for my brothers and me to deal with. I don't remember the name of the film, I only remember that –

> A man wakes in his apartment in the city to utter silence. He turns on the radio... nothing. He goes down the still hallways of the building and out into the empty sunshine. Cars are scattered in the city streets. There is no life. He opens a car door, and a man's body falls out. He runs to other cars, opens the doors and there is nothing but bodies. He is alone.

Hiding behind our knees was not protection enough. We crawled from our seats onto the floor where we crouched trying to use the back of the seats in front of us as a protective barrier from the visions on the screen. Cowering together, fingers in our ears, the eerie electronic music informing us of impending disaster pounded on us; so, we covered our heads with our jackets. This was too much for Mommie, and in disgust, she grabbed the three of us and marched from the show – the only time that she didn't stay to "get her money's worth".

The Forbidden Planet (1956) was one of my worst experiences. By today's standards, the film is a laugh. Watching the huge crushing footsteps of an invisible monster coming for the humans reached some intense atavistic fear when I saw the film at eight years of age. I lately discovered that the movie also intensely frightened my brother, Jack, who was twelve at the time. So much so, that he watched the film three times as an adult to discover that the monster was, in fact, the Id of a father trying to keep his daughter from the "strangers." I was so frightened by the film that I have never watched it again.

A part of my reality remains the aftertaste of fears experienced in the Del Oro. When I was ten or eleven, I would stand in our backyard, and, with a sense of dread look at the sky. Was *The Blob* (1958) or some other alien entity brought back from another planet going to insidiously take over our world? Or, were fire ants, like the army ants in *The Silent Jungle* (1956), going to come north from South America or Texas and threaten the relative safety of our existence? Not until I was a sophomore in High School and my biology teacher told me a cell could not grow larger than an ostrich egg did I lose my fears of *The Blob* (1958). And, not until I was in college and had learned to use anger to combat fear, could I walk alone at night. I was not afraid of people; it was always those seemingly intangible, imagined elements from science fiction films.

Repetition

ZAJONC (1980, 160) suggested that preferences are based first on emotion or affect rather than cognition, and that "preferences ... can be induced by virtue of mere repeated exposure". Emotion as basis for preferences, combined with the probability that repeated exposure to specific landscapes / places and stories may help explain preferences for specific images or places, and, if negative emotions were aroused, aversion to others.

A majority of movies we saw were Westerns, because those were what Mom enjoyed most. While Mom preferred Jeff Chandler because she thought he looked like Dad, Randolph Scott and Gary Cooper were my heroes – I'm still looking for my Gary Cooper. In Westerns, it was usually clear who the good guys and bad guys were. Good guys usually won, the hero and the heroine usually were married or engaged by the end. Only the bad guys – bank robbers, power hungry crooks trying to control the citizens of a town, or (of course) Indians – were killed. Killing was quick and usually amounted to someone looking startled and falling over, or, falling off a horse. Portrayal of Native Americans was through stereotypes and most often was jingoistic, as in the film *The Searchers* (1956). A large number of Westerns were shot in Monument Valley, Kanab Utah, or Old Tucson Studio – in Arizona and Southern Utah (Figure 6).

When I moved east from California to Arizona, I felt like I had moved to the West. After we chose to live on the Navajo Nation Reservation, we lived only about an hour from the Monument Valley featured in all the John Ford Westerns. These were the images from my childhood. Living on the reservation, my daughter, Mélisa, went to a Bureau of Indian Affairs boarding school at Teec Nos Pos, and I learned the difference between stereotypes and reality. Moving to Tucson also brought me to familiar landscapes. After all, it has saguaros, just like in the Coyote and the Roadrunner cartoons, and, the surrounding landscape was also "on location" for innumerable Westerns (Figure 7).

Figure 6. Landscape near Teec Nos Pos on the Navajo Nation, 1980. Photo by Tina Kennedy.

Figure 7. Mélisa and friend during "The Children are Beautiful" ceremony on the Navajo Nation, 1980. Photo by Tina Kennedy.

Introjection

Introjection, the internalization of experience of the world (IZOD 2000) including the experience of movies, the opposite of projection, is another avenue through which films can impact our emotions and lives. With film, introjection, subconscious identification and psychological alignment with a character or characters, and projection "occur with high intensity" and "bring about a two-way flow between screen and unconscious" (IZOD 2000, 272–273).

In the late 1940s to early 1950s, war films were a popular genre in the United States. As children, it seems we saw them all and incorporated many aspects of them into our daily lives. My brothers and I drew airplanes gunning down enemy planes. We played war with neighborhood kids, lobbing pinecone "hand grenades" from behind ridges in the tailing piles left from mining. That was fun. But, war movies, with their hard characters, violence and death frightened me.

Mike tried to teach me not to be frightened in war movies. *"It's not real, Tina." "It's just pretend." "That's not really blood."* Mike was my hero throughout childhood. My big brother – almost twin – my playmate while Jack lost himself in books. I liked what Mike liked, I echoed his opinions. "Fords are the best cars." "The New York Yankees are the only good baseball team." "The Marines are the very best!"

Mike didn't know any Marines as a child. Dad had been drafted into the Army Air Force in WWII, didn't leave the country, and was released on a medical discharge after three years. Dad distrusted or disliked authority, except his own. He never praised the military. How much did the movies we saw when we were small, *The Sands of Iwo Jima* (1949), or *The Halls of Montezuma* (1951), influence Mike's values, sense of patriotism, preferences, and concept of heroism?

Mike went to Vietnam. I went to Berkeley. Mike eventually became one of twelve Sergeant Majors in the U.S., and, eight years after he retired from thirty years as a Marine, killed himself with his *own* pistol. Had he not liked war movies, joined the Marines directly out of high school and built his identity upon being a Marine, would his life have been different? (Figure 8)

Figure 8. Scenes from The Sands of Iwo Jima. *Drawing by Tina Kennedy.*

Connection of Story to Place

The concept of connecting story to place connotes a "perception" or idea on the part of a viewer that the narrative and place in which the narrative occurs are, in essence, inseparable – a conscious or subconscious belief that, *"If I go to that place I will meet those types of people and experience or live that kind of story."* Perhaps the development of these perceptions are strongest for children with limited experience, or when the viewer has had little or no actual experience of a specific type of social or physical setting.

Film Noir strongly influenced my image of the city. Inhabitants of small towns in the 1950s traditionally had an anti-urban attitude. This attitude was strongly reinforced though movies. The city in the films I saw was filled with dark alleys, smoke filled rooms, detective's offices and night clubs. There weren't any clear heroes, just tough, misogynistic, bitter, homely men like Humphrey Bogart as a detective, or James Cagney as a nightclub owner. The women drank, smoked and, if they sang, sang the blues. "Love me or leave me, don't let me be lonely…" (*Love Me or Leave Me*, 1955). I still can't stand "club" or "lounge" music. Maybe the moral ambiguity of the films was too complex for my understanding; but I grew up knowing that I didn't want to be in any city. I mistrusted cities, and had no experience with them except through film.

When I became a geographer, I learned, over time, to enjoy cities. Still, many of those impressions remain. The following is an excerpt from my written impressions during my first trip to New York City to visit my daughter, Tiànna, eight years ago.

> The taxi stops. Surely this huge blocky building with graffiti on all its walls, in a line of other huge, dirty, graffiti sprayed square buildings is not a living space. We unlock then duck through a cast iron door and go up a darkened stairwell. Up four flights of cold, stained, filthy cement and brick. Neo Brutalism to the extreme. No. That is an architectural type. This, simply "old factory turned lofts…Later, we begin our hunt for groceries along a street where I expect a thug will slip from behind a wooden wall, slither around a pile of garbage, stab one or both of us, then walk on with no emotion – a job simply done. But that is an image from movies. The street is empty except for people not unlike us (Figure 9).

While Film Noir negatively influenced my image of cities, seeing *North to Alaska* (1960) when I was thirteen made me want to go to Alaska because I loved the landscape portrayed in the film, and the story was a funny, happy one. After one year studying at U. C. Berkeley, I quit college and headed for Alaska with friends. I thought Alaska would help erase the confusion and grayness of soul I found in Berkeley in the 1960s. Alaska's reality didn't match my expectations. I worked at a home for emotionally disturbed children and found the country beautiful, but not what I had pictured. Years later, I discovered that *North to Alaska* (1960) was actually filmed on the east side of the Sierra Nevada Mountains of California. The mountain viewed from the cabin was Convict Peak, the crest of the ragged mountains behind John Wayne, the crest of the Sierra, home of my heart, the place for which I experienced intense topophilia. The movie was filmed where I had worked and lived many years and which had started my interest in geography (Figure 10).

Figure 9. Tiànna outside her home in New York City, 2000. Photo by Tina Kennedy.

Figure 10. The "home of my heart", the crest of the Sierra Nevada. Photo by Tina Kennedy.

Symbolic Content

Cinema can be seen as a form of symbol play in which we can organize the symbols based on the unconscious, on the self (IZOD 2000). Some films such as the *Lord of the Rings* trilogy (2001, 2002, 2003) and *Lawrence of Arabia* (1962) touch the psyche of a wide audience because of their powerful symbolic content such as that of the Hero's journey (CAMPBELL 1949; KENNEDY 1994). I saw *Lawrence of Arabia* when I was sixteen. Despite my dislike of war films, violence and unhappy endings, "Lawrence" affected me powerfully. I returned the next day to see the film again. I think that, for me, this film combined affect; symbolic content of both the hero's journey and the desert as symbol of freedom, power, suffering; introjection; and connecting story with place in a powerful way. All I could think about was going to the desert, to Arabia, of adventure, of riding on a camel, and – okay, of meeting someone like Peter O'Toole. I've never made it to Arabia, but I moved to Death Valley and loved its stark beauty. The impact of *Lawrence of Arabia* was so strong that I saw it twice more when it was re-released to the wide screen and was then willing to watch it another thirteen times in order to write about it for my first paper on film geography (KENNEDY 1994).

Film Invading Memories

I've alluded to the probable influence of filmic place and narrative on the development of my image of places and to decisions and actions in the course of my life. What happens when the reverse occurs? We moved to Point Reyes National Seashore when my daughters were six weeks and two and a half years old. The house we lived in had three stories and the equivalent of seven bedrooms. It was located atop a cliff overlooking Drake's Bay. The nearest neighbor was two miles away, the nearest town, an hour. I spent a year and a half alone most of the time with an infant and a toddler. Although I have many good memories, I never felt quite at ease in that landscape or house. It was an isolated location, the ocean always overwhelming, the fog eerie, and the wind at times seemed unceasing. At night I was afraid to go down the stairs into the basement. Outside the wind roared through the cypress trees. Sometimes a family of great horned owls called or a great blue heron screamed. The setting was the nearest to gothic I have lived (Figure 11).

A couple of years ago, I rented *Village of the Damned* (1995) based on WYNDHAM's (1957) novel "The Midwich Cuckoos" set in a village in England in the 1950s. The 1995 version of the film was shot at the towns of Point Reyes Station (where I bought groceries and did banking), Inverness (where we received our mail), the National Park Service Headquarters (where we attended potlucks), and *in* my former home.

Seeing my home in the context of a horror story was intensely disturbing. The film's main characters lived in the house where I had spent so much time alone and isolated with my two small daughters. In the film, however, the innocent appearing infant living there is the spawn of extraterrestrial beings and through mind control forces her mother to stick her arm into boiling water and hold it there. This event

Figure 11. My former home at Point Reyes National Seashore. Photo by Tina Kennedy.

happens in "my kitchen", in "my home." Later in the film the child forces her birth mother, who is depressed by a growing understanding of her daughter's real nature, to walk to the cliffs edge in front of "my house" and jump – a cliff edge where I had stood alone many times looking at the rocks and water below. The power or horror of a "B" science fiction film was magnified by its invasion of my former home, life-space, and by its replication of a stage or time period of my life. My memories of a real place, my former home and environs, were twisted into symbols of a horror movie.

CONCLUSION

Film is an integral part of popular culture. Billions of dollars are spent each year on production and consumption of film. Yet, each person experiences these films through his or her own personal filters, including personality, past experiences, and emotions (ZONN 1990) and within a specific context, be it the back seat of a car at a drive-in, a video watched in the privacy of home or in a darkened theater – alone or with family and friends. There is a need for more information on how, or if, film affects audience preference, image of places, identity, and actions. I believe films can affect us deeply in both positive and negative ways.

In geographic research on film we critique films and discuss the effect of cinematic techniques. Psychoanalytic and social theories have proven useful in investigating film imagery, narrative, the director's intent, the role of the audience, as well as power relations as portrayed in film or found in the production of film itself. We argue that our lives are so entwined with film and representations that it is difficult to tell what is real and what a reflection of that learned in film (AITKEN and ZONN 1994). And, finally, we talk about how cinema impacts personal identity and our images of places (cf. CRESSWELL and DIXON 2002; AITKEN and ZONN 1994; LUKINBEAL and KENNEDY 1993; BURGESS and GOLD 1985). What is largely missing from our discussions is information on audience response to specific films or to film genres.

How can we learn about the impact films, and the emotions experienced, may or may not have on a person's life? We can project our own interpretation about the meanings and affect of film (which is primarily what has been done so far), or, we could survey audiences (which would at least give us superficial knowledge of audience reactions to specific films). A third option is to examine our own experience and search for patterns. Autobiography is one approach to the exploration of film's power to affect our everyday lives. In an attempt to say something "genuine" about the impact of cinema on everyday life, I told a story of cinema on my own life through an autobiographical, narrative-descriptive approach. How might cinema's impact differ for people in different age cohorts, geographical settings, and back-grounds?

My identity and life decisions seem deeply place-based. The Del Oro Theatre and movies I saw there were an integral part of my childhood and influenced my brothers and me. Films are no longer seen as mere images or "unmediated expressions of the mind, but rather the temporary embodiment of social processes that continually construct and deconstruct the world as we know it (CRESSWELL and DIXON 2002, 4)." As such, they helped construct the world I knew as a child and the world as I later experienced it. I married a man who seemed the embodiment of a Royal Canadian Mounted Policeman – except he couldn't sing. I grew up in a small town where people traditionally have a negative attitude toward cities. Grass Valley was in the foothills on the west side of the Sierra Nevada. Films I saw about mountains reinforced that sense of home, but introduced more magnificent landscapes and reinforced a sense of an "ideal" home. In my life I have sought the "home-land-scapes" I saw in film and have a propensity for living in little cabins in the mountains. The terror experienced watching science fiction films informed by McCarthyism permeated my childhood, had to be outgrown through scientific "facts" and life experiences. Still, I assiduously avoid horror films or films with realistic or excessive violence. Repetitive exposure to Westerns and the experience of watching *Lawrence of Arabia* gave me an affinity to deserts, "wide open spaces", and the landscapes and imagined cultures of the Southwest. This affinity was manifested in my choices to live in Death Valley, Teec Nos Pos on the Navajo Reservation, Tucson, and now Flagstaff. My search for my perfect landscape was fed both consciously and unconsciously by the movie *North to Alaska* and the Paramount icon. I didn't find that landscape in Alaska, but rather, had unwittingly already explored it in the home of my heart three years before fleeing to Alaska – the crest of the Sierra Nevada wherein also lies my sacred mountain, North Peak. And finally, films of war provided a model of "heroism" and identification with the Marines to my brother Mikel who became a "lifer" in the Marine Corps.

We talk about the willing suspension of disbelief. For young children and for some personalities, is there even the possibility of achieving psychic distance? Through film, I was introduced into many worlds and realities that, in some cases I wasn't ready or willing to experience and that, in others, appear to have influenced my life at an unconscious level far more than I had dreamed. Some of the patterns I found in writing this paper were disturbing and seemed far too deterministic for my comfort and concepts of "free will". But, who knows? This may, after all, be only my mythography.

REFERENCES

AITKEN, S. and L. ZONN (1994): Re-presenting the Place Pastiche. AITKEN, S. and L. ZONN (Eds.): *Power, Place, Situation, and Spectacle*. Totowa, 1–15.

BURGESS, J. and J. GOLD (Eds.) (1985): *Geography, the Media, and Popular Culture*. New York.

CAMPBELL, J. (1949): *Hero with a Thousand Faces*. Cleveland.

COOPER MARCUS, C. (1986): Remembrance of Landscapes Past. *Landscape*, 35–43.

CRESSWELL T. and D. DIXON (2002): Introduction: Engaging Film. CRESSWELL, T. and D. DIXON (Eds.): *Engaging Film: Geographies of Mobility and Identity*. Lanham, Maryland, 1–10.

CURRY, M. (1999): "Hereness" and the normativity of place. PROCTOR, J. and D. SMITH (Eds.): *Geography and Ethics: Journeys in a Moral Terrain*. London, 95–105.

FREEDMAN, D. and O. FREY (2003): *Autobiographical Writing Across the Disciplines: A Reader*. Durham.

IZOD, J. (2000): Active imagination and the analysis of film. *Journal of Analytical Psychology* 45 (2), 267–286.

JAY, P. (1994): Posing: Autobiography and the Subject of Photography. ASHELY, K., L. GILMORE, and G. PETERS (Eds.): *Autobiography and Postmodernism*. Amherst, 191–210.

JOHNSTON, R. (2000): *Reel spirituality: theology and film in dialogue*. Grand Rapids.

JONES III, J. P. (2004): *Mine the Gap, Strategies of Narrative*. Paper presented at Association of American Geographer's Meeting, Philadelphia.

KENNEDY, C. (1994): The Myth of Heroism: Man and the Desert in Lawrence of Arabia. AITKEN, S. and L. ZONN (Eds.): *Power, Place, Situation, and Spectacle*. Totowa, 137–160.

LEVINE, Linda J. and Martin A. SAFER (2002): Sources of Bias in Memory for Emotions. *Current Directions in Psychological Science* 11 (5), 169–173.

LUKINBEAL, C. and C. KENNEDY (1993): Dick Tracy's Cityscape. *The Yearbook of the Association of Pacific Coast Geographers* 55, 76–96.

LYDEN, J. (2003): *Myths, Morals, and Rituals: Film as Religion*. New York.

MAIO, G. and V. ESSES (2001): The Need for Affect: Individual Differences in the Motivation to Approach or Avoid Emotions. *Journal of Personality* 69 (4), 583–615.

MAST, J. (2004): Personal correspondence.

MAYER, T. (2004): *Narratives of Remembering the Jewish Past in Contemporary Israel*. Paper presented at Association of American Geographer's Meeting, Philadelphia.

NICHOLSON, Heather N. (2001): Seeing How it Was: Childhood Geographies and Memories in Home Movies. *Area* 33 (2), 128-140.

OKELY, J. (1992): Participatory experience and embodied knowledge. OKELY, J. and H. CALLAWAY (Eds.): *Anthropology and Autobiography*. London, 1–28.

PRICE, P. (2004): *Just stories: narrative, landscape, and the struggle for place*. Paper presented at Association of American Geographer's Meeting, Philadelphia.

REAVES, G. (2001): *Mapping the Private Geography: Autobiography, Identity, and America*. London.

RICHARDSON, L. (2004): Writing: A Method of Inquiry. HESSE-BIBER, S. and P. LEAVY (Eds.): *Approaches to Qualitative Research: A Reader on Theory and Practice*. Oxford, 473–495.
ROEBUCK, P. (1999): Meaning and Geography. PROCTOR, J. and D. SMITH (Eds.): *Geography and Ethics: Journeys in a Moral Terrain*. London, 19–29.
SELL, J. (2004): Personal Conversation, May 12.
SINGER, I. (1998): *Reality Transformed: Film as Meaning and Technique*. Cambridge.
SPRENGER, A. (2004): *The Geographical Life of Stories.* Paper presented at Association of American Geographer's Meeting, Philadelphia.
SMITH, S. (2001): Editorial: Emotional geographies. *Transactions of the Institute of British Geographers* 26, 7–10.
TAN, S. (1996): *Emotion and the structure of narrative film: film as an emotion machine*. Mahwah, New Jersey.
THYBONY, S. (1997): *Burntwater*. Tucson.
TUAN, Yi Fu (1991): Language and Place: A Narrative-Descriptive Approach. *Annals of the Association of American Geographers* 81 (4), 684–696.
TUAN, Yi Fu (1976): Humanistic Geography. *Annals of the Association of American Geographers* 66 (2), 266–276.
TUAN, Yi Fu (2001): Life as a Field Trip. *Geographical Review* 91 (1/2), 41–45.
WEATHERS, C. (2004): Personal conversation, June 18, 2004.
WYNDHAM, J. (1957): *The Midwich Cuckoos*. London.
ZAJONC, R. (1980): Feeling and Thinking: Preferences Need No Inferences. *American Psychologist* 35 (2), 151–175.
ZHU, J. and P. THAGARD (2002): Emotion and Action. *Philosophical Psychology* 19 (1), 19–36.
ZONN, L. (1990): Tusayan, the Traveler, and the IMAX Theatre. ZONN, L. (Ed.): *Place Images in Media: Portrayal, Experience, and Meaning*. Savage, Maryland, 1–5.

FILMOGRAPHY

Gone with the Wind (1939) Director: Fleming, V.
The Indian Love Call / Rose Marie (1936) Director: Van Dyke, W.
The Attack of the Crab Monsters (1957) Director: Corman, R.
The Forbidden Planet (1956) Director: Wilcox, F. Metro
The Blob (1958) Director: Yeaworth Jr., I.
The Searchers (1956) Director: Ford, J.
The Sands of Iwo Jima (1949) Director: Dwan, A.
The Halls of Montezuma (1951) Director: Mileston, L.
Love Me or Leave Me (1955) Director: Vidor, K.
North to Alaska (1960) Director: Hathaway, H.
The Lord of the Rings (2001, 2002, 2003) Director: Jackson, P.
Lawrence of Arabia (1962) Director: Lean, D.
Village of the Damned (1995) Director: Carpenter, J.

CONTRIBUTORS

Stuart Aitken: Professor of Geography in the Department of Geography at San Diego State University.

Mita Banerjee: Professor of English and American Literature at the University of Siegen.

Johnathan Bascom: Professor in the Department of Geology, Geography, and Environmental Studies at Calvin College.

Gerd Becker: Lecturer of visual Anthropology at the University of Hamburg and freelance filmmaker.

David B. Clarke: Professor of Human Geography at Swansea University.

Deborah Dixon: Senior Lecturer in the Institute of Geography & Earth Sciences at the University of Wales, Aberystwyth.

Marcus A. Doel: Professor of Human Geography at the University of Wales, Swansea.

Anton Escher: Professor and Chair in the Institute of Geography at the University of Mainz.

Christina Beal Kennedy: Professor of Geography at Northern Arizona University, Flagstaff.

Chris Lukinbeal: Assistant Professor at the School of Geographical Sciences at Arizona State University, Tempe.

Susan P. Mains: Lecturer in the department of Geography and Geology at the University of the West Indies at Mona, Jamaica.

Peter W. Marx: Junior Professor in the Institute of Theatre Studies at the University of Mainz.

Christopher M. Moreno: PhD student in the Department of Geography at San Diego State University.

Joseph Palis: Assistant Professor in the Department of Geography at the University of the Philippines, Diliman, Quezon City.

Stefan Zimmermann: Lecturer in the Institute of Geography at the University of Mainz.

Leo Zonn: Professor and Chair in the Department of Geography at the University of Texas, Austin.